Parliamentary Texts
of the Later
Middle Ages

Parliamentary Texts
of the Later
Middle Ages

NICHOLAS PRONAY

AND

JOHN TAYLOR

CLARENDON PRESS · OXFORD
1980

Oxford University Press, Walton Street, Oxford OX2 6DP

OXFORD LONDON GLASGOW
NEW YORK TORONTO MELBOURNE WELLINGTON
KUALA LUMPUR SINGAPORE JAKARTA HONG KONG TOKYO
DELHI BOMBAY CALCUTTA MADRAS KARACHI
NAIROBI DAR ES SALAAM CAPE TOWN

*Published in the United States by
Oxford University Press, New York*

© *Oxford University Press 1980*

British Library Cataloguing in Publication Data

Parliamentary texts of the later Middle Ages.
1. England. Parliament—History—Sources
I. Pronay, Nicholas   II. Taylor, John
III. Modus tenendi Parliamentum
328.42'09   JN515   79-40404

ISBN 0-19-822368-4

*Typeset by CCC,
printed and bound in Great Britain by
William Clowes (Beccles) Limited, Beccles and London*

Preface

In working upon this edition of the *Modus Tenendi Parliamentum* and other texts the authors have incurred a number of obligations. The study of the *Modus* was first prompted by the work of Miss M. V. Clarke and Professor V. H. Galbraith which did much to indicate the importance of this text for the history of the late medieval English parliament. The authors are also indebted to Professor S. B. Chrimes for his view, implicit in this book, that to understand the history of institutions we must appreciate the ideas which practical men held about them at the time. Professor J. S. Roskell and Professor Sir Richard Southern helped to improve considerably the shape and substance of the volume, and the authors wish to acknowledge also the assistance at various stages in the preparation of the book of Dr. C. E. Challis, Dr. J. L. Grassi, Dr. E. W. Ives, Professor Vernon F. Snow, and Professor E. L. G. Stones. For help with the Latin texts they are indebted to Mr. R. H. Martin, Mr. J. W. Cox and Mr. Ian Moxon; for help with the Middle English texts to Dr. Betty Hill; and they are indebted to Mrs. L. Carter for typing the manuscript. The extract from the manuscript of the Red Paper Book of Colchester is reproduced by permission of the Colchester Borough Council, and the account of the Speaker's Protestation by permission of Yale University Library. Finally they would like to acknowledge the assistance of the staff of the Oxford University Press in the preparation of this volume, and the help of the various libraries and colleges in England and the United States in answering queries and supplying microfilm of manuscripts in their possession.

Contents

Abbreviations

B.L.	British Library
B.I.H.R.	*Bulletin of the Institute of Historical Research*
B.J.R.L.	*Bulletin of John Rylands Library*
C.C.R.	*Calendar of Close Rolls*
C.P.R.	*Calendar of Patent Rolls*
Clarke	M.V. Clarke, *Medieval Representation and Consent* (London, 1936, reprinted New York, 1964)
E.H.R.	*English Historical Review*
R.S.	Rolls Series
Rot. Parl.	*Rotuli Parliamentorum*
T.R.H.S.	*Transactions of the Royal Historical Society*

I
General Introduction

In the course of the last decade the work of continental scholars has demonstrated beyond reasonable doubt that the emergence of effective parliamentary institutions during the later Middle Ages was a common feature of the countries comprising Latin Christendom. It was not, as has been previously thought, confined primarily to England and to a lesser extent to Aragon, the Netherlands, and Sweden but rather it was a general European development. In summing up the work of continental historians since the Second World War, Professor Myers has drawn this picture of the representative institutions of medieval Europe. 'They first emerge clearly towards the end of the twelfth century in the Spanish kingdom of Léon, in the thirteenth century in Castile, Aragon (and also Catalonia and Valencia), Portugal, Sicily, in the Empire and some of its constituent states such as Brandenburg and Austria, England and Ireland. In the fourteenth century parliaments developed in France (in many of the provinces and for a large part of the realm), the Netherlands, Scotland, more of the German states and Hungary, in the fifteenth century representative estates appeared in Denmark, Sweden and Poland.'[1] During the fourteenth and fifteenth centuries the majority of these parliaments were conceived of as being representative of the whole population of the state and embraced in any event those elements that mattered in the political life of the country. It was only later that the majority of them degenerated into strongholds of minorities of one kind or another.

Contrary to older views concerning the history of the parliament of England, the majority of these European sister-parliaments were also effective political institutions during the later Middle Ages. It was not the exception but rather the rule amongst them to possess that multiplicity of functions which has sometimes been seen as the distinguishing feature of the English parliament. In their heyday the majority of these European parliaments participated in legislation, in taxation, and in the rendering of justice as a court of law. They too developed their rights as the body which might grant or deny extraordinary taxes to the Crown and they too used this right

[1] A. R. Myers, 'The Parliaments of Europe and the Age of the Estates', *History* 60 (1975), 16. For further references and a full discussion see A. R. Myers, *Parliaments and Estates in Europe to 1789* (London, 1975). An interesting introduction to this subject is found in R. B. Lord, 'The Parliaments of the Middle Ages and the Early Modern Period', *Catholic Historical Review* 16 (1930), 125–44.

successfully as a means of obtaining the redress of 'grievances'. At times of governmental weakness they too claimed a variety of powers and asserted their right to have a say in high matters of policy. Seen in the full European context the exception in the general trend of development towards a well established constitutional position for a representative parliament in the state, was not England but rather Capetian France.[2] In France, and to some extent also in Castile, the idea of a representative parliament appeared late, developed least, and was eclipsed the soonest. By comparison it gave a misleading impression of English developments for it has long been customary to look chiefly to France when seeking 'continental' parallels or contrasts to English developments. Hence the atypical failure of the representative idea to take roots in French soil helped to give the impression that its successful implantation in England had been an exceptional development.[3] In fact, in the matter of developing a representative parliamentary institution, it was England rather than France which was in the mainstream of European ideas between the thirteenth and the fifteenth centuries.

The explanation for the emergence and development of the English parliament drawn from the *specific* needs and conditions of the English monarchy needs therefore to be set against the fact that similar institutions embodying similar ideas emerged at about the same time in most of the other monarchies of Latin Christendom, and in often very different *specific* local circumstances. It may be necessary therefore to reconsider the significance ascribed to political expediency in our view of the development of the English parliament. The fact is that during the two centuries and ten reigns which lay between 1300 and 1500 (a period which encompassed great differences in the personalities of the Kings as well as in the nature of the political problems which they faced), there were at least 101 parliaments summoned and held in England.[4] Day-to-day political expediency might indeed have made it desirable for the King at times to summon various groups of his subjects through some form of representative process or even, and more occasionally, it might have appeared to him advantageous to meet

[2] See Myers, 'The Parliaments of Europe', pp, 14–20.

[3] For an instructive comparison see A. R. Myers, 'The English Parliament and the French Estates General in the Middle Ages', *Album Helen Maud Cam* (Louvain, 1961) (Studies Presented to the International Commission for the History of Representative and Parliamentary Institutions) II, 139–53.

[4] This excludes not only all those assemblies which were not described as parliaments, but also those which according to the records that survive did not contain a full 'representative' complement, and also those assemblies concerning which the records are ambiguous.

them all at once, yet manifestly it cannot account for the frequency and regularity of fully representative parliaments during this period. The inherent unlikeliness of a purely local and pragmatic political explanation is rendered even less credible by the need to postulate that the same necessity appears to have been felt by most of the fellow monarchs of Christendom for equally local and pragmatic reasons.

It may still be said that in the case of the especially effective English monarchy parliament 'was born of the irresistible will of the king'[5] but we can no longer regard this as comprising the whole story. Parliament also was manifestly born of and nurtured by a new climate of political ideas permeating the whole of Europe, a political phenomenon wider and more sustained than the mere administrative convenience or political expediency of the English (or any other particular) western monarchy. In order to understand more fully the development of parliament in England, we need to see it therefore in a broader context, as an institution arising in local response to the emergence of a new set of political expectations in a still homogeneous Christian Europe. In particular we need to consider more seriously than before the ideas which were held by the people themselves who came to acquire a new political status through the acceptance of representative institutions. We should note that the emergence of a system in which they came to be consulted derived in some measure from the emergence of the belief that they ought to be so consulted. For evidence of what Englishmen thought about parliament, and what general expectations it embodied for them, we must look outside the official records. It is the purpose therefore of this volume to present an edition of the one treatise about parliament (the *Modus Tenendi Parliamentum*) which was written in England during the later Middle Ages, and with it to include one or two other parliamentary items relevant to the history of the *Modus* which indicate how parliament appeared to contemporaries and how it was seen by those people who were sufficiently interested or involved in its affairs to write about it.

The amount of surviving material which indicates either what contemporaries thought about parliament or what actually happened or was discussed within a parliament is relatively small, though in fact it is far from insignificant in quantity or importance. The later Middle Ages was a period in which political debates were not much conducted in writing. As yet neither the intellectual habit, nor lay literacy were

[5] S. B. Chrimes, *English Constitutional History*, 3rd edn. (London, 1961), p. 109, and S. B. Chrimes, *English Constitutional Ideas in the Fifteenth Century* (Cambridge, 1936), p. 66.

fully adequate, and what pamphleteering or newsletter writing did exist, had a relatively small chance of surviving. Unlike the keeping of royal or ecclesiastical records it was nobody's particular job or interest to preserve such materials. Moreover parliament was a lay institution from which the church had separated itself at least on the representational level. Parliament therefore made relatively little appeal to monastic chroniclers though they might in certain cases have contact with the knights and burgesses who attended parliament.[6] Yet even if chroniclers did have a substantial interest in politics and in political arguments they tended not to be too well informed upon the technicalities of parliament and of parliamentary procedure.[7] The one exception, the famous account of Good Parliament in the *Anonimalle Chronicle,* underlines the point. It is almost certain that this account is an interpolation, perhaps from a contemporary newsletter which was incorporated into the chronicle, thus proving that there was indeed a new sort of political literature, embodying a new lay interest in parliament, outside the normal purview of the monastic chroniclers.[8]

As far as lay writers were concerned the later Middle Ages witnessed the slow emergence of two lay sub-cultures, those of the lawyers and of the citizens. It is from these two circles that our two most important texts originate. The *Modus Tenendi Parliamentum* almost certainly comes from the legal fraternity and, appropriately since the lawyers could be expected to have had a sustained interest in the theory and practice of parliament, it is the most important single treatise on parliament. For

---

[6] See A. Goodman, 'Sir Thomas Hoo and the Parliament of 1376', *B.I.H.R.* 41 (1968), 139–49. Sir Thomas Hoo, member for Bedfordshire, may have been Walsingham's source for his account of this parliament.

[7] This can be illustrated by contrasting Walsingham's account of the Good Parliament found in the *Chronicon Angliae* (R.S., 1874), 68–100 with the much better account found in the *Anonimalle Chronicle* which appears to come from a lay source.

[8] The manuscript of the *Anonimalle Chronicle* is now in the FitzWilliam Museum, Cambridge (Bradfer Lawrence Collection) B.L. 6. (see Phyllis M. Giles, 'A Handlist of the Bradfer-Lawrence Manuscripts Deposited on Loan at the FitzWilliam Museum', *Transactions of the Cambridge Bibliographical Society* 6:2. (1973), p. 88). The chronicle was edited by V. H. Galbraith, *The Anonimalle Chronicle, 1331–81* (Manchester, 1927, reptd 1970). It is possible that the original account of the Good Parliament found in this chronicle was in the form of a newsletter written in the middle of the proceedings of parliament, for it ceases to give accurate dates after 25 May 1376 (we are indebted to Professor J. S. Roskell for this suggestion). The author had an eye for detail, and an ear for direct speech. He may well claim to be, therefore, the ancestor of that long and important line of parliamentary correspondents, through whom people at home could come to identify with parliament. Another example of such newsletters finding their way into northern sources is cited by Constance M. Fraser, 'Some Durham Documents Relating to the Hilary Parliament of 1404', *B.I.H.R.* 34 (1961), 192–9.

that reason it is treated at some length in the following section.[9] For the student the significance of the *Modus* derives from the conjunction of two separate elements: the fullness of its treatment of parliament, which is unparalleled, and the fact that this treatise was purchased, owned, and thus presumably read by contemporaries from the late fourteenth century onwards. The owners of the *Modus* were lawyers, officials, and others who in one capacity or another had a practical connection with parliament. This fact alone indicates that the treatise could not have been thought of as being utterly removed from the parliaments which they actually knew. The continuing circulation of the *Modus*—both as part of the standard law-books of the later Middle Ages and as part of various collections of the laws and usages pertaining to particular communities within the realm—indicates that while some of its specific information might have become outdated, its general concept of what parliament was, its emphasis upon the representative element in parliament, remained relevant throughout the period. Did parliamentary reality come in fact to conform to the view expressed by the *Modus,* and if so did the long reading life of the treatise itself have an influence upon that outcome?[10] In any event, the *Modus* offers the student a unique insight into what knowledgeable contemporaries, expecially the important class of lawyers in the service of the Crown, could read about parliament during its formative years.

The second lay sub-culture to develop in England was that of the citizens, the merchants and administrators of the franchise towns. It was from this culture—which was slow to develop speculative writing and whose chronicles in particular are characterized by a paucity of interpretative material[11]—that the first parliamentary diary emerged towards the end of the fifteenth century. The Colchester account was a day to day report by the two burgesses who represented the town in the parliament of 1485.[12] Its chief significance lies in the manner in which it demonstrates how far parliament had developed by the end of the Middle Ages. It shows how very far the Commons in particular were from being that routine-bound, rubber-stamping, formal assembly

---

[9] Section II. Inevitably any account of the English *Modus* must deal also with the Irish version of the text which is given in the third section.

[10] See the interesting comments of G. L. Harriss in his important study, *King, Parliament and Public Finance in Medieval England to 1369* (Oxford, 1975), in particular pp. 268–9.

[11] Illustrative of the late development of an urban culture is the curious dearth of late fourteenth-century London town chroniclers. The fifteenth-century London chroniclers when they do appear seem to belong to a different tradition.

[12] Section V.

which the official records can so easily lead one to believe. It also shows another important historical element: how deeply the usage and procedures of the modern English parliament were already developed by the later Middle Ages. The account emphasizes the fact that by the end of the Middle Ages parliament had developed a recognizable pattern and a parliamentary language which links it to the Tudor and the Stuart age and even to some of the still living aspects of parliament today. The Colchester account at the very end of the period confirms as living reality the concepts, and perhaps hopes, ascribed to parliament as a representative institution and a partner in government by the author of the *Modus* at the very beginning of our period.

We should note that the diary of the Colchester burgesses is not only the earliest account to be written by members of the Commons, but is also the first account of parliament written in the English language. It has therefore a special significance for the understanding of parliament at the end of the Middle Ages. There are many phrases in the text which not only foreshadow the parliamentary usage of the seventeenth century but are indeed still with us today. 'Bills' are 'read', 'acts' are 'passed', 'questions' are 'moved' and bills are 'sent down' from the King and the Lords. These phrases indicate how well settled was the procedure of parliament and how well established was the Commons' routine within it by this time. They show something else as well; how deeply parliamentary usage is imbedded in the English language and that very close, indeed *sui generis*, relationship between the English people and their most distinctive institution, which far antedates the Elizabethan period. Overall, this parliamentary diary of 1485, written by ordinary men with no pretence whatever to be constitutional savants, reinforces the impression derived from the theoretical writings of Sir John Fortescue. That by the close of the Middle Ages parliament was too well established for its fate to be still in the balance during the Tudor period[13]

---

[13] A 'literary' account of parliament written in English is the well known description of an imaginary parliament in the 1390s which survives among the manuscripts of the B text of Piers Plowman. This is the only hostile account of the Commons of any length which has survived. It shows that parliament and the Commons were important enough in the scheme of politics at the end of the fourteenth century to be at the centre of an attack. It also reinforces the view presented by the *Modus* that parliament was a *political* assembly much engaged in debating with the magnates and the King the 'grosses busoignes' of the realm. The poem is found in Cambridge University Library LI. IV. 14 and in B. L. Add. 41666. It is printed in *Political Poems and Songs*, ed. T. Wright (R.S. 1859), I. 368–417; *The Vision of William Concerning Piers the Plowman, Richard the Redeles*, ed.

The *Modus* and the Colchester account are both to some extent more than merely personal expressions; the *Modus* because it came to be a part of the lawbooks, and the Colchester account because it is meant to be the conjoined report to the town's authorities. Whilst, therefore, these two texts share an element of corporate status, the Rochester item in the volume is purely private in origin representing an individual viewpoint.[14] The Rochester account concerning disputes during the parliament of 1321 describes the arguments amongst the Lords at a time when the transition from the notion of parliament as an assembly of the nobility was giving way to the concept of parliament as a representative assembly. In this description the magnates still conceive of parliament as a full and formal meeting of the baronage which can settle all disputes by the 'judgement' of peers. The appearance of the representative idea expressed in the *Modus*, written at precisely this time, and the older notion of parliament as a 'high court' of the baronage illustrates the co-existence of these two ideas in 1321. It also serves to illustrate the point that the impetus for developing the representative aspect of parliament came from social groups below the baronage.[15]

The last item in this volume contains an account of the process of 'electing' the Speaker of the parliament in 1504.[16] The significance of this account lies, firstly in the fact that this is the earliest extant report of what *actually* happened in the course of the formal process of electing and presenting the most important official of the Commons, as opposed to the highly stereotyped version entered in the rolls of parliament. Secondly the report gives, or at any rate purports to give, for the first time the actual words used by a Speaker-elect in his customary 'protestation' and of the responses of the King and the Chancellor. Thirdly it offers a rare chance of comparing the formalized account on the rolls of parliament with an extraneous report of a procedural

W. W. Skeat, (Oxford, 1886), I. 603–28 (627–8); *Mum and the Sothsegger*, ed. Mabel Day and Robert Steele, Early English Text Society (Oxford, 1936), pp. 23–6. See also Helen. M. Cam, 'The Relation of English Members of Parliament to their Constituencies in the Fourteenth Century: a Neglected Text', *Liberties and Communities in Medieval England* (London, 1963), pp. 230–1.

[14] Section IV.

[15] Much of the significance of the *Modus* lies in its insistence upon the importance of the middle elements of society, i.e. the clerics, knights, and burgesses. We should note that it was in the middle years of Edward II's reign that the responsibility for the running of parliament was passing to the higher chancery clerks.

[16] Section VI.

exchange showing how far the actual words may on occasion have differed from the identical formula repeated by the Chancery clerks in the rolls. It adds, as the other reports in this volume add, a glimpse of the living and human institution behind the gothic formularity of the late medieval rolls of parliament. In adding a little of the human and practical reality to the rolls' description of the unvarying formulae dictated by long evolved principles, this external account balances the official version in a perhaps surprising way. In reading the official words of the Speaker's protestation in the rolls of parliament, there emerges a picture of a rather stern encounter between the King and the Speaker of the Commons. We hear the Speaker politely but firmly reminding the King that he represents the powerful privileges of the Commons of the realm in parliament assembled who might, through his mouth, speak freely to the King. This report of what actually was said on one such occasion shows that the words spoken at least by this particular Speaker were a good deal more muted and circumspect *almost* to the point of complete dilution of the message. If we may picture the scene through the words used, they appear to have been spoken in a much more supine pose by the worthy Speaker, knees at least half bended, than the words officially entered on the rolls would suggest. The principles are understood, they can be duly recorded in the time honoured words in the rolls; they need not be emphasized by this particular Speaker as a verbal irritant for this particular King.

This account shows finally in a poignantly practical form that at the end of the Middle Ages, after more than a century and half of development and co-habitation between the monarchy and the Commons, in a normal parliament held in normal times, the rule was co-operation and not confrontation between the King, the Lords and the Commons. It was this kind of good sense and pragmatic maturity which, by this time, had set the parliament of England on a course vastly and fatefully different from those of all the other formerly sister institutions of the continent.

II

Modus Tenendi Parliamentum

I. THE AGE OF THE *MODUS*

(1)

Among historians, views on the *Modus Tenendi Parliamentum* have generally been of two main kinds. From the time of Stubbs one school of historians has regarded the *Modus* as a document of little historical value, at best a historical curiosity, to be put in much the same category as the spurious *Mirror of Justices*. A second and increasingly influential school of thought has suggested that the *Modus* is of some value, that it contains information relevant to, and of importance for the parliaments of the later Middle Ages, but that it is to be regarded chiefly and perhaps wholly within a political context. Among studies of this kind, the fullest and most complete is still that by Miss Clarke.[1]

Whatever their viewpoint, however, all previous studies of the *Modus* have been based largely upon particular conceptions either of the role of parliament, or of the political purpose of the work. In this context it is particularly useful to consider the use of the *Modus* in the fifteenth and sixteenth centuries, the period of its greatest vogue, and to examine the numerous fifteenth- and sixteenth-century codices in which the *Modus* survives, and which provide the firmest evidence as to the nature of the work.[2] The most cursory examination of these codices reveals at the outset the strength of the medieval manuscript tradition, a tradition totally at variance for example with that of the spurious *Mirror of Justices* which survives only in a single copy.[3] The numerous medieval copies of the *Modus*, to say nothing of the later transcripts, reveal in fact that the work was widely distributed, and therefore presumably regarded as being of some consequence during the later Middle Ages.

A detailed examination of the codices reveals, moreover, that as

[1] *Medieval Representation and Consent* (London, 1936, reptd New York, 1964) (cited as Clarke). See also the valuable articles by V. H. Galbraith, 'The *Modus Tenendi Parliamentum*', *Journal of the Warburg and Courtauld Institutes* 16 (1953), 81–99, and J. S. Roskell, 'A Consideration of Certain Aspects and Problems of the English *Modus Tenendi Parliamentum*', *B.J.R.L.* 50 (1968), 411–42, Stubbs described the *Modus* as 'worthless', but he printed excerpts in his *Select Charters and Other Illustrations of English Constitutional History*, edns 1–8 (1870–1905); reptd in 9th edn. by H. W. C. Davis (Oxford, 1929), pp. 500–6. G. T. Lapsley referred to the *Modus* as 'this *ignis fatuus* of parliamentary history' in his article on 'The Interpretation of the Statute of York', *E.H.R.* 56 (1941), 22–49, 411–46.

[2] For an examination of the codices see N. Pronay and J. Taylor, 'The Use of the *Modus Tenendi Parliamentum* in the Middle Ages', *B.I.H.R.* 47 (1974), 11–23.

[3] *The Mirror of Justices*, ed. W. J. Whittaker, Selden Soc. vii (1895). All printed copies of the *Mirror* derive from a fourteenth-century manuscript, Corpus Christi College, Cambridge, 258.

regards its use the treatise must be viewed not against a political but rather against a legal background. Almost invariably the *Modus* is found as part of a legal codex; rarely is it found as an isolated text.[4] The codices in which the *Modus* is discovered can be shown to have been manufactured for lawyers for everyday use in the courts. These codices served a completely practical purpose, and were used by lawyers who practised in the field of the Common Law, as well as by lawyers involved in the procedure of the Courts of Chivalry and Claims. The fifteenth-century owners of the codices in which the copies of the *Modus* are found were lawyers, magnates, and members of baronial councils. In addition copies of the *Modus* were owned by borough corporations, by the Speaker of parliament, and by the clerk of parliament. Apart from the one abortive attempt in Ireland, there is no evidence that during the Middle Ages the *Modus* was ever used in a political context, or quoted in the field of political controversy.[5] Indeed the *Modus* became a controversial document in England only in the late sixteenth and early seventeenth centuries.[6] The *Modus Tenendi Parliamentum*, as its use in the fifteenth century clearly shows, was in its origins a parliamentary treatise or manual, written it appears principally for the use of lawyers, and incorporated by them in their working libraries. To understand its form and purpose we must look at the nature of English legal literature between the time of Bracton and the 1340s.

(ii)

Towards the end of the thirteenth century a new kind of legal literature came to succeed the works of Bracton and Hengham in England. This new kind of literature has been called 'the minor treatises', though it might perhaps more accurately be termed the law manuals or technical treatises.[7] The distinctive feature of these treatises was not only their

---

[4] The exceptions where the *Modus* is found apart from a legal codex are (1) MS. 163 in the Beinecke Rare Book Library at Yale University where the *Modus* (A recension) appears together with a draft of the Protestation of the Speaker in what seems to be a volume of family miscellanea, see p. 197; (2) Bodleian Library Rawlinson C. 398 where the (B) recension of the *Modus* appears as part of a collection of extraneous legal material collected by Sir John Fortescue whose scholarly interests extended to legal systems other than the Common Law; (3) A manuscript in the Newberry Library, Chicago, drawn to our attention by David M. Sills since the completion of this edition.

[5] For an account of the Irish *Modus* see pp. 117–52.   [6] See pp. 55–9.

[7] On the 'minor treatises' see T. F. T. Plucknett, *Early English Legal Literature* (Cambridge, 1958), ch. V.; *Radulphi de Hengham Summae*, ed. W. H. Dunham (Cambridge, 1932); for the history of one particular treatise see *De Prerogativa Regis*, ed. S. E. Thorne (New Haven and London, 1949).

brevity in comparison with the works of the preceding epoch, but more significantly the fact that they dealt with specific courts or specific legal tastes and did not aim to give a comprehensive description of the law as a whole. Their authors took for granted the great *Summae* of the twelfth and thirteenth centuries, and did not seek to emulate the scholarly width and structured logic of the great expositions of the principles of law. Though in depth of scholarship they bear no comparison with the *Summae*, these treatises were undoubtedly of greater practical value to the literate but unscholarly practitioners of law who earned their living as pleaders of the courts.

The development which changed the legal profession, and which eventually came to have an effect upon the law itself, that is to say the change from a technically ecclesiastical to a lay profession organized along the lines of a guild, had itself much to do with the appearance of this new kind of 'technical literature'.[8] By the end of the thirteenth century the legal profession had gained the right of training its own members, and eventually they were given the monopoly of the courts. The 'technical treatises' belong to this period, that is to say to the end of the thirteenth and to the early fourteenth century. The last 'ecclesiastical' Chief Justice, Hengham, was also the last composer of the *Summae*. Despite all the claims made later for the 'universities' of the Inns of Court, even in the fifteenth century which was the golden age of the Inns, they did not give that type of scholarly education which an appreciation of the *Summae* would have required.[9] In the early part of the fourteenth century, the period of the technical treatises, the training was even less extensive than it was to become later. It is clear therefore that at this time unpretentious practical manuals on such subjects as *Modus Componendi Brevia*, *Modus Levandi Finem*, or *Modus Tenendi Curiam Baronis* would have found a ready market among the practitioners of law.[10]

To look at this development in general terms it can be said that the disappearance of a scholarly breadth of vision from amongst the

---

[8] For the early development of the legal profession see T. F. T. Plucknett, *A Concise History of the Common Law*, 5th edn. (London, 1956), pp. 215–51.

[9] The early history of the Inns of Court is very obscure, T. F. T. Plucknett, 'Inns of Court', *Encyclopaedia Britannica*, XII (1970), 267–9, W. Blake Odgers, 'Sketch of the History of the Four Inns of Court', in *Essays in Legal History*, ed. Paul Vinogradoff (London, 1913).

[10] See the comments of G. D. G. Hall on the *Modus Componendi Brevia* in *Early Registers of Writs*, ed. Elsa de Haas and G. D. G. Hall, Selden Soc. lxxxvii (1970), pp. cxxxviii–cxxix.

lawyers has its parallels in the world of Canon and Civil Law, for the work of the Glossators and the school of Practical Jurists at the universities reveals essentially the same factors at work that we can see in the case of the 'technical treatises'. In most fields of medieval thought, after the great debates of the twelfth and thirteenth centuries the fundamental tenets had been established, and some kind of agreed synthesis had been achieved. The next generation had therefore no need to reopen these questions. Their task was rather to work out the details, and to add new 'chapters' when some fresh development, such as the appearance of a new court, made this necessary. The Middle Ages were moreover, in the textual as in the governmental field, innocent of the notion of 'supercession', and no difficulty was experienced over the fact that a great *Summa,* or a minor treatise, was out of date on a few points of detail. The whole system was based, in fact, on a combination of a veneration of 'great texts' and a considerable flexibility in interpretation, which often resulted in startling departures from the spirit of the text.

The manuals of the late thirteenth and early fourteenth centuries were therefore an expression both of the appearance of a new lay professional class and of the current state of medieval thought. During the late thirteenth and early fourteenth centuries manuals of every description were produced ranging from those on estate management, accounting, and banking, to others on various aspects of the Common Law or Chivalry. All were concerned with providing guidance to the appropriate class of practitioner. With this in mind we can say that they were strictly practical guides avoiding all pretence to scholarship. They are a concrete illustration of the transition from a legal system based on fundamental dictums into one based upon detailed legislation and technical rules.

It is against the background of this technical literature that we must consider the *Modus Tenendi Parliamentum.* The *Modus* is written in the form of a technical treatise, and just as the *Modus Tenendi Curiam Baronis* was a guide to the baronial court, so the *Modus Tenendi Parliamentum* was a guide to the last great council of the realm to be defined, the 'court of parliament'. We should note that before the *Modus* parliamentary literature had been practically non-existent. In *Fleta* (*c.* 1290), a treatise which is a good example of the transition from *Summa* to manual, in that it is constructed along the lines of the *Summa* though in terminology and style it was designed to appeal more to the practising lawyer than to the scholar, we find the first reference to parliament: 'Habet enim

Rex curiam suam in consilio suo, in parliamentis suis, presentibus prelatis, comitibus, baronibus, proceribus et aliis viris peritis. . . .'[11] In *Fleta*, however, the reference is very much an after-thought and parliament is clearly seen as a court which would be of little interest to practitioners. We should note in this connection that ten years earlier Hengham's *Summae* did not mention parliament at all.

Both in England and France, however, the early fourteenth century was an important period of parliamentary development, and one likely to produce a legal literature of parliament. In France there was produced about 1330, the *Stilus Curie Parlamenti*, an authoritative guide to the French parlement, written by Guillaume du Breuil, proctor of Edward II at the court of the King of France in 1314 and 1318.[12] The *Stilus* was written in the same manner, and for much the same reasons as the *Modus Tenendi Parliamentum* was written in England, that is to say as a parliamentary manual, and a general guide to parliamentary procedure. In contrasting the *Modus* with its French counterpart, the *Stilus Curie Parlamenti*, we should note that both belong to much the same period, and both have a similar manuscript tradition. The *Stilus* however undoubtedly contains a fuller and more detailed account of parliamentary procedure than does the English *Modus*, but the explanation of this is to be discovered in the fact that it found a better author, and also that during this period the French parlement itself was more highly developed than its English counterpart.[13]

We should note also in connection with the *Modus Tenendi Parliamentum* (and the other treatises of which it is a representative member) that there was the same absence of any notion of revision which has been mentioned already in connection with the *Summae* of the thirteenth century. The *Modus* was not revised.[14] Having absorbed the rules of parliament, as of any court, the practitioner was expected to keep in touch with the practical work of the courts. Because of

---

[11] *Fleta*, ed. H. G. Richardson and G. O. Sayles, Selden Soc. lxxii (1953), Lib. II. cap. 2. p. 109. See the comments of F. Pollock and F. W. Maitland, 'the so-called *Fleta* is little better than an ill-arranged epitome . . .' *The History of English Law Before the Time of Edward I* (Cambridge, 1968) I, 210. Its authorship is discussed by N. Denholm-Young, 'Who wrote Fleta?', *Collected Papers of N. Denholm-Young* (University of Wales Press, Cardiff, 1969), pp. 187–98.

[12] *Guillaume du Breuil, Stilus Curie Parlamenti*, ed. F. Aubert, Collection de textes pour servir à l'étude et à l'enseignment de l'histoire (Paris, 1909).

[13] The *Stilus* survives in some twenty-two manuscripts of which six belong to the fourteenth century, and none are earlier than 1366. *Ibid.*, pp. xviii–xlvii.

[14] Some manuscripts of the second recension omit certain passages, possibly because these parts of the text did not accord with the prevailing situation. J. Taylor, 'The Manuscripts of the *Modus Tenendi Parliamentum*', *E.H.R.* 83 (1968), 681–2.

political exigencies parliament developed more rapidly and along a more unpredictable course than did most of the other courts of law. Yet as far as the practising lawyers were concerned, whether they offered professional advice to peers or made pleas before parliament, the essential principles of parliament did not change. The *Modus Tenendi Parliamentum* expressed these principles, and hence the tract remained an item in the 'working libraries' of lawyers despite the fact that the statements of the *Modus* on certain matters, for example on clerical representation, bore little resemblance to contemporary practice after the reign of Edward III.[15] Only when fundamental changes took place in the Tudor period was the *Modus* finally superseded as a manual of authority for parliament, and even then its influence was to endure for a further century over the form of parliamentary guides.[16]

(III)

The *Modus* appears to belong therefore to a particular type of legal literature written in the early part of the fourteenth century. Certainly the codices in which it is found testify to the fact that it was used by, and possibly written by lawyers. Its terminology is completely legal. To understand its character fully, however, some comment should be made about certain of the codices in which the *Modus* is found. Most copies of the second recension of the *Modus* which is known as (A) are a part, or were once a part of the 'working libraries' of lawyers.[17] These 'working libraries' were essentially collections of treatises, tables, statutes, formularies, etc., which were relevant to the professional needs of practitioners, and which were gathered together into one, or more usually two, volumes.[18] The second recension of the *Modus* is almost always found as a part of such a collection, i.e. as part of a lawyer's library. These collections of legal materials may be further distinguished as Part I and Part II volumes. A Part I volume, or collection of *Vetera*

---

[15] See pp. 41–3.   [16] See pp. 52–5.

[17] On the versions of the *Modus* see pp. 59–63, and Appendix IV. For a detailed analysis of the texts, Taylor, 'The Manuscripts of the *Modus Tenendi Parliamentum*'. There are two principal recensions of the text which are known as (A) and (B). The two recensions contain not only textual differences, but represent differences in provenance and use. The (A) recension is found only in codices which were manufactured for the use of common lawyers; the (B) recension is found in codices which were compiled to facilitate proceedings in which the higher nobility only were involved.

[18] There is evidence of ownership in several of the codices which contain the (A) recension of the *Modus*. MS. 9 in the Free Library of Philadelphia belonged, for example, to the Molyneux family of Nottingham. On the difficulty of identifying the precise member of this family in the fifteenth century see *Readings and Moots at the Inns of Court in the Fifteenth Century*, ed. S. E. Thorne, Selden Soc. lxxi (1954), pp. xxxix–xl.

Statuta, contained treatises and statutes up to the end of Edward II's reign.[19] A Part II volume, or collection of *Nova Statuta,* contained legislation from the beginning of Edward III's reign up to the date of the purchase of the volume. Occasionally a single volume might contain the items both of Part I and Part II. None the less of whatever kind they were, all such volumes formed a part or the whole of the 'working libraries' of lawyers during the later Middle Ages. We should note that the *Modus* is found in every kind of collection of this type.

As regards these different kinds of collections there were good reasons for the division into two volumes. Legislation up to the end of Edward II's reign consisted of statutes such as Magna Carta in its 1297 reissue, the Statutes of Winchester, Westminster I and II, which laid down the basic principles of the law. Upon these statutes had been raised the whole immense edifice of the Common Law. They were not subject to the rule that parliament could revoke by an Act any previous Act of parliament. Such legislation together with supplementary items formed the contents of the Part I volumes of the lawyers' libraries. The contents of the Part II volumes were somewhat different, for although a few further statutes of the same basic character were made such as, for example, the Statute of Treasons of 1352, the vast majority of Edward III's legislation, like that of his successors, was to be of a more limited and less fundamental kind. The principal reason for this was that Edward I working in conjunction with the great Hengham himself had already laid down the principles of English law, as surely as Aquinas or Innocent III had fixed the principles of medieval theology or canon law.

Though the *Modus* is found in other codices and in other contexts a main tradition associates it therefore with these 'working libraries' of practitioners of the Common Law. In the fifteenth century the production of such 'working libraries' appears to have become a flourishing concern.[20] From the copies that survive it appears likely that a lawyer ordered his codex or volume to meet his own requirements.[21] Anyone who wished to specialize in conveyancing, for

---

[19] On the complicated question of the fundamental 'legislation' before Edward III see T. F. T. Plucknett, *Statutes and their Interpretation in the First Half of the Fourteenth Century* (Cambridge, 1922).

[20] Pronay and Taylor, 'The Use of the *Modus*', p. 15.

[21] This can be illustrated in the case of Cotton Vespasian B. vii, which contains the *Modus.* It appears to have been made for a lawyer who hoped to specialize in work relating to the councils of magnates and perhaps obtain a law office under the crown. Pronay and Taylor, 'The Use of the *Modus*', pp. 13–14.

example, would have had included in his codex all the treatises and acts relating to that subject, but only the major pieces of legislation on other topics. The extent of the lawyer's resources might well have determined the quality of the parchment and binding, and whether the work was illuminated or not. For our purposes the point to note is that the *Modus* formed a part of such 'libraries'. The inclusion of the *Modus* in these volumes, as well as in other legal collections, and in volumes pertaining in part to the Courts of Chivalry and Claims is the surest indication of its legal character, and of its use by lawyers during the later Middle Ages.

The use of the *Modus* by the practitioners in the common law courts did not exhaust its use as a legal treatise. The earliest recension of the *Modus* known as (B) is almost always found as a part of a codex which formed part of the corpus of the developing law of chivalry.[22] The basic codex of this type (Cotton Nero D vi) was possibly compiled for Thomas Mowbray during his tenure of the office of earl marshal in the 1380s, but in the course of the fifteenth and sixteenth centuries other codices of a similar type were manufactured on a not insubstantial scale. These volumes were probably meant to be used as direct authorities in the same manner as the volumes of *Nova* and *Vetera Statuta*. In these codices, which were primarily of value to members of the higher nobility and their legal officers, the *Modus* appears to have been included as a manual of authority which could be referred to on parliamentary matters, and which might be cited before assemblies such as the Court of Claims.[23] In certain cases items in this codex would appear to have been of some interest to officials in the lord chamberlain's office for supplementary material relating to court etiquette appears in certain of the later codices.[24]

Although the *Modus* survives basically in two recensions which were compiled for two different courts, a third version known as (C) appears to have been a lay version of the *Modus,* and is found associated with legalistic though non-professional material. This version is found in a fourteenth-century lay cartulary, a law book belonging to Durham priory, a fifteenth-century register of writs, and a collection of legal

---

[22] For the items in this codex see note at the end of this section.

[23] For a more detailed discussion of the use of the (B) version see Pronay and Taylor, pp. 16–19.

[24] An example of this is Pepysian MS. 2516, a sixteenth-century codex, which contains a variety of items relating to court etiquette, and to the offices of the Queen's household.

material belonging to a bencher of the Inner Temple. This version only was translated into French.[25]

The manuscript tradition of the text suggests therefore that the *Modus* was a legal treatise in the possession of various branches of the legal profession. It appears moreover to belong to that variety of legal treatise which was incorporated not only into the volumes of *Vetera* and *Nova Statuta,* but also into cartularies, registers of writs, and municipal by-laws.

Note on the Codex in which the (B) recension is found

The earliest known recension of the *Modus* is always found in a standard form of codex which contains the following items:

1. The coronation order of Richard II.
2. The order of precedence among peers at the coronation of Richard II.
3. The treatise on the office of the Marshal/Constable.[26]
4. The Ordinances of 1385 promulgated by the Steward.

As well as these items it may contain a selection of the following:

1. Treatises on the rules of judicial combat such as the *Modus Faciendi Duellum.*
2. Ordinances governing precedents and rights at royal funerals.
3. The *Chronica Bona et compendiosa* which was used for its information on royal coronations.
4. The Household Ordinances of Edward II.
5. Regulations relating to the coronation procedures and the funerals of the kings of France.
6. Items relating to other aspects of chivalry such as Regulations of the Order of the Garter.

It should be noted that the Household Ordinances of Edward II are found only in those codices which contain the (B) recension of the *Modus.*[27] Also found among these items is a detailed itinerary of Edward

---

[25] See Appendix IV, 'Minor Versions of the English *Modus*'.

[26] For a valuable comment on the statement of the rights of the Marshal (found in those codices which contain the (A) recension) and the treatise on the offices of the Marshal and Constable (found in those codices which contain the (B) recension) see Michael Prestwich, *War, Politics, and Finance under Edward I* (Faber, 1972), p. 263. n. 3.

[27] See T. F. Tout, *The Place of the Reign of Edward II in English History,* 2nd edn. (Manchester, 1936), pp. 241–84.

I's movements during the Scottish campaign of 1296, which was written in French by someone who was with him.[28]

2. PROBLEMS OF THE *MODUS*

Before considering what the *Modus* says about parliament certain of the problems connected with this work must first be examined. Among other matters we must know of what stage of parliamentary history the author is writing. We must examine the hypothesis that the *Modus* was in origin a political pamphlet of a highly biased and controversial kind. Finally we must consider the evidence for the authorship of the treatise.

(1)

As regards the date of the *Modus* written in England, an increasing weight of evidence would assign the earliest version of the Latin *Modus* to a date in Edward II's reign, and possibly to a period in the early 1320s.[29] One important reason for dating the *Modus* to the early part of the fourteenth century is that the general description of parliament in that treatise accords more with the conditions of the earlier than of the later fourteenth century. 'The arrangement of the members of parliament into six *gradus* . . . would be a hopeless anachronism by the

[28] E. L. G. Stones and Margaret N. Blount, 'The Surrender of King John of Scotland to Edward I in 1296. Some New Evidence', *B.I.H.R.* 48 (1975), 94–106. It may be, as Professor Stones has suggested, that Edward's itinerary was included because it was by far the best guide to Scotland that was available.

[29] The principal works on the date of the *Modus* are W. A. Morris, 'The Date of the *Modus Tenendi Parliamentum*', *E.H.R.* 49 (1934), 407–22, who argued for a date in 1321; Clarke, pp. 153, 202, 367, who dated the *Modus* 1322; Galbraith, 'The *Modus Tenendi Parliamentum*', p. 84, who suggested 1316–24 as the probable time of compilation. On the other hand J. H. Round argued that the mention of the earl marshal, a title not conferred until 1386, was proof that the *Modus* belonged to the reign of Richard II, *Commune of London* (London, 1899), pp. 302 ff. Round's views are no longer accepted, and scholars have demonstrated that the title earl marshal was used in the reign of Edward II, Clarke, pp. 353–5; Morris, p. 408. Other dates have been given for the composition of the *Modus*, but apart from Round, whose views have been stated, they are based upon little definite evidence. T. F. Tout, *Chapters in the Administrative History of Medieval England* (Manchester, 1928), III. 139, n. 2. dated the work to a period soon after 1340. H. G. Richardson in *History* 22 (1937), 66–9; *Irish Historical Studies* 3 (1942), 137 ff., and H. G. Richardson and G. O. Sayles, *The Irish Parliament in the Middle Ages* (Philadelphia and Oxford, 1952), p. 137, have argued for the priority of the Irish version, and dated both the Irish and English *Modus* to the reign of Richard II. Their arguments which are brief, and based mainly upon the tariff of amercements set out in the *Modus*, have been fully answered by Galbraith, pp. 95–9, who has convincingly demonstrated the priority of the English over the Irish text. It is possible, none the less, that the Irish version, which was taken from an English original, was compiled during the reign of Richard II. See p. 121.

end of Edward II's reign'.[30] There is no mention in the *Modus* of the office of the Speaker, or of intercommuning between Lords and Commons, all of which parliamentary developments belong to the period after 1330.

The work of scholars over the last thirty years suggests that the tract belongs in fact to the early 1320s, and at the outside limits to the period 1316–24.[31] Here we need notice only some of the principal arguments which have been used to support this general conclusion. In the first place the emphasis in the *Modus* on the attendance of clerical proctors in parliament and by a summons supplementary to the *praemunientes* clause suggests a time near the period 1311–22 when this question was under review.[32] Clerical proctors ceased to attend parliament after 1330, though the clergy were on occasion as in the 1390s represented in parliament by lay proctors.[33] The *Modus* says that the rolls of parliament were to be delivered to the Treasury, but we know in fact that between 1322 and 1330, the custody of the rolls passed from the Treasury to the Chancery.[34] The rolls are stated to be ten inches wide as they were in the reign of Edward II.[35] In the *Modus* the wages of the representatives are shown to be variable, though they were in fact fixed after 1327.[36]

The *Modus* exists in two recensions which are known as (A) and (B). As already mentioned the (A) recension of the *Modus* is always found as a part of the 'working libraries' of lawyers;[37] the (B) recension is

---

[30] Galbraith, p. 84, n. 2.

[31] See Galbraith, p. 84; G. P. Cuttino, 'A Reconsideration of the *Modus Tenendi Parliamentum*', *The Forward Movement of the Fourteenth Century*, ed. F. L. Utley (Columbus, 1961), p. 33.

[32] This is fully dealt with by Clarke, pp. 125–53, and Morris, pp. 414–16.

[33] B. Wilkinson, *Constitutional History of Medieval England, 1216–1399* (London, 1958), III. 381. note 5; E. C. Lowry, 'Clerical Proctors in Parliament and Knights of the Shire 1280–1374', *E.H.R.* 48 (1933), 443–55.

[34] Clarke, pp. 211–13; Galbraith, p. 88.

[35] Clarke, p. 215; Galbraith, p. 88.

[36] *Modus Tenendi Parliamentum*, ed. T. D. Hardy (London Record Commission, 1846), pp. vii–x, xxviii–xxix; Morris, p. 417. The *Modus* appears to give maximum, and perhaps to some extent hypothetical figures for payment of members. The manuscripts of (A), which appears to be the later text, states that *now* they are to be paid four shillings a day. This rate was fixed in 1327, Helen Cam, *Liberties and Communities in Medieval England* (London, 1963), p. 237.

[37] There are eleven surviving Latin manuscripts of (A). These are B.L. Vespasian B. vii, Nero C. i., Lansdowne 522, Julius B. iv., Add. 24079; Bodleian Library, Oriel 46; Holkham Hall, 232; Boston, Harvard Law Library, 21, 29–30; Pennsylvania, Free Library of Philadelphia, Rare Book Collection 9; Yale University, Beinecke Rare Book and Manuscript Libr. 163. To these add now Newberry MS. 32.1.

found in chivalric codices, which were compiled to facilitate proceedings in which the higher nobility only were involved.[38] In both cases the *Modus* was regarded as an authoritative text and was copied unchanged, as were other venerable tracts of the Common Law and the law of Arms respectively. In addition to these two recensions, other minor versions were compiled at a later date from the texts of (A) and (B). One of these, known as (C), appears to have been a kind of lay version of the *Modus*, which endeavoured to reproduce the gist of both standard versions.[39] It is the only version which was translated into French.[40] At a later date a copy of the *Modus* found in the House of Lords Journals, which precedes the Journals for 1510, was a copy constructed from (A) and (B).[41]

Of the two main recensions there is some evidence to suggest that (B) contains the earlier text. The reference in (B) to the chamberlain among the official members of the King's Council appears to refer to Hugh Despenser the younger who was chamberlain from 1318 until his banishment in August 1321.[42] The paragraph *Concerning Difficult Cases and Decisions* in the (B) recension which contains the famous proposal for a committee of twenty-five, mentions disputes between parliament, the King, and certain magnates. This has sometimes been taken as referring to conditions in the mid-summer of 1321 when parliament met to banish the Despensers who were supported by the King. In the paragraph *Concerning the Barons of the Ports* all the manuscripts of the (B) recension open with the phrase 'the King is bound to send his writs to the warden of the Cinque Ports', and not with the phrase found in the other opening paragraphs of the *Modus* and also in (A), 'the King used

[38] There are eight Latin manuscripts of the (B) text. In addition to Bibliothèque Nationale, Paris Lat 6049, these are B.L. Nero. D. vi., Domitian A. xviii., Add. 32097, Add. 29901, Vitellius C. iv., Tiberius E. viii. Bodleian Library, Rawlinson C. 398 is not a codex.

[39] See Appendix IV. The text of (C) is found in London, Inner Temple, Petyt 511; California, Huntington Library, E.L. 35. B. 61; Durham, Dean and Chapter, Registrum I, Part I; Dublin, Trinity College, E.4.5.

[40] The French version is found in B.L. Add. 49359 (Courtenay Cartulary), and the Finch-Hatton Roll (Northampton Record Society). It was printed by T. D. Hardy, *Archaeological Journal* 19 (1862), 259 ff. For its influence on the Irish version see pp. 120–1.

[41] See Appendix IV. Professor A. F. Pollard first drew attention to this copy in his paper, 'The Authenticity of the "Lords' Journals" in the Sixteenth Century', *T.R.H.S.* 3rd ser. 8 (1914), 36–7. As he wrote, 'the fact that a clerk of the Parliaments thought it incumbent upon him in 1510 to prefix to his record the *Modus* . . . does show that it was considered authoritative on parliamentary procedure in Tudor times'. See also G. R. Elton, 'The Early Journals of the House of Lords', *E.H.R.* 89 (1974), 505.

[42] Morris, p. 418; Clarke, pp. 204–5.

to (*solebat*) send his writs'.[43] The phraseology in (B) may well derive from the fact that the barons of the Cinque Ports were not summoned to parliament regularly until 1322,[44] and at the time of writing the word *solebat* could not appropriately have been used in connection with the representation of the Cinque Ports.

A number of comments in the (B) recension appear therefore to refer to conditions in 1321.[45] However, even if this precise date be disputed, there is other evidence to suggest an early origin for the (B) recension. The (B) recension speaks of clergy being summoned to parliament as proctors of the clergy, though the attendance of clerical proctors as a group ceased after about 1322.[46] In the paragraph *Concerning Transcripts of Records* the (B) recension mentions the rolls of parliament where (A) has the roll of parliament. It is known that before 1341 there was not generally one parliament roll, and that records of parliamentary business are to be found elsewhere.[47]

(II)

We must now consider the evidence for assuming, as most earlier writers have assumed, that the *Modus* is a political pamphlet of a highly biased and incorrect kind that somehow slipped unnoticed into the corpus of English law by the reign of Richard II. Though we cannot entirely discount the possibility that the *Modus* was a political pamphlet

[43] The *solebat* phrase is of some importance in the construction of the *Modus* being used in the early paragraphs as an appeal to antiquity as opposed to the formula of the later and more contentious paragraphs which employ the expression the King ought to or is bound to.

[44] Clarke, p. 202. The first parliament they attended under Edward II was that of 1322. See also K. M. E. Murray, *The Constitutional History of the Cinque Ports* (Manchester, 1935), p. 205.

[45] The reference in paragraph XVII to the steward, the constable, and the marshal arranging for the committee of twenty-five also appears to refer to the conditions of 1321, Roskell, pp. 411–12. This section of the *Modus* was omitted from the Irish version.

[46] Where (B) speaks in the chapter on *The Summoning of the Parliament* of clergy summoned to parliament as proctors of the clergy, (A) does not specify the type of person elected. It is known that the attendance of clerical proctors as a group in parliament ceased after about 1332 though the clergy were on occasion represented by lay magnates who acted as proctors. See Wilkinson, *Constitutional History*, III. 381, n.5; Lowry, 'Clerical Proctors in Parliament', *E.H.R.* 48, (1933), 443–55; E. W. Kemp, *Counsel and Consent* (London, 1961), p. 105. An important part of Miss Clarke's book is concerned with clerical representation. See *Clerical Representation in the Modus*, below pp. 41–3.

[47] None the less it is possible that the words *rotulus* and *roluti* were interchangeable before 1341. We are grateful to the Public Record Office for information on this point. On the development of the parliament rolls see H. G. Richardson and G. O. Sayles, 'The Early Records of the English Parliaments', *B.I.H.R.* 6 (1929), 129–55. The (A) recension may also have been written before 1330. See p. 60.

in origin, for we know virtually nothing about the treatise until some fifty years after the date of its composition, the evidence such as it is, suggests that the *Modus* was originally a legal or quasi-legal treatise.

In the first place if the *Modus* was a political treatise no evidence of this has survived. It is quoted in no political controversy of Edward II's reign, nor is there any evidence that it was ever regarded as a controversial document during the Middle Ages.[48] The view that it was a political treatise, although perhaps implicit in the statements of Stubbs,[49] appears to have originated with C. Bémont in his contribution to *Mélanges Julien Havet* where he wrote of the *Modus* that apart from its procedural value, 'il prend parfois les allures d'un manifeste politique'.[50] Bémont's qualified suggestion that the *Modus* was a political treatise secured considerable acceptance, but it was a suggestion only, and Bémont's own comments came in a brief article which contained a pioneering survey of certain of the manuscripts, and no detailed analysis of the internal evidence. Bémont himself stated that he could not at that time undertake the lengthy researches necessary to sustain his suggestions.[51]

A political treatise must, however, come out of a current political situation in which it was designed to operate, and as a political treatise the message of the *Modus* is so obscure that since the time of Bémont scholars have been unable to agree to which political faction of Edward II's reign it should be ascribed. Indeed the political affiliations of the *Modus* are so uncertain that it has been assigned both to the Lancastrian faction and to other political groups. Tout, who devoted a footnote only to the treatise, appears to have been the first to describe the *Modus* as a Lancastrian tract.[52] In his footnote he limited himself to the suggestion that 'the stress laid on "peerage" and the closed character of the "baronial gradus"' were evidence of its Lancastrian character. This view of the *Modus* as a Lancastrian document, again based solely on

[48] The one possible reference to it in 1386 at the time of Richard II's absence from parliament describes it as an 'ancient statute', *Chronicon Henrici Knighton*, ed. J. R. Lumby, R.S. (1895) II. 219. Gloucester and Ely suggested to Richard at Eltham quoting 'ancient statute' that if a king withdraws himself from parliament for 40 days, then it is permitted to all and singular of them to return home.

[49] In his *Select Charters*, reptd in 9th edn. by H. W. C. Davis (Oxford, 1929), p. 500, Stubbs described the *Modus* as 'a somewhat ideal description of the constitution of parliament'.

[50] *Mélanges Julien Havet* (Paris, 1895), p. 478.

[51] *Ibid*, p. 479. Among these suggestions was one that the *Modus* was written during Richard II's reign.

[52] T. F. Tout, *Chapters in the Administrative History of Medieval England* (Manchester, 1928), III. 139. n. 2.

internal evidence, was elaborated by W. A. Morris who stated that 'the writer shows attachment to the personal interest of Thomas of Lancaster'.[53] Maude Clarke, however, writing principally from the textual evidence of the *Modus,* but with a fuller awareness of the manuscript tradition, suggested that the *Modus* was written in 1322 in order to expound and define the parliamentary theory and practice upheld by moderate men of that time.[54]

The underlying assumption that the *Modus* was a political treatise was not subject to serious examination until the work of V. H. Galbraith. His article on the *Modus* suggested that the treatise was 'a close description of procedure', 'as important in its way as the *Dialogue Concerning the Exchequer,* for the other half of our central institutions', and that it was probably the work of a Chancery clerk.[55] This attempt to free the *Modus* from a strictly political setting finds some support in Professor Roskell's suggestion of an Exchequer origin.[56] If not a 'political pamphlet' the *Modus* may be a 'procedural treatise' with a certain amount of special pleading written by someone well acquainted with parliamentary procedure.

Textual evidence alone has been unable to determine the nature of the *Modus.* An examination of the complete manuscript tradition, and particularly the codices in which the *Modus* is found gives on the other

---

[53] W. A. Morris, p. 408. The view that the *Modus* was a Lancastrian treatise has been restated by J. R. Maddicott, *Thomas of Lancaster 1307–1322* (Oxford, 1970), pp. 289–92.

[54] Clarke, p. 367. Although Miss Clarke noted the so-called association of the *Modus* with the Tract on the Steward, she did not assume from this that the *Modus* was a Lancastrian treatise. The dangers of associating the *Modus* with one particular item in the codices in which it is found is well illustrated in the case of the Tract on the Steward. Because the *Modus* is found together with this treatise in certain of the common law volumes this has sometimes been taken as an indication of the Lancastrian and political origin of the *Modus.* Yet if we examine the tradition of the *Modus* (A recension) in the common law volumes, the *Modus* is never found alone with the Tract on the Steward in the earliest volumes of *Vetera Statuta.* There it appears either by itself or with *both* the Marshal Tract and the Tract on the Steward, as in B.L. Cotton Vesp. B. VII. In the collections of legal material belonging to local corporations the *Modus* is again found by itself (Cotton Julius B. IV). It is only in certain of the later volumes of *Nova Statuta* that the *Modus* is found together with the Tract on the Steward. In one such volume, however, it is found not with the Tract on the Steward, but with the 1297 reissue of Magna Carta (Harvard Law Lib. 21).

[55] Galbraith, pp. 81–99. Although he did not himself subject the *Modus* to a detailed examination A. F. Pollard in his *The Evolution of Parliament* (1920) described it as 'the official handbook to parliaments', p. 12. At his suggestion Miss Hodnett and Miss White produced their valuable study of the manuscripts of the *Modus,* 'The Manuscripts of the *Modus Tenendi Parliamentum*', *E.H.R.* 34 (1919), 209–24.

[56] Roskell, 'A Consideration of Certain Aspects and Problems of the English *Modus Tenendi Parliamentum*', pp. 435–42.

hand weighty evidence against its being a purely political treatise. No copy of the *Modus* has been found in association with materials other than the technical texts of the law of the land and the procedure at court. It is equally significant that no copy of the *Modus* is found in any of the collections and chronicles which preserve the records of the political crises of the fourteenth century.[57] In particular we should note that the *Modus* is not found in the collections at Canterbury or Lambeth from which our knowledge of much of the crisis of 1321 derives.[58] A full examination of the surviving texts of the *Modus* shows moreover that there is no foundation for the view which assumes that the *Modus* is exclusively associated with the Tract on the Steward, an association which has been produced as the main textual evidence of its Lancastrian and political origin.[59] On the contrary there is no hint in any of the codices of which the *Modus* forms a part, that they contained at any time, any political material whatsoever. The textual tradition of the *Modus* stands therefore in the clearest possible contrast to the manuscript tradition of all the political pamphlets, poems, and prophecies of the fourteenth century.[60]

Finally it is unlikely that a political treatise which never obtained official sanction, or the political backing of a powerful section of the community, would have been incorporated in lawyers' books by the last quarter of the fourteenth century. From what we know about the legal profession in the fourteenth century it is to say the least unlikely that they would have included a 'political pamphlet' in the corpus of law. In the fourteenth century many of the Judges, the Benchers of the Inns, and a number of the Serjeants had already been in the profession for some thirty or forty years. Through their own former colleagues and teachers there must have been a living memory stretching back at least to the reign of Edward II. The whole system of the Common Law was built around the organic and organized continuity of legal tradition and memory. The profession moreover was trained to distill legal memory in their network of precedents, and was equipped with the aide-memoire of the Year Books. In the light of this it is difficult to

[57] This militates against the view that the *Modus* might have been in origin a type of 'paper constitution'.

[58] B. Wilkinson, 'The Sherburn Indenture and the Attack on the Despensers, 1321', *E.H.R.* 63 (1948), 1–28. For a recent comment on these documents, Maddicott, pp. 270–87.

[59] See above, p. 27. n. 54.

[60] The codices in which it is found are all without exception fundamentally different in kind from those in which the political pamphlets and literature of the time have been preserved.

believe that in the small, tightly-knit, self-perpetuating community of the lawyers, who were intimately concerned with everything that went on around the Court and the Council, someone could have produced a 'political pamphlet' as an authority of the law, and secured its acceptance by *c.* 1380. Such a situation might just conceivably have occurred in the thirteenth century, before the profession had acquired the right to train its own entrants through the apprenticeship method of the Inns, but it would have been quite impossible during the reign of Edward III. The very ossification of the system, and its excessive reliance on precedents and refusal to admit new writs ruled out the emergence of any new (and even less of a doubtfully conceived) addition to its ancient and venerated corpus of authorities.

The evidence of the codices suggests therefore that during the reign of Richard II the *Modus* was one of a number of standard texts used by the legal profession. This together with the fact that the *Modus* is never found outside the law books, and the absence of any evidence of a political origin or a political use all suggest that the treatise was written for lawyers in the first instance. If the *Modus* had a legal origin, this in its turn has some light to cast upon the manuscript history of the work, a question which has always presented difficulties to students of the treatise. The fact that the earliest surviving manuscripts of the *Modus* derive from a period some fifty years after the generally accepted date of composition, might suggest to some that the circumstances of the composition of the treatise were exceptional, and set the *Modus* apart from the rest of the legal literature with which it is found. Yet had the *Modus* been conceived as a political pamphlet during the reign of Edward II, fallen into disfavour, and then been incorporated in the legal literature of Richard II's reign, its manuscript history would indeed be truly astonishing. From the point of view of legal manuscripts, however, there is nothing exceptional about the relatively long interval in time between the date of composition of the work and the date of the earliest surviving manuscripts. The majority of the manuscripts of Hengham's *Summae*, for example, derive from the early part of the fourteenth century.[61] The *Stilus Curie Parlamenti*, composed about 1330, survives in a manuscript no earlier than the late 1360s, and possibly later in point of time.[62] We need not assume therefore that the 'disappearance' of the *Modus* in Edward III's reign is necessarily to be explained in political terms. The lack of an early manuscript of the

---

[61] *Radulphi de Hengham Summae*, ed. W. H. Dunham (Cambridge, 1932), pp. lxxi–lxxviii.
[62] Ed. F. Aubert, pp. xviii–xlvii. The earliest manuscript is *c.* 1366.

Modus, like the lack of an early manuscript of the *Stilus,* is more easily explicable by the fact that we are dealing with a lawyer's codex, which stood less chance of surviving than other manuscripts. The antiquarians to whom we owe the preservation of so many sources, were less interested in retaining copies of the *Vetera* and *Nova Statuta,* than they were in preserving other manuscripts.

To conclude these comments, though evidence that the *Modus* was in origin a legal manual stops short of complete proof, its use by lawyers from the late fourteenth century onwards, the nature of the English legal tradition, as well as the complete absence of any evidence of a political use or a political purpose, all make it probable that the *Modus* was conceived for a legal purpose, and was accepted as a legal treatise throughout the Middle Ages. As evidence of its complete acceptance within legal circles, we should note that the treatise excited no controversy and no comment among the lawyers of fifteenth-century England who owned copies.[63]

(III)

The problem of the authorship of the *Modus* is one that is unlikely to be solved with complete certainty. In order to identify the author the provenance of the work must first be decided. As we have seen the *Modus* is unlikely to have been in origin a 'political tract', written that is to say in order to further the aims of one of the main baronial groupings of Edward II's reign. It is more probable that the tract originated as one of the 'minor treatises' written for the benefit of lawyers in Edward II's reign. It is not impossible, however, that the *Modus* may have originated as a type of 'procedural tract' constructed by a Chancery or Exchequer clerk, which then became incorporated in a legal tradition. Certainly to have written this treatise the author of the *Modus* must have been someone thoroughly acquainted with parliamentary practice and procedure. The bureaucracy run by the Crown was at the centre of new ideas and new thinking in the reign of Edward II, and a Chancery or Exchequer clerk with a legal training is a possible author.

High up on any list of such candidates must be William Ayreminne, a Yorkshireman, who was Keeper of the Rolls of Chancery from 1316 to 1324, and probably clerk of the parliament.[64] Ayreminne was one of that large, close-knit group of clerks from the diocese of York who were a dominant influence in the royal administration during Edward II's

---

[63] See Appendix I.   [64] Galbraith, pp. 89–93.

reign.[65] He was probably responsible for the transfer of the rolls from the Treasury to the Chancery, and was the author of the unique roll of the Lincoln parliament of 1316 which gives a more or less consecutive account of proceedings in parliament, and which anticipates the form of the parliament rolls as they emerge after 1330.[66] As Professor Cuttino has said, 'few people can have been in so strategic a position for understanding parliament or for knowing what people were thinking and saying about parliament'.[67] Indeed the author of the *Modus,* given its date, must have been in almost as central a position to the institution which he described as Richard FitzNeal was to the Exchequer in the twelfth century, both authors having an intimate knowledge of the institution whose proceedings they described.

It is not impossible, however, that the *Modus* was the work of an Exchequer clerk. If an Exchequer origin is postulated then the author of the *Modus* might well have been someone in the circle of Walter Stapeldon, treasurer of the Exchequer from April 1320 to August 1321, and a statesman whose career showed a constant concern for parliament.[68] In his circle was Master William Maldon, one of the chamberlains of the Exchequer. As Professor Roskell, who has suggested Maldon as a possible author, says: 'Formerly a public notary, he (Maldon) had been a chamberlain of the Exchequer since September 1315. He had certainly some proper experience of parliament: he had been one of the two receivers of petitions of Gascony, Wales, Ireland, and Scotland in the Lincoln parliament of January 1316, when he must have been made well aware of the adverse affects of the delayed arrival of some of the magnates and the failure of several others to appear at all. . . . More recently (since August 1320) as chamberlain of the Exchequer, Maldon had been directly associated with Stapeldon in a great overhaul of Exchequer and Treasury and other records.[69]

None the less as Professor Roskell himself remarks, the attribution of the authorship of the *Modus* to any single individual must in the end be largely a matter of conjecture.[70] All we can say with certainty is that the author was most likely a lawyer, and certainly a person well acquainted with the working of parliament.

[65] J. L. Grassi, 'William Airmyn and the Bishopric of Norwich', *E.H.R.* 70 (1955), 551–2.
[66] *Rot. Parl.* I. 350 ff. See the comments of Galbraith, p. 92, and T. F. Tout, *The Place of the Reign of Edward II in English History* (Manchester, 1936), p. 166. For a different view see Richardson and Sayles, 'The Early Records of the English Parliaments', p. 129 ff.
[67] Cuttino, p. 36.   [68] Roskell, pp. 437–8; Clarke, pp. 134–6.
[69] Roskell, p. 439.   [70] *Ibid.*, p. 441.

3. THE *MODUS* AND PARLIAMENT

(I)

What light does a legal tract written during the second half of Edward II's reign have to cast upon the nature and working of the English parliament? To start with, the form of the *Modus* must be borne in mind. It is a treatise containing a great deal of procedural information designed it seems partly as a handbook to parliament for the use of contemporary readers. Because of the manner in which it is written it does not, however, provide information on several questions to which historians today would like answers.[71] The author does not tell us, for example, what the precise relationship of the King's Council to parliament was.[72] His statements on the role of the Commons come in the paragraph, *Concerning Aids to the King* and occupy little more space than the description in the paragraph, *Concerning the Doorkeepers of Parliament.* For all his perspicacity the ability of the author of this treatise should not be overestimated. In many ways he did not possess a penetrating mind. Even for its time the information given in the treatise is not well balanced, apart from the fact that there may well be errors in the text.[73]

In addition to the form of the treatise we must remember also that the *Modus* was probably never intended to be an exact description of a particular parliament, but rather that it stated in the manner of legal tracts the lines along which parliament was to be guided. It was a statement of how a properly organized parliament ought to be held as the author understood it.[74] It is because in many cases the author of the *Modus* states what he regards as parliamentary principles, distilled from the practice of many different parliaments, that the *Modus* appears not to correspond to the practice of any one parliament during the reign of Edward II. The author clearly sought to select from previous

[71] 'What the manual of infantry training is to the young soldier, that was the thirteenth-century law tract to the lawyer. They both tell a man what to do, not why he should do it.' Percy H. Winfield, *The Chief Sources of English Legal History* (New York, 1925), pp. 268–70. We might add that they do not discuss the nature of war.

[72] On the strong professional element in the Council as described by the *Modus* see J. F. Baldwin, *The King's Council in England in the Later Middle Ages* (Oxford, 1913), pp. 70–3. See pp. 93–4.

[73] The account of the election of clerical proctors may well be the result of confusion. See pp. 41–3.

[74] For example in the paragraph concerning the representatives of the Cinque Ports the (B) recension of the *Modus* says that they *ought* to be summoned to parliament, and not that they were summoned to parliament, see p. 93.

practice those examples which he thought were most favourable to the functioning of parliament. By writing down what he regarded as the essence of parliamentary organization he would help future parliaments to function better. Yet by attempting to rationalize and codify what was a far from settled procedure he introduced to some extent an element of falsification into his work, for flexibility and a capacity to change were themselves essential features of parliament during this period.

Again as regards its contents, the *Modus* came out of a context of ideas current in Edward II's reign not all of which were destined to have a parliamentary future. Thus one of the more 'hypothetical' parts of the *Modus*, the suggestion for a committee of twenty-five to settle disputes, has certain similarities with the suggestion for a committee in the Tract on the Steward.[75] That some such notions were current in the parliaments of the early fourteenth century is likely.[76] The *Modus* is further a part of contemporary modes of thought in that it takes a static view of society and of government and institutions. The author did not have a concept of evolution and change, and was therefore badly placed for describing an institution which was in fact very much in the process of evolution at the time that he was writing. As a result he defines the rules and structure of parliament much more rigidly and finitely than someone with a more historical viewpoint would have done.

In considering how accurately the treatise reflects the practice of existing parliaments, it should also be remembered that we know relatively little about the parliaments of this early period. Much of the detail concerning procedure and organization with which the *Modus* deals is simply not recorded elsewhere. We must therefore treat the *Modus* with caution. None the less it is possible that some of its 'misstatements' are true. It is possible, for example, that the procedure described in the paragraph, *Concerning the Five Clerks*, assigning a special clerk to each of the five estates of parliament might have been tried in some of the earliest parliaments of the fourteenth century.[77] In general it may be said that some of the statements in the *Modus* on the composition of parliament have been borne out, while others stand

[75] See p. 96.
[76] There is evidence of a committee of twenty-six appointed in the Lincoln parliament of 1301, and the use of the committee of estates in 1327 is well known, Clarke, pp. 173–95.
[77] A. Redlich, *The Procedure of the House of Commons* (London 1908), I. 10. n. 4.

uncorroborated rather than disproved by contemporary evidence.[78]

Another difficulty about comparing the views of the *Modus* with parliamentary practice during the 1320s, is that to talk about 'parliamentary practice' itself in this period is misleading. We can only talk about the practice of each of the assemblies which met the King before 1327. The period when the *Modus* was written was a period of unconscious experimentation,[79] when the constituent parts of parliament varied considerably, and when the amount of information which we have about individual parliaments also varies.[80] The names used to describe assemblies composed of various representatives of sections of the community again varies to such an extent as to make it clear that there was no settled definition or constitution concerning the calling and the function of the assembly to which the King summoned certain of his subjects. When the *Modus* says, therefore, that proctors of the clergy attended parliament, we do find in fact that clerical proctors were present at certain assemblies during the opening and middle part of Edward II's reign.[81] Thus it is clear that a man closely acquainted with the assemblies of Edward II's reign, and wishing to compile a manual of this court, would have been entirely justified in assuming that a particular assembly which included clerical proctors was in fact a full and properly constituted parliament. No doubt he was aware that there had also been parliaments in recent years in which the clerical proctors had failed to appear. As a 'medieval man' our author would, however, have been used to institutions falling short of their ideals. He had little concept of the modern notion that institutions could change their basic rules through habitual usage tending away from them.

Inevitably not all the judgements of the author, many of which were in the nature of generalizations of past practice translated into rules for the future, were justified. In some cases development took a turn away from what the author anticipated. He was successful none the less in

[78] Galbraith, p. 83, n. 4.

[79] S. B. Chrimes has warned against extending the nineteenth-century notion of conscious political experimentation, a product of modern scientific ideas, to the Middle Ages i.e. 'the Lancastrian constitutional experiment', *English Constitutional Ideas in the Fifteenth Century*, pp. xvi–xix.

[80] See the list of assemblies in 'English and British Parliaments and Related Assemblies to 1832', *Handbook of British Chronology*, ed. F. M. Powicke and E. B. Fryde (London, 1961), p. 492 ff. The best account of parliament in the fourteenth century covers a slightly later period, T. F. T. Plucknett, 'Parliament, 1327–36', in *The English Government at Work, 1327–36*, ed. J. F. Willard and W. A. Morris (Cambridge, Mass., 1940), I. 82–128 (cited as Plucknett).

[81] Powicke and Fryde, pp. 513–16.

discerning many of those features of parliament which were to last. Had he not been, the *Modus* would not have become and remained a regular item in the legal manuals until Tudor times.

(II)

In considering the picture of parliament presented in this treatise we should first of all note that according to the author of the *Modus* 'parliament' is an assembly which comprises the King, the Lords, and the representatives of the various communities. He is emphatic that without the presence of these representatives there can be no 'parliament'. The point is repeatedly made that together with the King the representatives of the commonalty of the realm are the essential part of parliament. Without them there is no parliament, nor can some of the functions of parliament be discharged at all. This is a point of obvious importance yet it is one that has none the less been invested by modern scholars with a degree of revolutionary intention which on closer examination it appears not to have. What the author does is to state that of all the possible forms of assemblies in which the King may choose to meet his subjects, 'parliament' is the one in which *all* the representatives of the communities meet the King for such business as lies between them. To this kind of assembly which he calls 'parliament', the Lords are obliged to come, but their presence is not the characteristic element of the assembly. Having defined parliament in this way he can safely state that although all the Lords may be present, yet without the representative element there is no 'parliament'. Thus it follows that according to the *Modus,* parliament is the representative assembly of the kingdom, a statement possessing more semantic than constitutional significance. There can be no doubt that there were many assemblies, going back to the reign of Edward I at least, which did indeed contain all the representatives as defined by the *Modus.* There is no doubt also that there were many other assemblies which did not. All our author is claiming is that the term 'parliament' describes the fully representative kind of assembly. There can be no doubt that contemporaries must have been aware that there was some difference between the representative and the non-representative type of assembly, if only because of the number of members involved. Within at most a generation of the writing of the *Modus* the Chancery also standardized the term 'parliament' for that kind of assembly which contained all the representatives. The furthest extent to which the author's definition of parliament can be said to be a claim ahead of its time, therefore, is that it anticipated Chancery usage by a couple of decades. No more political significance need be read into it, and it was not in fact a claim to increase the share of the Commons in what by definition was their particular assembly for meeting the King.[82]

Turning now to the business of this representative assembly a similar caution should be exercised. According to the *Modus* the business of parliament is the settling of questions which are of common concern to the King, the magnates, and the commonalty. These are questions involving war and peace, the affairs of the King, Queen, and their children, and other matters 'of common concern to the kingdom', which according to the commonly accepted notions of the time involved the consent of all. In modern terminology we may say therefore that the author of the *Modus* sees parliament as a 'political assembly'.[83] Yet apart from its political business parliament deals with legal matters. Legislation 'against the defects of customary law, the law of the Courts (Common Law) and of the executive' is also an important function of this assembly. It is the business of parliament to consent not only to the clarification and changing of the law, but also to support individual pleas for justice in cases where the ordinary courts have either failed or been unable to render justice. The rendering of justice in individual cases, i.e. petitions from individuals or from individual corporations are therefore according to the *Modus* to be taken up by parliament.

We should note, however, that the functions of parliament as described by the *Modus* are not predominantly those of a court of law. Although the representatives who form the Commons take part in the legislative function of parliament by assisting in the clarification of the law they do not themselves constitute a court. The development whereby the long accepted idea of trial by peers (including the right of magnates to be tried by fellow magnates in parliament) grew into a procedure in which the Commons could themselves form and present an indictment against an individual to be tried by the Lords had not yet taken place when the *Modus* was written.[84] Nor had the procedure by

[82] At the same time it is important to note that the author assumes a corporate identity for the representatives, and in so far as they do come from all the identifiable corporate bodies below the Lords, there is a sense of a national assembly.

[83] For a view that the *grosses busoignes* of the realm were of equal interest to the King and his officers as was justice, J. G. Edwards, 'Justice in Early English Parliaments', *B.I.H.R.* 27 (1954), 41; *Historians and the Medieval English Parliament* (Glasgow, 1960), p. 18 ff.

[84] On the development of the procedure of impeachment the various articles by T. F. T. Plucknett are of particular importance, in particular, 'The Origin of Impeachment', *T.R.H.S.* 4th ser. 24 (1942), 47–71.

which the Commons would assent to a bill of attainder and thereby effectively pass judgement over individuals. Arguably it was this development culminating in the process of impeachment which gave rise by the end of the century to a new form of the concept of parliament as a high court.[85]

In any case we should not expect the author of the *Modus* who regards the Commons as the central element of parliament to view that assembly primarily as a high court, as indeed he does not. As far as parliament acting in the manner of a court was concerned, proceeding in accordance with the rules of judicial trial, that aspect of parliament was always confined to the Lords. It was for example only the Lords who at any time during the life of the medieval parliament could form themselves into a properly constituted court. It was only in the Lords that the Crown's judicial officers sat, and it was only there that the necessary procedural machinery was found for a properly conducted trial. From the point of view of the Commons therefore parliament neither was nor became during the Middle Ages a court of law. The use of the phrase 'the high court of parliament', in so far as it refers to what was actually done, refers only to the Lords. None the less in so far as it described metaphorically the highest court of the King in which all his lieges were present, the phrase has an appropriate ring.

Thus although parliament as a whole, with the Commons as an integral part, was not a law court in which trials took place, it was as the author of the *Modus* implied, a last resort for those who could not get justice through the judicial procedure of the ordinary courts. When in common justice or in common humanity within the spirit of the law a person had a good case against another man it was the function of parliament to see that justice was done. The proportion of time spent by parliament on judicial matters, i.e. responding to petitions, varied with the efficiency of the judicial system of the time. In periods of corruption, excessive legalism, or political disturbance, when the judicial system was more prone to fail those who came before it, a very great deal of parliament's time and attention would have to be given to the settling of petitions. Such a time was during the aftermath of the Barons' War. During such a period the main function of parliament in practical terms was to supplement the judicial system.[86] This should not,

[85] 'We have to note the comparatively late emergence of a distinct and explicitly formulated theory of parliament as the King's high court.' S. B. Chrimes, *English Constitutional Ideas in the Fifteenth Century* (Cambridge, 1936), p. 70.

[86] This would accord with the view of Professor Sayles, *The King's Parliament of England* (London, 1975), that in the early period of parliamentary history the dispensation of

(continued)

however, obscure the fact that there was no automatic right for bringing a case to parliament. It was the task of the receivers and triers of petitions to prevent parliament's time being spent on cases which could be dealt with by other courts, including the Council. Parliament was only the last resort. The judicial function of parliament was therefore to see that justice was not denied in particular cases where ordinary process failed. The main purpose of parliament was predominantly political in that it settled issues which required consultation and consent between the King and his lieges.

(III)

The author's views on the role of the Commons in parliament have been taken by most scholars as the crucial part of this treatise. We have already seen that the author describes parliament as that assembly which contains the Commons. This particular assembly, whose distinguishing feature is the presence of *all* the elected representatives,[87] is the assembly with whose functions and procedure he alone deals, and therefore we should remember that when he states that 'in all matters which have to be confirmed or admitted, granted or denied or done by parliament they ought to be proceeded upon by the commonalty', he does not claim a large role for the Commons in all great matters of State. All he says is that *in parliament* (which he in effect defines as the assembly which contains the elected Commons) those particular matters which are to come before a 'parliament' need to go through the Commons—as if by definition. He makes a point of stating that matters of high politics, that is to say discord between the King and some magnates or between the magnates themselves, are only to come to parliament if the King and Council think it profitable in that particular

justice was the central task of parliament. Professor Sayles does not deny, however, that 'public affairs' and 'high politics' were also prominent in the work of the King's parliament.

[87] In considering the views of the author of the *Modus* on parliament we should also recognize the existence at this time of assemblies other than parliament in which the King might consult or obtain the consent of certain of his lieges for purposes where consent was thought to be necessary. The King for example held meetings with his tenants-in-chief, formally distinguished in the course of time as Great Councils, in which matters affecting common affairs between King and magnates were settled. The King would also hold meetings with representatives of particular towns, or merchants, in which regulations relating to trade could be settled, and in which representatives might assent to making financial grants on behalf of those whom they represented. Assemblies therefore corresponding to the central idea of parliament, namely consent through representation, existed alongside parliament for at least forty years after the date of the *Modus*.

Modus Tenendi Parliamentum   39

instance. In fact the practice, and perhaps even the theory of parliament, at least from the time of the statute of York, was larger than this legalistic definition.

As regards the particular role of the Commons the author's comments occur principally in the paragraph entitled *Concerning Aids to the King*. This paragraph states that the King used not to demand aid except for an impending war, knighting his sons, or marrying his daughters, and that these aids ought to be requested in full parliament. It further states that these requests should be delivered in writing to each grade of peers of parliament, and given a written reply.[88] The paragraph also emphasizes 'that two knights who come to parliament for the shire have a greater voice in granting and denying than the greatest earl of England.'[89]

Although this passage, which has perhaps attracted the greatest interest, applies to 'everything that ought to be granted, denied, or done by parliament', the reference is primarily to taxation, and the assumption is that the Commons speak in that field with a greater authority than the Lords because they 'represent the whole community of England and not the magnates, because each of these is in parliament for themselves in their own person and for no other.' With some qualification this statement of the *Modus* is true of the period in which it was written.[90] 'Doubtless the Commons by themselves could not claim to represent the whole community of England as the author (of the *Modus*) asserts, but it was an entirely defensible (though not entirely verifiable) assertion that in rendering the assent of that community the unanimous voice of the representatives had greater weight than the individual voices of the Lords. At the very least their assent had become a sine qua non.'[91]

Two points may be raised finally. In the use of the terms 'community' and 'commonalty' we are dealing with one of the most vexing of medieval expressions. Once their modern senses have been fully developed 'community' and 'commonalty' are crucially different expressions. At the time when the author wrote the separation had indeed begun, but was not yet completed. Some contemporaries used *communitas* in the old sense of the community as a whole, some in the

---

[88] See pp. 77, 89–90.
[89] See pp. 77, 89–90.
[90] See in particular the comments of G. L. Harriss, *King, Parliament, and Public Finance in Medieval England* (Oxford, 1975) for the background to the position in the 1320s, pp. 81–4.
[91] *Ibid.* p. 84.

newer sense of only the common people within it. We would be inclined to believe that the author of the *Modus* when he speaks of the community of England used the term in the latter rather than the former sense, although there is no way of proving that he was fully aware of the eventual separation of the two expressions.[92]

A different but related point is that we should be careful not to read into the passage claiming a specific and essential role for the Commons in 'parliament', a claim to political power which may be challenging the power of the Lords. We should note that the *Modus* says nothing about the influence which individual Lords exercised over particular members of the Commons, nor of the influence of the Lords as a body over the Commons as a whole. This was not its purpose. Concerned as it was with the general principles of parliament, the *Modus* does not deal with the realities of political action. Its author sought to define parliament, and was not concerned with analysing the structure of power behind that body.[93]

It may be observed finally that in defining parliament and in particular the role of the Commons the author does not exaggerate the position which each individual representative might have. The celebrated passage in the paragraph, *Concerning Aids to the King* which states that if the Commons refuse to come, the King may not proceed, must be set against the passages on non-attendance and the passage in the final paragraph *Concerning the Grades of Peers of Parliament* which states that if any of the five grades below the King be absent provided that they have been summoned correctly, parliament shall still be considered complete. What the author of the *Modus* states, in fact, in the passage *Concerning Aids to the King* is that if the Commons having been summoned collectively decide not to attend parliament (which pre-supposes that they held a meeting to arrive at such a collective decision) then the King cannot simply ignore their absence and proceed to make parliamentary ordinances and grants as if consent had been granted. If on the other hand, as is stated in the paragraph, *Concerning the Grades of Peers of Parliament*, summons has been duly sent out but few or no members of a particular grade have actually appeared, i.e. the proctors

[92] There is an interesting discussion of the use of the term 'community of the realm' by J. R. Strayer, 'The Statute of York and the Community of the Realm', *American Historical Review* 47 (1941), 1–22.

[93] At the same time a strong case can be advanced for minimizing the influence of the Lords over the Commons in the late fourteenth and early fifteenth centuries, J. S. Roskell, *The Commons in the Parliament of 1422* (Manchester, 1954); A. L. Brown, 'The Commons and the Council in the Reign of Henry IV', *E.H.R.* 79 (1964), 1–30.

of the clergy or the burgesses (who constitute the third and sixth grades) have absented themselves, this should not prevent the King and the remainder from proceeding with their business, while at the same time putting into effect the penal provisions for non-attendance.

Clerical Representation in the Modus

One of the most puzzling features in the *Modus* is the account of clerical representation contained in the treatise. The author omits the middle clergy normally summoned as individuals and states that clerical proctors are to be elected not by dioceses but by archdeaconries, which would have had the consequence of considerably increasing the numbers of elected proctors in parliament. Because of these statements the *Modus* has been regarded as an 'ecclesiastical manifesto'. In particular it has been suggested that the central argument of the treatise was in the nature of a plea for shifting 'the balance of the representation of the clerical order in parliament away from the dignitaries to the rank and file of the Church' and (implicitly) for 'co-ordinating the parliamentary representation of the lower clergy with that of the lay folk of the communities of the shires'.[94] On the other hand it has been maintained that the difficulties of this part of the *Modus* derive simply from an error, and from telescoping the procedure of election.[95]

As regards the situation in the Church during the reign of Edward II the statement in the *Modus* that clerical proctors are to be elected by archdeaconries and not by dioceses corresponded to practice in the northern province and to some dioceses in the south.[96] In most parts of the southern province proctors were elected not by archdeaconries but by dioceses, although in the case of Winchester, and possibly Chichester, which had only two archdeaconries, one proctor from each archdeaconry was elected directly to parliament. In five other dioceses in the southern province there was only one archdeaconry and therefore 'the proposal of the *Modus* to have proctorial representation by archdeaconries would have meant no actual change'.[97] As regards the basis of proctorial representation therefore there was no uniformity of practice, and had the author of the *Modus* been searching for a unifying principle, and for a territorial basis to clerical representation the most

[94] Roskell, 'A Consideration of Certain Aspects and Problems of the English *Modus Tenendi Parliamentum*', pp. 420–2. See Clarke, p. 20.
[95] Clarke, pp. 151–2.
[96] Roskell, pp. 421–2; Clarke, pp. 326–9.
[97] Roskell, p. 422.

natural basis he could have selected was the archdeaconry. This may well be the explanation of a passage which occurs in a treatise which is in part 'theoretical'.[98]

In writing this part of his treatise, however, it is evident that the author was dealing with a complicated situation. In addition to the difference in the basis or representation between one diocese and another, there was more than one stage in the election of proctors in certain dioceses. In these dioceses 'the clergy of each rural deanery elected a proctor, the proctors thus chosen in one archdeaconry together elected a representative to meet those from other archdeaconries; by the proctors of archdeaconries the final choice for the diocese was made'.[99] In addition the whole situation was rendered more complex by the attitude of the clergy towards representation in parliament. Although during the reign of Edward II the clergy still in theory attended parliament on a representative basis, in practice their attendance was irregular, and the whole body of the clergy were in fact in the process of withdrawing from that assembly.[100] There was therefore no established pattern of clerical election and representation which the author of the *Modus* could successfully describe in the 1320s.

It was the opinion of Miss Clarke that the author of the *Modus* with this background in mind was thinking 'rather carelessly of the primary stages (of election)', and that when he wrote of representation by proctors from archdeaconries he confused the system of pre-election in archdeaconries with the final diocesan election.[101] Evidence of possible confusion on the part of the author is to be found in the fact that there is no mention in the *Modus* of the proctorial representation of cathedral chapters, nor of the personal attendance of archdeacons and cathedral deans. Professor Roskell maintains, however, that the statement describing representation by proctors from archdeaconries was 'no slip'. The omission of deans of cathedral chapters and of archdeacons was according to Professor Roskell probably deliberate and intended

[98] 'There are actually a few cases where a single archdeaconry sent up two proctors independently to parliament: Salop in 1307, Hereford in 1309, and Stafford (one of the five archdeaconries in the diocese of Lichfield) in 1309'. Roskell, p. 422. In any event the author of the *Modus* was searching as much for principles as for practice.

[99] Clarke, p. 152.

[100] On the question of clerical representation see Lowry, 'Clerical Proctors in Parliament', *E.H.R.* 47 (1933), 443–55; Kemp, *Counsel and Consent*, p. 105. For the best discussion see Clarke, pp. 15–32.

[101] Clarke, pp. 151–2.

'to exclude the more important of the king's clerks from parliament in their capacity as proper members of the lower clergy'.[102]

Whatever the truth of this particular argument there is no evidence to suggest that the *Modus* as a whole was written primarily as an ecclesiastical treatise. Had the *Modus* been a treatise of this kind almost certainly it would have noted such matters as the frequent absences of the higher clergy, and of the proctors of the lower clergy from parliament, as well as noting the fact that the Church as a whole was trying to deal with the King directly through Convocation instead of through parliament. Yet the *Modus* says nothing of these matters and apart from this one short and inexact passage ignores the Church altogether. Once again this suggests a Common Law authorship. The point can be further illustrated by the fact that clerical proctors in the numbers described in the *Modus* were hardly consistent with the notions and aims of the Church as seen by the episcopal hierarchy or by the clergy as a whole in 1320. Had it continued, the system of clerical proctors would have ensured not the separation of the Church from the lay state, but rather its integration into the body-politic under the King. In fact the Church adopted a different policy during the reign of Edward II. At that time the hierarchy protested at the involvement in parliament, held Convocations for granting aid to the King, and made other attempts to have the King deal with the Church as a sovereign body. The success of this evasionary campaign is well illustrated by the situation after the Lincoln parliament of 1316. After the proceedings in parliament had been vitiated by the number of absentees, the Archbishop was obliged to summon a Convocation to give general approval to the grant because the numbers of clergy attending the parliament had been so few.[103]

In all it may be said that the *Modus* deals entirely with the Church in its lay capacity. The higher clergy are to be summoned because of their tenure as lay-lords only; nothing is said about other claims, sacerdotal or spiritual, and no reference is made to clerical privileges, or indeed to any other of the standard provisos and qualifications with which the Church hedged its participation in lay affairs. While the treatment given to the Church in the *Modus* could hardly have satisfied a churchman, it is very consistent with the tone and attitude which we find illustrated time and again in the Year-books.

[102] Roskell, p. 430. The scheme as outlined in the *Modus* might have had the effect of inducing the lower clergy 'to return to parliament willingly by reforming the system of their direct representation.' *Ibid.*, p. 419.

[103] Clarke, pp. 135–6.

The Tariff of Amercements

The tariff of amercements is a notable feature of the English, although not of the Irish *Modus*.[104] Though the rules of amercement as set out in the *Modus* have been questioned we know that as regards the magnates at least there were amercements for non-attendance at the English medieval parliaments. Amercements were also a well-known feature of the medieval parliaments held in Ireland.[105] In an age when parliaments meant, in Professor Roskell's phrase, 'travel and travail' rather than a privilege, especially with no less than thirty-four parliaments or *colloquia* being held between July 1290 and January 1327, the problem was how to ensure the presence of those summoned.[106]

One obvious method was the imposition of fines or amercements for non-attendance such as are listed in the *Modus*. The *Modus* states that for absence from parliament an archbishop or earl will be fined £100, a bishop or baron 100 marks, counties will be fined £100 if their member does not appear, and boroughs 100 marks. The elaborate description of checks on attendance and fines in the case of default has been cited as 'evidence' that the *Modus* did not describe parliament as it was. The author's proposals have been held to be 'unreal' partly because attendance was, in the opinion of some historians, thin amongst the Commons, and because the Lords were also known to have been infrequent attenders. Yet again we have to remember the scope of the treatise which was 'rules' and not the extent to which they were observed in any one parliament.

Legally there can be no doubt that a writ of summons to parliament (or to any other court, including the Curia Regis) had the force of law, and secondly, that all writs of command of this kind had to have in law an ultimate fine attached in case of default. In any case this problem was not confined to parliament. All courts waged a continuous battle to secure attendance, and, conversely, a great deal of the time and ingenuity of the legal fraternity was expended on the art of essoins, a subject so fraught with technicalities and so buttressed with an attitude

---

[104] It is a curious feature that the tariff of amercements is found only in the English version of the text, Galbraith, p. 99.

[105] Richardson and Sayles, *Irish Parliament in the Middle Ages*, pp. 137–44.

[106] J. G. Edwards, 'The Personnel of the Commons in Parliament under Edward I and Edward II', *Essays in Medieval History Presented to Thomas Frederick Tout* (Manchester, 1925), p. 198. 'In the fourteenth century, parliament was summoned to meet, on an average every eleven months', J. S. Roskell, 'The Problem of the Attendance of the Lords in Medieval Parliaments', *B.I.H.R.* 29 (1956), 155.

of accepted lying that it was a veritable jungle.[107] In the case of parliament, the solution available to the Common Law, appearance by attorneys, was objected to by the Crown. The frequency with which this was re-stated indicates that the Crown took personal attendance at parliament very seriously.[108]

Though not numerous, there were occasions in the English parliament when, as regards the Lords at least, fines or amercements were threatened or actually levied. In the parliament of 1344 non-attendance among the Lords was such that a written list of absent Lords was required to be forwarded to the King, who could then ordain such punishment as he saw fit.[109] Whether any fines were actually levied on this occasion we do not know. In 1454 fines were actually imposed for non-attendance among the Lords and 'this was to be the only occasion in the history of the medieval parliament on which there is record evidence of fines being actually imposed on lords for non-attendance'.[110] These fines exacted in 1454 were fixed according to rank. An archbishop or duke had to pay £100, and a bishop or earl a 100 marks. As Professor Roskell remarks, 'the fines bear some resemblance, at least regarding the upper ranges of parliamentary society, to those tariffs proposed in the English *Modus Tenendi Parliamentum*, where the fines were £100 for an archbishop or earl, and 100 marks for bishop or baron.[111]

As regards the Commons, we have no evidence of fines imposed on absent representatives in English medieval parliaments. Whether the heavy fines listed in the *Modus* were ever exacted we have no means of knowing. It may be that as regards the Commons in the medieval parliaments these fines remained more theoretical than practical. Evidence of financial penalties for non-attendance among the Commons however is found in the act of 1515 which 'penalised unauthorized absence with loss of wages'.[112] Later in the sixteenth century, there is evidence of fines for non-attendance on those members absent the whole session without license, 'twenty pounds for county, and ten pounds for borough members. . . . How the fines were collected we are

---

[107] For examples of difficulties which even the Council had in enforcing the attendance of those whom it summoned see N. Pronay, 'The Chancellor, the Chancery, and the Council at the End of the Fifteenth Century', *Studies Presented to S. B. Chrimes,* ed. H. Hearder and H. R. Loyn (Cardiff, 1974), p. 98.

[108] Amercements for non-attendance at parliament were the subject of a statute by Richard II, *Statutes of the Realm.* 5 Richard II. 2.4.

[109] *Rot. Parl.* II. 147. Roskell, 'The Problem of the Attendance of the Lords', p. 167.

[110] Roskell, p. 190.   [111] *Ibid.,* p. 190. n. 2.

[112] J. E. Neale, *The Elizabethan House of Commons* (London, 1954), p. 413.

not told; presumably they were certified into the Exchequer, and so enforced.'[113]

From this evidence, slight as it is, we cannot say that the tariff or amercements set out in the *Modus* was too far removed from contemporary reality.[114] Although so far as we know, fines were seldom imposed in the English parliament, on the one occasion when they were imposed, in 1454, they bore a remarkable resemblance to the figures set out in the *Modus*. In the case of the county and borough members the sums mentioned are undoubtedly high, but as in other parts of the *Modus* these could have been conceptual figures, and possibly were not meant to be taken too literally. In any event the sums mentioned in the *Modus* would have required to have been revised in a later period.

Finally it is entirely fitting that a treatise written for the legal fraternity should devote so much space to providing in detail the rules and the fines for non-appearance since that was a very central, almost obsessive preoccupation for practitioners in the Common Law courts though it would hardly have occupied a political analyst to quite the same extent. Yet just as a system of courts based on the right of the parties to be fully and fairly represented would break down if either of the parties were allowed regularly to fail to appear, so it was essential for an institution based on the idea of representing the whole community to ensure that no one could say that his consent had not been given. Perhaps one of the reasons why parliament in England did not degenerate into impotence as so many of its continental sisters did was the maintenance, indeed compulsion, of attendance by the government. The manner in which this compulsion was exercised as described by Lambarde in the Tudor period reflects so much the spirit of the *Modus* that it may be appropriate to recount it here. 'It is common policy', says Lambarde 'to say upon the Wednesday that the House

---

[113] Neale, *Elizabethan House of Commons*, p. 414.

[114] Of the fines for absence in the Irish parliament Richardson and Sayles say that 'there was no scale of fines relating to rank or precedence in parliament, but at the same time (the fines in the Irish parliament) point ... to the source which suggested to the redactor of the English *Modus Tenendi Parliamentum* the scale of fines he incorporated in his text', *Irish Parliament*, p. 142. Although we may believe that the reverse process occurred, and that the English *Modus* was the source for the scale of fines in the Irish parliament, the fact is that there was some general correspondence between the level of fines proposed by the *Modus* and the practice in the Irish parliament. It should also be noted that in the Perth parliament of July 1427 some of the tenants-in-chief who 'contumaciously absented themselves' were to pay an amercement of £10 each. Ranald Nicholson, *Scotland: The Later Middle Ages* (Edinburgh, 1974), p. 302.

shall be called on Saturday and on Saturday to say that it shall be called on Wednesday, and so from day to day, by fear thereof to keep the company together.' As Professor Neale says, 'In 1566 after several roll calls during the session, at the end the House was called on two successive days. . . . In 1581 the policy of keeping members on tenterhooks described by Lambarde was practised, and then at the end of the session came swingeing fines on those absent the whole session without license.'[115]

4. THE *MODUS* IN THE MIDDLE AGES

What was the value of the *Modus* to the lawyers and members of parliament of the later Middle Ages? Here we must identify two functions in the role of a work that was partly a parliamentary handbook and partly a treatise on parliament. As a parliamentary handbook the *Modus* was in the possession of officials such as the Speaker and the clerk of parliament who were concerned in a practical way with the procedure of parliament. As a treatise, however, the *Modus* was of wider interest to fifteenth-century lawyers and to all who had to do with the business of parliament.[116] The *Modus* functioned therefore on at least two levels and because of its twin functions its text was in reasonably wide circulation in legal and parliamentary circles during the later Middle Ages.

The evidence of the codices and manuscripts suggests that during the later Middle Ages the *Modus* was regarded as a useful guide to the past functioning of parliament.[117] One copy almost certainly belonged to the Speaker of one of Henry VII's parliaments and is found together with a draft of his Protestation.[118] Another copy was in the possession of the clerk of parliament in the early sixteenth century.[119] Other copies are known to have been owned by members of the nobility who occupied the office of Steward.[120] Yet another version prefaced the

[115] Cited by Neale, *Elizabethan House of Commons*, p. 414.
[116] For the evidence of ownership see Appendix I.
[117] Although the bulk of the evidence on this point comes from the very beginning of the sixteenth century, it may be regarded as relating substantially to the late medieval parliament before the changes of Henry VIII's reign.
[118] See Section VI for the evidence of dating, which may be 1487 or more likely 1504. As Speaker, Edmund Dudley was directly connected with the procedure of parliament. See the comments of Neale, *Elizabethan House of Commons*, p. 394.
[119] The copy is B.L. Harley 930.
[120] A copy was in the possession of Edward Seymour (1506–52) who was High Steward of England at the time of Edward VI's coronation. *Hist. Mss. Comm.* 6th Report, p. 301.

continued

Lords Journal of 1510.[121] Later in the sixteenth century an ornamental copy of the *Modus* appears to have been used as a ceremonial guide to parliament for it contains as an insert the order of procession for the opening of parliament in Elizabeth's reign.[122]

In the procedural field the influence of the *Modus* is suggested by the circumstance that in the period before the first printed parliamentary manuals it was the one text in the possession of those who had to do with procedure in parliament. Its influence in this field is even more evident after the Middle Ages for when the first parliamentary manuals or histories of parliament were written in the sixteenth and seventeenth centuries they were either modelled upon the *Modus* or considerably indebted to that work.[123] In a very real sense, therefore the *Modus* was the ancestor of all later parliamentary guides, and in the late Middle Ages and the early modern period it is encountered first and foremost in a procedural tradition.

During the later Middle Ages the procedural value of the *Modus* probably consisted chiefly in its background information. Essentially it contained a basic set of ancient precedents to which reference could be made. As the oldest parliamentary treatise in existence (a role enhanced by its reference to a pre-conquest institution) it provided the best precedents for the parliamentary clerks.[124] The *Modus* told medieval officials concerned with parliamentary procedure what it appeared to tell Hooker and Elsyng later, namely how the parliaments of an earlier period had been organized. It was probably consulted on such subjects as who had been summoned to parliament in an earlier period and in what way, the times at which earlier parliaments had been held, what the seating arrangements had been, and what the procedure was for ending a particular assembly. Despite the fact that the *Modus* gave a far from accurate statement on these matters, and that during the later

---

The *Modus* says that the Steward is responsible for the seating of members. One of the Steward's duties was certainly to supervise the roll call of members.

[121] See Appendix IV. See the comments of A. F. Pollard and G. R. Elton on this version, p. 24. n. 41. According to Pollard its presence in the *Journal* 'does show that it was considered authoritative on parliamentary procedure in Tudor times'.

[122] Huntington Library, E.L. 35. B. 61. Certain late medieval copies of the *Modus* were furnished with an index (B.L. Add. 15091). This suggests that they were intended to be used in a practical way.

[123] See pp. 52–5. The comments of Catherine Strateman, *The Liverpool Tractate* (New York), pp. xxx–xxxvi, are particularly valuable in this context.

[124] Professor Elton accordingly believes that it was for such procedural/precedental purposes that the *Modus* was copied into the front of the Lords Journal. G. R. Elton, 'The Early Journals of the House of Lords', *E.H.R.* 89 (1974), 505.

Middle Ages parliamentary procedure differed considerably from that outlined in the treatise, the *Modus* still constituted the one work of reference available to fifteenth-century parliamentarians.[125] Because it was the only treatise of this kind available, it continued to be used as a type of 'parliamentary handbook' until the time of Elsyng.[126]

Apart from the practical use made of the *Modus* or of parts of the *Modus* by parliamentary officials, the treatise also provided, to those interested, a rationale of parliament. This was its second main function during the later Middle Ages. Whatever its practical value on matters of procedure, the treatise alone provided an over-all view of parliament, of its history and functions, and of why its members were summoned to this assembly. As the one text in existence which described the origins and nature of parliament the view of the *Modus* on that assembly must have been very much in the minds of fifteenth-century parliamentarians. It can be said moreover that as a treatise which offered a justification for parliament the *Modus* helped to preserve and buttress parliament during the later Middle Ages. It offered a coherent case for a parliament in England, and this at a time when there was no equivalent case being offered for absolute government. At the very least we must say that the *Modus* as part of the political literature of fifteenth-century England was pro-parliamentary, and the bias is important in view of the situation prevailing, for example, in contemporary France.

Within the form of a treatise on parliament the *Modus* provided therefore the only picture of parliament then available. A part of that picture was necessarily historical, for the question had to be asked was parliament a new or an ancient institution? The *Modus* which traced the origins of parliament back to the pre-Conquest period provided the answer, and in doing so provided also a form of parliamentary history. The *Modus* was in fact the one history of parliament available to contemporaries during the later Middle Ages. In the absence of any critical examination of parliamentary records, and at a time when men

[125] At no time during the later fourteenth and fifteenth centuries did the *Modus* correspond to parliamentary 'reality', yet it might equally be said that the first edition of Erskine May would be of limited practical help for parliamentary procedure today. In the course of its nineteen editions it has been revised beyond recognition. Erskine May itself displaced John Hatsell's, *Precedents of Proceedings in the House of Commons*, 4th edn (1818).

[126] A. F. Pollard who was the first modern historian to take the *Modus* seriously, and who encouraged the study of its manuscript tradition (see p. 27 n. 55), described it as 'the official handbook to parliaments', *Evolution of Parliament*, p. 12. With some qualification this may be regarded as the correct description.

would believe literally *anything* about the past, it must be assumed that the lawyers of fifteenth-century England believed what the *Modus* stated, namely that there had been parliaments since before the Norman Conquest, in which the representative element had been important, and which were competent to deal with all the great affairs of the land.[127]

The myth of an ancient constitution did not therefore originate in the sixteenth and seventeenth centuries. To a large extent the common lawyers of the later Middle Ages believed in an ancient constitution, and certainly the Middle Ages expected all its institutions to be of ancient origin. To contemporaries the fifteenth-century parliament must have appeared to have existed always in that form, and the *Modus* gave written support to that belief. A Commons petition of 1414 said that the Commons 'ever had been a member of parliament as well assentors as petitioners'.[128] Fortescue himself believed that the body politic which included parliament had come into being in the time of Brutus.[129] We should not be surprised therefore that the lawyers of fifteenth-century England believed in a representative parliament which pre-dated the Norman Conquest.

Yet the manner in which this view was held is as important as the belief itself. The fifteenth-century view of the antiquity of parliament was a traditional and static belief with little element of political or partisan bias. In the fifteenth century the political demands of parliaments were relatively modest, popular interest in parliament was not great, and in the field of 'political literature' the *Modus* alone rescued parliament from almost complete neglect.[130] It is against this kind of background that we must consider not only the use of the *Modus* but also its views on the antiquity of parliament. Against such a background its views were not so much revolutionary as commonplace. Claims that parliaments were of ancient origin and pre-dated the Crown were to assume a quite different character when put forward in a period of parliamentary evolution to support parliament's claims during the late sixteenth and early seventeenth centuries.

---

[127] For the idea of an ancient constitution in the sixteenth and seventeenth centuries see J. G. A. Pococke, *The Ancient Constitution and the Feudal Law* (Cambridge, 1957).

[128] *Rot. Parl.* IV. 22.

[129] Chrimes, *Constitutional Ideas*, p. 322.

[130] This situation is reflected in the scarcity in the fifteenth century of good contemporary descriptions of particular parliaments. By way of contrast see the fourteenth-century descriptions mentioned by T. F. Tout, 'The English Parliament and Public Opinion, 1376–88', *Collected Papers* (Manchester, 1934) II, 173–90.

Yet we should not for all that minimize the importance of the *Modus* during the later Middle Ages. The *Modus* was the first and the only treatise on parliament written in England during this period. Enjoying a monopoly in this field, it identified parliament throughout almost the whole of its medieval history with the view that parliament was a representative assembly and not simply a High Court. Parliament it has been said 'was observed to have extraordinary features of which no simple court, however high, could possibly boast. It had a unique capacity for binding all and sundry, essentially because it represented all and sundry, which no ordinary law-court could be supposed to have or to do'.[131] As a parliamentary treatise, in use during a period of parliamentary consolidation rather than of parliamentary advance, the *Modus* must have helped therefore to disseminate ideas about the scope and nature of parliament.[132]

5. THE *MODUS* AFTER THE MIDDLE AGES

The history of the *Modus* in the later sixteenth and seventeenth centuries forms the last but not the least interesting aspect of its story. Precisely because the *Modus* had been incorporated in a long line of workaday legal collections which were in daily use in the courts its influence was in many respects greater than that of most other medieval tracts. The *Modus* in the sixteenth century was a text in common, although decreasing, use and unlike the controversies created by such 'sensational discoveries' as the *Mirror of Justices* the statements of the *Modus* were not therefore subjected to scrutiny until the time of Selden.[133] It is an ironical commentary upon the history of the *Modus* that its use in the seventeenth century as a weapon in contemporary controversy, and in particular the use of its preamble assigning

[131] Chrimes, *Constitutional Ideas*, p. 76.
[132] It can be argued that the doctrine of the *Modus* had become the consensus of the knights and burgesses in parliament by 1340. See the comments of G. L. Harriss, pp. 268–9. As early as the 1390s the text of the *Modus* appears to have been quoted in the Commons. '. . . . les ditz Chevalers sont a chescun Parlement pur tout la Commune des countees et les seignurs des franchises soulement pur lour mesmes . . .', *Rot. Parl.* III. 293. This was noted by Helen Cam, *Liberties and Communities in Medieval England* (London, 1963), p. 242.
[133] *The Mirror of Justices*, ed. W. J. Whittaker, Selden Soc. vii (1895). See the introduction by F. W. Maitland. The *Mirror* had a considerable influence on the thought of the seventeenth century.

parliament to the reign of Edward the Confessor, were the factors which turned the work into a controversial source. In the Middle Ages, by way of contrast, there is no evidence to suggest that the *Modus* was ever regarded as a suspect or a controversial text.[134]

It must be emphasized that after the Middle Ages the status of the *Modus* inevitably changed. With the end of Henry VII's reign, the age of the Codices and the Year Books was over, a new age of the Printed Statutes and the Printed Reports began, and the *Modus* ceased to exist as part of the corpus of the law. Although ended as a living legal text, however, the *Modus* survived as an independent treatise, and in the dying world of the Court of Chivalry it still had some relevance. None the less at the beginning of the sixteenth century the main era of the *Modus* was over. Despite this the *Modus* had a precedental life in the later sixteenth and seventeenth centuries which should be described here even if in the briefest detail. In particular the *Modus* exercised a dominant influence over the first post-Reformation handbooks and histories of parliament. Something of its form and structure was adopted by a writer such as Hooker who copied it not only because it was the only parliamentary handbook in existence, but also because he thought it a sensible way of writing such a work.[135]

The first parliamentary manual to be written after the *Modus* was John Hooker or Vowell's *The Order and Usage of the Keeping of a Parlement in England* (1572).[136] Hooker, who was a lawyer by training, sat in the Irish parliament of 1569, and in the English parliament of 1571.[137] His experiences in the Irish parliament appear to have convinced him of the necessity of compiling some handbook of parliamentary procedure. With this in mind he published in 1572 *The Order and Usage* to show how parliament functioned in his own day together with a translation of the (B) recension of the *Modus* to show how parliament had been held in

---

[134] See pp. 47–9.

[135] Writers of parliamentary guides such as Hooker did not have to use the *Modus*. The form of other medieval legal works was not necessarily adopted in the post-Reformation period. Coke did not, for example, copy the form of the *Nova* and *Vetera Statuta*. For the influence of the *Modus* on later parliamentary handbooks see the valuable comments of Catherine Strateman, *The Liverpool Tractate* (New York, 1937), pp. xxx–xxxvi.

[136] The following comments are indebted to Vernon F. Snow, *Parliament in Elizabethan England* (Yale University Press, 1977), which contains an edition of Hooker's *Order and Usage*. The references are to this edition, and are cited as Snow.

[137] Hooker kept a diary of these parliaments. That for the parliament of 1569, published in the *Proceedings of the Royal Irish Academy* 25.C. (1904–5), is the first parliamentary diary of its kind.

previous centuries.[138] Hooker's treatise which was intended as a practical guide for M.P.'s in the English and Irish parliament took 'the *Modus* very much as its model'.[139]

Writing more than two centuries after the reign of Edward II Hooker described a tricameral assembly of Lords, Commons and Convocation House that was different from the fourteenth-century assemblies known to the author of the *Modus*. None the less the chapters of Hooker's treatise bear such familiar titles as 'Of the degrees of parliament', 'Of the Days and Hours to Sit in Parliament', 'The order of the beginning and the ending of parlement', and at least a part of the contents of certain chapters derives from the *Modus*. Passages from the *Modus* concerning the composition of parliament, the function of the King, and even the cost of the text of a bill (ten lines for one penny) were worked into Hooker's treatise.[140] It is possible that the prominent role which the *Modus* gives to the proctors of the clergy as well as the prelates 'may explain the *Orders* treating Convocation straightforwardly as the fourth degree or component, or the third house of Parliament'.[141] In particular the stress on representation, and the view that the Commons constituted the essential element in parliament was restated by Hooker in words which clearly derive from the earlier treatise. 'Again every Baron in Parlement dooth represent but his owne person, and speaketh in the behalf of him self alone. But in the knights, Citizens and Burgesses: are represented the Commons of the whole Realme, and every of these giveth not consent only for himself: but for all those also for whom he is sent'.[142]

Although in Ireland *The Order and Usage* appears to have been adopted as a practical guide for use in the Irish parliaments, in England its function is less certain.[143] In the late sixteenth century procedure in

---

[138] Hooker may have translated a (B) recension of the *Modus* because the (B) text survived longer in general use in chivalric codices than did the (A) text in the common law volumes, Pronay and Taylor, p. 19. Hooker's translation was the first printed text of the *Modus*, see Snow, pp. 29–38. His translation was reprinted in *Somers' Tracts* (1751), and in Sir Walter Scott's edition of 1809. See Appendix V. Hooker's own treatise was printed in the second edition of Holinshed's *Chronicles* (London, 1586) in the section relating to Ireland. It was reprinted in the 1808 edition of Holinshed's *Chronicles*, VI. 345–62.

[139] *William Lambarde's Notes on the Procedures and Privileges of the House of Commons (1584)*, ed. Paul L. Ward (London Stationery Office, 1977), p. 15. The introduction is cited as Ward.

[140] Snow, pp. 147–52, 179–80.   [141] Ward, p. 15.

[142] Compare Hooker's translation of the *Modus* (Snow, p. 142) with his own account, *ibid.*, p. 182.

[143] For the situation in Ireland see pp. 124–5.

the English parliament was governed rather by unwritten rules and 'orders' than by any official guide. *The Order and Usage* is not cited in the *Journal of the House of Commons* nor do parliamentary diarists refer to it as such.[144] None the less in a manner similar to the *Modus* in an earlier period Hooker's treatise appears to have served as a type of unofficial guide to parliament, and copies of his work circulated among members of parliament.[145]

Hooker's guide to parliamentary procedure was the first in a series of procedural and historical works which during the next half century or so were indebted to the *Modus*. *William Lambarde's Notes on the Procedures and Privileges of the House of Commons* mentions the *Modus* in first place in its bibliography, but does not refer to the treatise as such in the text.[146] The reason for this may be that the *Modus* says 'little that pertains in detail to the Commons, except on the summoning of members and their recompensing or fining for absence'.[147] Hakewill's account of Commons' procedure, written *c.* 1610 but only published in 1641 by parliamentary authority, began with a translation of the *Modus*, to which Hakewill added 'Some Additions to the Privileges of Parliament'.[148] The influence of the *Modus* is most clearly seen in the work of Henry Elsyng, clerk of the parliaments, 1621–35, and an official intimately involved with the procedure and records of that assembly.[149] Elsyng's treatise, *The Manner of Holding Parliaments in England*, named in Latin *Modus tenendi parliamentum apud Anglos*, was an historical account of how parliaments had been held from the time of Henry II to the seventeenth century. Elsyng probably intended, according to Professor Elizabeth Read Foster, 'that his work . . . should replace the medieval *Modus Tenendi Parliamentum* which, whatever

---

[144] Snow, pp. 92–3.

[145] These sometimes included copies of Hooker's translation of the *Modus*, see Appendix I.

[146] See the edition of Lambarde by Ward which is taken from Exeter College, Oxford 139. Lambarde also used Hooker's treatise.

[147] *Ibid.* p. 14. Lambarde was well acquainted with manuscripts of the *Modus*. Lawrence Nowell left Cotton Domitian xviii with him in 1567 (Ward, p. 35 n. 4.). See also Appendix I. A copy of the *Modus* B.L. Add. 32097 was given to Lambarde by Richard Atkins, of Lincoln.

[148] Hakewill's work was entitled in some editions, *Modus tenendi parliamentum* or *The Old Manner of Holding Parliaments in England* (London, 1671). An (A) version of the *Modus* prefaces this work. See Snow, p. 90. Hakewill's work was first published in 1641 in an unauthorised edition.

[149] See the account of Elsyng by Elizabeth Read Foster, 'The Painful Labour of Mr. Elsyng', *Transactions of the American Philosophical Society*, new ser., 62. part 8 (Philadelphia, 1972), 1–69.

modern historians may think of it, had long been considered an authoritative guide to the past'.[150] Although only Book I of Elsyng's work was published in 1660, it is clear from this and from other portions which have since been printed that Elsyng regarded the *Modus* as an important source of parliamentary precedents.[151] In his draft of an unpublished chapter on Subsidies he began with the *Modus*.[152] Elsewhere he consulted the treatise on such matters as who had been summoned to parliament, where they had sat, whether Lords and Commons had originally sat together, when parliament was to be summoned, and the problems of parliamentary attendance. Elsyng's use of the *Modus* illustrates the manner in which the text helped in the establishment of precedents for the holding of parliament, and this was the manner in which presumably it had been consulted in earlier periods.[153]

In the sixteenth and seventeenth centuries the *Modus* was perhaps of the greatest value to Hooker and Elsyng, men concerned with parliamentary procedure, and interested in the practical organization of that assembly. They looked upon the *Modus* sometimes as a model for their own work, but more particularly as a valuable source of parliamentary precedents. In the later sixteenth and the seventeenth centuries the *Modus* is therefore encountered first and foremost in a procedural tradition and through the writings of Hooker, Hakewill and Elsyng something of its contents were absorbed into the practical parliamentary thought of the time.[154]

None the less in the use made of the *Modus* in this period a distinction should be made between the writings of Hooker and Elsyng, where the *Modus* was put to a practical and historical purpose, and more polemical

[150] *Ibid.*, pp. 6–7.

[151] Elsyng completed the first book of his work in 1625, but it was not published until 1660. A manuscript copy now in the Huntington Library, California is in a mixture of Latin and French with many quotations 'from the auntient manuscript *de Modus tenendi parliamentum*'. Chapter 5 of Book Two was edited by Catherine Strateman Sims, *Expedicio Billarum Antiquitus* (Louvain, 1954). Professor Elizabeth Foster has printed drafts of Book Two in 'The Painful Labour of Mr Elsyng'.

[152] Foster, pp. 38–9. She suggests that Elsyng may have come to have had doubts about the *Modus*, *ibid.* p. 45. Elsyng almost always contrasted the statements of the *Modus* with the evidence of the rolls and records of parliament.

[153] See pp. 48–9.

[154] It is noteworthy that the *Modus* was not so valuable to a more theoretical writer such as Sir Thomas Smith who wrote his *De Republica Anglorum* (London, 1583) in France 'to emphasise the contrast between French and English forms of government', Ward, p. 42.

writings occasioned by the conflict between Crown and Commons.[155] It was inevitable in a period such as the seventeenth century when fundamental arguments were being advanced about the nature of the English constitution that the *Modus* together with other material should have been put to polemical purposes.[156] The *Modus* was in fact used by antiquaries and lawyers in defence of the antiquity of parliament, and in this respect its preamble assigning its procedure to the age of the Confessor furnished ammunition to those who argued that parliament out-dated or co-dated the King. It was division within the ranks of the 'parliamentarians', notably through the writings of William Prynne, which more than anything else was to turn the *Modus* into a 'controversial' text.[157]

In the writings of those who supported the claims of parliament in the late sixteenth and early seventeenth centuries a strong belief was expressed that parliament including the Commons had been an original element of government existing long before the Norman Conquest. This belief, fortified by Hooker's publication of the *Modus* in its English form in 1572, was to be of immeasurable value to a body increasing in power and self-confidence during this period.[158] One of the most notable exponents of the antiquity of parliament was Lord Chief Justice Coke who owned several copies of the *Modus*.[159] When he was Speaker of the House of Commons in 1592–3 Coke announced in the House that 'there were Parliaments before the Conquest. This appeareth in a book which a grave member of this House delivered unto me which is intituled *Modus Tenendi Parliamentum*.'[160] Although Coke was influenced

---

[155] See the comments of Catherine Strateman Sims on the work of Elsyng, *Expedicio Billarum Antiquitus*, p. li. The distinction is not perhaps absolute, for Hooker himself had 'an uncritical Saxonist bias', Snow, p. 27.

[156] For a valuable account of the background of this literature see J. G. A. Pococke, *The Ancient Constitution and the Feudal Law* (Cambridge, 1957). It is perhaps worth noting that John Milton accepted the *Modus* as a genuine document. See Snow, pp. 90–1.

[157] See pp. 58–9.

[158] The *Modus* appears in English versions from the fifteenth century onwards. Pollard's remarks on Magna Carta are worth noting, 'the popular claim for Magna Carta would be more convincing if there could be found a single thirteenth, fourteenth or fifteenth century version of the charter in the English language.' *Evolution of Parliament*, p. 10.

[159] Cambridge University Library, Pepysian MS. 2516; Holkham Hall 678. There was another copy of the *Modus*, No. 333 in his library. W. O. Hassall, *A Catalogue of the Library of Sir Edward Coke* (Yale, 1950), p. 26.

[160] S. D'Ewes, *Journals of all the Parliaments during the Reign of Queen Elizabeth* (London, 1682), p. 515. The 'grave member' may have been Hooker, Snow, p. 89. n. 35. D'Ewes himself owned two transcripts of the *Modus*. They are in Latin and French in B.L. Harley 305.

in his views by other writings, notably by the *Mirror of Justices*, there can be no doubt that the *Modus*, with its preamble, helped to shape his view that parliament dated from Anglo-Saxon times.[161] Coke's prestige gave his opinion an authority which historically it did not deserve.[162] Yet his use of the *Modus*, 'the *Modus* misunderstood', was of some significance. It helped to strengthen the case for an ancient constitution against the King, and in assisting seventeenth-century scholars and statesmen to trace parliament back beyond the Conquest to the Saxon Witan Coke's use of the *Modus* furnished ammunition to those who were to shape the classical Whig view of English history.

Coke was not alone in quoting the *Modus* in support of parliament's antiquity. If William Lambarde did not intend his note in the 1579 fragment on parliament to be a defence of the pre-Conquest origins of that assembly, there were others who did defend that position.[163] In 1572 the Society of Antiquaries was formed which had close associations with the parliamentary opposition. At their meetings held between 1572 and 1604 antiquaries such as Tate, Holland, Agard, Camden and Dodderidge found among other sources convincing proof for the pre-Conquest existence of parliament in the *Modus*.[164] As evidence of this belief several transcripts of the *Modus* made in the seventeenth century contain notices of 'parliaments' held in the Anglo-Saxon period.[165] In the parliament of 1610 Henry Finch argued from the *Modus* that parliament had existed from the time of the Norman Conquest.[166]

The defence of the antiquity of parliament was bound up with the ancient position of the Commons in that assembly, and the especial importance of the lower House. Here again the *Modus* furnished

[161] Coke treated the notion of the immemorial antiquity of the Commons as 'solemn dogma' in 1593 when presenting the Bill of Subsidy, Ward, p. 19. See also the chapter on 'The Norman Yoke' in C. Hill's *Puritanism and Revolution* (London, 1958). Although the *Mirror of Justices* stated that there was a parliament before the Conquest, it did not associate the Commons with the parliaments of that time.

[162] E. Evans, 'On the Antiquity of Parliaments in England: Some Elizabethan and Early Stuart Opinions', *History* 23 (1938), 209.

[163] Lambarde wrote 'there is an ancient written treatise, entituled Modus tenendi Parliamentum tempore Regis Edwardi filii Ethelredi, to be seen in many hands, purporting the very order, form, and manner of this stately Court and solemn Assembly'. Ward, p. 44. See also *Archeion*, ed. C. H. McIlwain and P. L. Ward (Harvard University Press, 1957).

[164] E. Evans, p. 208; T. Hearne, *Curious Discourses* (London, 1771) I. 281–310; Hill, 'The Norman Yoke', pp. 58, 125; Snow, p. 109.

[165] For example, B.L. Harley 1576. 'In the ligier booke of the late Abbot of St. Edmonds Bury in Suffolk which is in the hands of Sir Edward Coke is cited a parliament holden in the first year of Canute's reign ....' See p. 212.

[166] *Proceedings in Parliament 1610*, ed. Elizabeth R. Foster (Yale, 1966), II. 231.

welcome 'evidence'. Its text suggested that a bi-cameral parliament had existed from Anglo-Saxon times, and that in this assembly the Commons were the essential element. *A Discourse upon the Exposicion and Understandinge of Statutes* (March 1569), possibly the earliest commentary upon the statutes belonging to the renaissance of legal studies during the reign of Elizabeth, states that as regards parliament the Lords are superfluous, 'the King with his Commonalty may keep the Parliament alone, for the Commons have every one of them a greater voice in Parliament than hath a Lord or Bishop'.[167] Undoubtedly this view came from the *Modus* which is quoted in the chapter entitled 'Parlyament and Acte de Parlyament'. Coke expressed a similar viewpoint, 'his Majesty and the Nobles being every one a great person, represented but themselves; but his Commons, though they were but inferior men, yet every one of them represented a thousand men'.[168] Opinions of a similar kind, based upon the *Modus*, were put forward during the Commons' debates of 1621. During the course of the debate in this parliament Sir Edward Peyton said, 'and there is a book called the *Modus Tenendi Parliamentum* which shows that there cannot be a parliament without the Commons, but there may be by the King and Commons without the Lords'.[169]

To seventeenth-century parliamentarians, and to Coke in particular the *Modus* was an important document. Its 'proof' of the fact that the House of Commons had been established long before the Norman Conquest, assisted the argument for the 'continuity' of English history which parliamentarians and lawyers used to oppose the Stuart conception of monarchy. Even in Coke's lifetime, however, a reaction was setting in against his views, and even among those who supported the parliamentary cause. In the case of the *Modus* the preamble professing to describe what the author believed to have been the manner of holding parliaments under the Saxon government which had appeared so important to Coke and his contemporaries was the cause of increasing criticism of the document. John Selden, who supported the parliamentary opposition, suggested in his *Titles of Honour*

---

[167] *A Discourse upon the Exposicion and Understandinge of Statutes*, ed. S. E. Thorne (San Marino, California, 1942), p. 113. 'The influence of the *Modus* on the *Discourse* . . . is evidence of its repute among lawyers, for the *Discourse* was competently done, and Thomas Egerton of Lincoln's Inn (the later Lord Chancellor Ellesmere) may indeed have been its author.' Ward, p. 14. The spelling has been modernized in this passage.

[168] S. D'Ewes, *op. cit.* p. 515.

[169] *Commons Debates 1621*, ed. W. Notestein, F. H. Relf and H. Simpson (New Haven, 1935) II. 352–3. See also II. 403; III. 138 n. 53, 192, 332 n. 41, 340 n. 18; IV. 388.

that the *Modus* was no older than the reign of Edward III.[170] In the case of the Irish *Modus* Selden's caution was reinforced by the fact that he did not see the copy exemplified under the Great Seal.[171]

The main critic of the *Modus* was, however, William Prynne who 'faced with a subversion of the whole parliamentary structure ... was intelligent enough to see that the root of the trouble was in his own house's claim to virtual sovereignty'.[172] Prynne's criticisms, though politically motivated, and, despite his greater knowledge of the records of parliament as prejudiced and ill-informed as Coke's earlier comments had been, were none the less damaging to the reputation of the *Modus*. The notion that the *Modus* were 'a meer Forgery' begins with Prynne's writings.[173] Prynne's criticisms had no sound historical foundation. He believed that the *Modus* was written in the reign of Henry IV or Henry VII, and he held the view that a parliament consisting of King and Lords where the Lords sat 'by right of peerage and tenure' existed centuries before the Conquest. 'In his mind all he had proved was that the constitution was immemorial, that the King and Lords were immemorial, but that the Commons were not.'[174] Yet as Hardy was to write in his introduction to the first scholarly edition of the *Modus*; 'In impeaching its authority as a correct exposition of the mode of holding Parliament during any stated period, Prynne had been betrayed into a misconception of the real character of the treatise, and he impairs the value of his objections to its authority in endeavouring to destroy its authenticity.'[175]

THE TEXT

The Latin text of the *Modus* was first printed by D. L. D'Achery, (*Spicilegium* (Paris, 1675), xii, 577 ff.) from a manuscript in the Bibliothèque Nationale (Lat. 6049). This manuscript came into the possession of the Bibliothèque Nationale from the Gruthuyse collection, and may well have been acquired by Louis de Gruthuyse (1422–92), governor of Holland, on one of his several visits to England during the fifteenth century.[176] T. D. Hardy's edition of the *Modus*, printed for the

---

[170] *Titles of Honour* (London, third edn. 1672), p. 611. Selden had doubts about the *Modus* as early as 1614.

[171] Clarke, p. 74.

[172] Pococke, p. 157.

[173] *A Brief Register of Parliamentary Writs* (London, 1664) IV, 560, 604. See also his preface to *An Exact Abridgement of the Records in the Tower of London* (London, 1657).

[174] Pococke, pp. 159–60.

[175] T. D. Hardy, *Modus Tenendi Parliamentum* (London, 1846), pp. iv–v.

[176] Pronay and Taylor, p. 18.

Record Commission in 1846, was taken from this same manuscript which preserves an early although corrupt version of that text which is now known as the (B) recension. Hardy published his edition before it had been established that there were in fact two main recensions of the *Modus*, and his earliest readings often refer to the second and more official version.[177] Miss Clarke who published her edition after the existence of the two recensions had been established printed her text from the second and better recension (A) using as the basic manuscript B. L. Vespasian B. VII.[178] None the less Miss Clarke's edition was not entirely based upon this recension for it also contains readings from (B).[179]

Although something of its character may be deduced from existing versions no original text of the *Modus* survives. It has been said that 'all surviving texts of the English *Modus* descend from a much earlier original and are already somewhat corrupt'.[180] The two principal recensions appear almost simultaneously in manuscripts which were written some fifty years or so after the probable date of the composition of the text and they may well have been compiled within a few years of each other. The first recension (B) was possibly compiled *c.* 1321, while the second recension (A) may belong to a slightly later period in the 1320s. The (A) recension seems to have been constructed somewhat later than (B) because while (B) contains what appear to be references to the political situation in 1321, these have for the most part been excised or revised in (A).[181] Yet (A) also may have been compiled before 1330, for it too retains traces of the Edward II origin of the *Modus*. Thus like (B) it says that the parliament rolls shall be kept in the Treasury, a situation which had changed after 1330.[182] If the (A) version had been compiled later in the century, it would almost certainly have been revised more thoroughly. Yet although (B) is probably the earliest known recension its text is clearly corrupt, and it

---

[177] Hardy's text was reproduced by W. Stubbs, *Select Charters and Other Illustrations of English Constitutional History*, edns 1–8 (1870–1905), and reptd in 9th edn. by H. W. C. Davis (Oxford, 1929).

[178] The existence of the two recensions was established by D. K. Hodnett and W. P. White, 'The Manuscripts of the *Modus Tenendi Parliamentum*', *E.H.R.* 34 (1919), 209–24, which contains a pioneering but valuable survey of the manuscripts.

[179] Clarke, pp. 374–84.

[180] Galbraith, 'The *Modus Tenendi Parliamentum*', p. 99.

[181] For the evidence of dating see pp. 22–5. A fuller examination of the manuscripts and of the evidence for dating the different versions is to be found in Taylor, '*The Manuscripts of the Modus Tenendi Parliamentum*', pp. 673–88.

[182] See p. 23.

appears to derive from a still earlier version (A1) closer in arrangement to (A). Proof of this lies in the arrangement of paragraphs. In the (B) recension after the paragraph *Concerning the Burgesses* (VII) a group of paragraphs or clauses appear to be displaced. They are found in the following sequence:

Concerning the Principal Clerks of Parliament (XV)
Concerning the Five Clerks (XVI)
Concerning Difficult Cases and Decisions (XVII)
Concerning the Order of Business of Parliament (XVIII)
Concerning the Days and Hours of Parliament (XIX)
Concerning the Grades of Peers of Parliament (XXVI)
Concerning the Manner of Parliament (VIII)

The sequence of paragraphs in (B) is therefore, I, II, III, IV, V, VI, VII, XV, XVI, XVII, XVIII, XIX, XXVI, VIII, IX, X, XI, XII, XIII, XIV, XX, XXI, XXII, XXIII, XXIV, XXV (numeration of the (A) recension).

It is clear that this is not the original sequence. In the (B) recension the paragraph, *Concerning the Manner of Parliament* (VIII) which occurs as the fourteenth paragraph describes the paragraphs or clauses dealing with the clerks of parliament as coming *later* although in fact they appear in the (B) recension as the eighth and ninth paragraphs. This error suggests an original arrangement closer to (A), where the two paragraphs on the parliamentary clerks occur after the paragraph *Concerning the Manner of Parliament.* The whole argument of the *Modus* as set out in this paragraph required moreover a sequence of paragraphs similar to (A). As Miss Clarke has said this is 'the logical order, treating of Parliament from its opening to the dissolution'.[183] Apart from its textual errors and its omissions to print only the (B) recension as it stands would be to mis-represent the whole argument and structure of the *Modus*.[184]

To print the text of the (A) recension alone would in turn fail to give weight to the manuscript tradition of the *Modus*. Although the (A) recension is found in the common law volumes and the parliamentary copies, to print only the (A) recension together with the variant readings of (B), would not reveal fully the text of the (B) version with

---

[183] Clarke, p. 349.
[184] Obvious examples of errors and omissions in the (B) recension are found in the paragraphs *Concerning the Days and Hours of Parliament, Concerning the Doorkeeper of Parliament,* and *Concerning the Sermon to Parliament.*

its different paragraph sequence. The (B) recension which is found in chivalric codices possibly connected with the newly established offices of the Heralds of the College of Arms, survived in a distinct manuscript tradition until after the end of the Middle Ages. Illustrative of the significance which was attached to this version is the fact that it was combined with (A) to construct other minor versions of the *Modus*.[185] To reconstruct the text of the original (A1) behind both (A) and (B) would again present difficulties. Such a reconstruction would necessarily be conjectural, and the result might well appear to be an artificial text rather than a proper historical original.

In view of these considerations it has been thought desirable to print both the (A) and the (B) recensions, and in that order because of (A)'s more logical arrangement of paragraphs. The variant readings of (A) and (B) are given below each text, and a complete translation of (A) has been provided. In association with the variant readings of (B) a translation of these has been supplied where necessary.

The text of the (A) recension is based upon the earliest text which is found in B.L. Vespasian B. VII, although occasionally readings have been preferred from other copies of (A).[186] Vespasian B. VII is a lawbook belonging to some member of the profession in Richard II's reign. Apart from the *Modus* it contains a number of standard texts such as the Statute of the Forests as well as other items necessary to a practising lawyer. The number of items which refer to matters concerning royal and seigneural administration indicates perhaps that the lawyer who ordered this particular volume was engaged in or hoped to specialize in work relating to the councils of magnates.

The text of the (B) recension of the *Modus* has been taken from the earliest copy of that recension which is found in B.L. Cotton Nero D. VI. It is possible that the codex in which this copy of the *Modus* is found was once in the possession of Thomas Mowbray while occupying the office of earl marshal, and that it was intended for the use of the Court of Claims. Other copies of the (B) recension differ only slightly from this text, and they may all have been manufactured in a common scriptorium. It should be noted that the (A) and (B) recensions represent not simply differences in the text, but more fundamentally differences in provenance and use.

Although there is no numeration of paragraphs in the medieval copies of the *Modus* it has been found useful for purposes of reference to

[185] See Appendix IV.
[186] In one or two cases of obvious error (B) readings have been preferred.

retain the system of numeration adopted by Miss Clarke. The numeration of the (A) recension which almost certainly preserves the original sequence of chapters is indicated in (B). Where appropriate the punctuation and treatment of abbreviations in Miss Clarke's edition have been preserved in the (A) version.

The title *Modus Tenendi Parliamentum* is found only in the (B) recension, the (A) recension having a variety of titles. None the less as the title *Modus Tenendi Parliamentum* has passed into general usage that title has been retained throughout the present edition.

RECENSION 'A'

SIGLA

Vesp	B.L. Vespasian B. vii.
N	B.L. Nero C. i.
L	B.L. Lansdowne 522.
J	B.L. Julius B. iv.
A	B.L. Add. 24079.
O	Oxford, Oriel College. 46.
H	Holkham Hall 232.
E	Harvard Law Library, No. 21.
F	Harvard Law Library, Nos. 29, 30.
B	Free Library of Philadelphia No. 9.
C	Yale University, Beinecke Library, 163.
codd	codicum consensus recensionis A.

De Modo Parliamenti

Hic describitur modus, quomodo Parliamentum regis Anglie et
Anglorum suorum tenebatur temporibus regis Edwardi filii Etheldredi
regis; qui modus recitatus fuit per discetiores regni coram Willielmo
duce Normannie conquestore et rege Anglie, ipso conquestore hoc 5
precipiente, et per ipsum approbatus, et suis temporibus ac etiam
temporibus successorum suorum regum Anglie usitatus.

I Summonitio Parliamenti

Summonitio Parliamenti precedere debet primum diem Parliamenti
per quadraginta dies. 10

II De Clero

Ad Parliamentum summoneri et venire debent archiepiscopi, episcopi,
abbates, priores et alii maiores cleri, qui tenent per comitatum vel
baroniam, ratione huiusmodi tenure, et nulli minores nisi eorum
presentia et eventus aliunde quam pre tenuris suis requiratur, ut si sint 15
de consilio regis, vel eorum presentia necessaria vel utilis reputetur ad
Parliamentum; et illis tenetur rex ministrare sumptus et expensas suas
in veniendo et morando ad Parliamentum; nec debent huiusmodi
clerici minores summoneri ad Parliamentum, sed rex solebat talibus
pariter mandare brevia sua rogando quod ad Parliamentum suum 20
interessent.

Item, rex solebat facere summonitiones suas archiepiscopis, episcopis,
et aliis exemptis personis, ut abbatibus, prioribus, decanis, et aliis
ecclesiasticis personis, qui habent iurisdictiones per huiusmodi exemptiones et privilegia separatas, quod ipsi pro quolibet decanatu et 25
archidiaconatu Anglie per ipsos decanatus et archidiaconatus eligi
facerent duos peritos et idoneos procuratores de ipso archidiaconatu ad
veniendum et interessendum ad Parliamentum, ad respondendum,
subeundum, allegandum et faciendum idem quod facerent omnes et
singule persone ipsorum decanatuum et archidiaconatuum, si ipsi et 30
eorum omnes et singuli personaliter interessent. Et quod huiusmodi

---

1 titulus nullus in *H B F N L*; De Modo Parliamenti *Vesp C J*; De Modo Tenendi
Parliamentum *E add A*; Modus tenendi parliamentum Anglie *O*.
6 ac etiam—7 temporibus *om B H C F*.
17 tenetur—19 minores *om O*.
22 facere *om Vesp*; suas *om B H F*.
30 ipsorum—31 personaliter *om F*; et archidiaconatuum *om Vesp J O*.

procuratores veniant cum warantis suis duplicatis, sigillis superiorum
suorum signatis, quod ipsi ad huiusmodi procurationem electi et missi
sunt, quarum litterarum una liberabitur clericis de Parliamento ad
irrotulandum et alia residebit penes ipsos procuratores. Et sic sub istis
duobus generibus summonicionum debet totus clerus summoneri ad 5
Parliamentum regis.

III *De Laicis*

Item, summoneri et venire debent omnes et singuli comites et barones,
et eorum pares, scilicet illi qui habent terras et redditus ad valentiam
comitie integri, videlicet viginti feoda unius militis, quolibet feodo 10
computato ad viginti libratas, que faciunt quadringentas libratas in
toto, vel ad valentiam unius baronie integre, scilicet tresdecim feoda et
tertiam partem unius feodi militis, quolibet feodo computato ad viginti
libratas, que faciunt in toto quadringentas marcas; et nulli minores
laici summoneri nec venire debent ad Parliamentum, ratione tenure 15
sue, nisi eorum presentia aliis de causis fuerit utilis vel necessaria ad
Parliamentum, et tunc de illis fieri debet sicut dictum est de minoribus
clericis, qui ratione tenure sue ad Parliamentum venire minime
tenentur.

IV   20

Item, rex solebat mittere brevia sua custodi Quinque Portuum quod
ipse eligi faciat de quolibet portu per ipsum portum duos idoneos et
peritos barones ad veniendum et interessendum ad Parliamentum suum
ad respondendum, subeundum, allegandum, et faciendum idem quod
facerent baronie sue, ac si ipsi de baroniis illis omnes et singuli 25
personaliter interessent ibidem; et quod huiusmodi barones veniant
cum warantis suis duplicatis, sigillis communibus Portuum suorum
signatis, quod ipsi rite ad hoc electi attornati sunt et missi pro baroniis
illis, quarum una liberabitur clericis de Parliamento, et alia residebit
penes ipsos barones. Et cum huiusmodi barones Portuum, licentia 30
optenta, de Parliamento recessuri fuerant, tunc solebant habere breve
de magno sigillo custodi Quinque Portuum, quod ipse rationabiles

---

3 litterarum *om J*; una deliberabitur *O*.
4 et sic—**6** regis *om J*.
7 *titulus* De Laicis *om Vesp*.
9 habent terras tenementas *C*; redditus comitive integre *add O*.
20 *titulus* De Baronibus Portuum *om codd*; Custodibus Quinque Portuum *add C*.
26 quod *om N L A B H F*.
31 tunc solebat Rex mittere *O*.

sumptus et expensas suas huiusmodi baronibus habere faceret de communitate Portus illius, a primo die quo versus Parliamentum venerint usque ad diem quo ad propria redierint, facta et expressa mentione in brevi illo de mora quam fecerint ad Parliamentum, et de die quo venerint, et quo licentiati fuerint redeundi; et solebat mentio 5 aliquando fieri in brevi quantum huiusmodi barones capere deberent de communitatibus illis per diem, scilicet aliqui plus et aliqui minus, secundum personarum habilitates et honestates, nec solebat poni pro duobus baronibus per diem ultra viginti solidos, habito respectu ad eorum moras, labores et expensas, nec solent huiusmodi expense in 10 certo reponi per curiam pro quibuscumque personis sic electis et missis pro communitatibus, nisi persone ipse fuerint honeste et bene se habentes in Parliamento.

V *De Militibus Comitatuum*

Item, rex solebat mittere brevia sua omnibus vicecomitibus Anglie, 15 quod eligi facerent quilibet de suo comitatu per ipsum comitatum duos milites idoneos, honestos et peritos, ad veniendum ad Parliamentum suum, eodem modo quo dictum est de baronibus Portuum, et de warantis suis eodem modo, sed pro expensis duorum militum de uno comitatu non solet poni ultra unam marcam per diem. 20

VI *De Civibus*

Eodem modo solebat mandari maiori et vicecomitibus Londoniarum, maiori et ballivis vel maiori et civibus Eboraci et aliarum civitatum, quod ipsi pro communitate civitatis sue eligerent duos idoneos, honestos et peritos cives ad veniendum et interessendum ad Parliamentum 25 eodem modo quo dictum est de baronibus Quinque Portuum et militibus comitatuum; et solebant cives esse pares et equales cum militibus comitatuum in expensis veniendo, morando et redeundo.

VII *De Burgensibus*

Item, eodem modo solebat et debet mandari ballivis et probis hominibus 30 burgorum, quod ipsi ex se et pre se eligant duos idoneos, honestos et peritos burgenses ad veniendum et interessendum ad Parliamentum

---

3—5 venerint et si licentiati fuerunt ad redeundum et solebat mentio *J*.
11 personis *om N L A H*.
16 quilibet *om* J.
17 ad veniendum—**32** peritos *om O*.
20 et nunc per diem viiis videlicet pro quolibet eorum quatuor solidos *add N L A B H C F*.

regis eodem modo quo dictum est de civibus; sed duo burgenses non
solebant percipere per diem pro expensis suis ultra decem solidos et
aliquando non ultra dimidiam marcam, et hoc solebat taxari per
curiam, secundum magnitudinem et potestatem burgi et secundum
honestatem personarum missarum.   5

VIII

Ostensa primo forma qualiter, cuilibet et a quanto tempore summonitio
Parliamenti fieri debet, et qui venire debent per summonitionem, et qui
non; secundo est dicendum qui sunt qui ratione officiorum suorum
venire debent, et interesse tenentur per totum Parliamentum, sine   10
summonitione; unde advertendum est quod duo clerici principales
Parliamenti electi per regem et concilium suum, et alii clerici secundarii
de quibus et quorum officiis dicetur specialius post, et principalis
clamator Anglie cum subclamatoribus suis, et principalis hostiarius
Anglie, que duo officia, scilicet officium clamatorie et hostiarie, solebant 15
ad unum et idem pertinere, isti duo officiarii tenentur interesse primo
die; cancellarius Anglie, thesaurarius, camerarii et barones de scaccario,
iusticiarii et omnes clerici et milites regis, una cum servientibus ad
placita regis, qui sunt de concilio regis, tenentur interesse secundo die,
nisi rationabiles excusationes habeant ita quod interesse non possunt, et 20
tunc mittere debent bonas excusationes.

IX *De Inchoatione Parliamenti*

Dominus Rex sedebit in medio maioris banci, et tenetur interesse
primo, sexto die Parliamenti: et solebant cancellarius, thesaurarius,
barones de scaccario et iusticiarii recordare defaltas factas in   25
Parliamento sub ordine qui sequitur. Primo die vocabuntur burgenses
et cives totius Anglie, quo die si non veniant, amerciabitur burgus ad
centum marcas et civitas ad centum libras: secundo die vocabuntur
milites comitatuum totius Anglie, quo die si non veniant, amerciabitur
comitatus ad centum libras: tertio die Parliamenti vocabuntur barones 30
Quinque Portuum, et postea barones, et postmodum comites: unde si
barones Quinque Portuum non veniant, amerciabitur baronia illa unde
sunt ad centum marcas; eodem modo amerciabitur baro per se ad
centum marcas et comes ad centum libras; et eodem modo fiet de illis

6 *titulus* De Modo Parliamenti *om codd.*
15 proclamatoris *N L A H.*
18–19 una cum servientibus ad placita regis *om C.*
27 cives comitatum *J.*

qui sunt pares comitibus et baronibus, scilicet, qui habent terras et
redditus ad valenciam unius comitatus vel unius baronie, ut predictum
est in titulo de summonitione: quarto die vocabuntur procuratores
cleri; qui si non veniant, amerciabuntur episcopi sui pro quolibet
archidiaconatu qui defaltam fecerit ad centum marcas: quinto die 5
vocabuntur decani, priores, abbates, episcopi et demum archiepiscopi,
qui si non veniant, amerciabitur quilibet archiepiscopus ad cenᵗum
libras, et quilibet tenens integram baroniam ad centum marcas, et
eodem modo de abbatibus, prioribus et aliis. Primo die debet fieri
proclamatio, primo in aula vel in monasterio, seu alio loco publico ubi 10
Parliamentum tenetur, et postmodum publice in civitate vel villa quod
omnes illi qui petitiones et querelas liberare voluerint ad Parliamentum,
illas deliberent a primo die Parliamenti in quinque dies proximo
sequentes.

X *De Predicatione ad Parliamentum* 15

Unus archiepiscopus, vel episcopus vel unus magnus clericus discretus
et facundus, electus per archiepiscopum in cuius provincia Parliamentum tenetur, debet predicare uno istorum primorum quinque dierum
Parliamenti et in presentia regis, et hoc quando Parliamentum fuerit
pro maiori parte adiunctum et congregatum, et in sermone suo 20
consequenter subiungere toti Parliamento quod ipsi cum eo humiliter
Deo supplicent, et ipsum adorent, pro pace et tranquillitate regis et
regni, prout dicetur specialius in sequenti titulo de pronuntiatione ad
Parliamentum.

XI *De Pronuntiatione pro Parliamento* 25

Post predicationem debet cancellarius Anglie vel capitalis iusticiarius
Anglie, ille scilicet qui tenet placita coram rege, vel alius idoneus,
honestus et facundus iusticiarius, vel clericus, per ipsos cancellarium et
capitalem iusticiarium electus, pronunciare causas Parliamenti, primo
in genere, et postea in specie, stando: et unde sciendum est quod omnes 30
de Parliamento, quicumque fuerit, dum loquitur stabunt, rege excepto,
ita quod omnes de Parliamento audire valeant eum qui loquitur, et si

---

3 procuratores cleri—**6** priores *om A.*
8 episcopus tenens *codd recensionis* (B).
12 querelas deliberare *J.*
23 predicatione *H E O*; departacione *B C F.*
28 iusticiarius—**29** electus *om E.*

obscure dicat vel ita basse loquatur dicat iterato, et loquatur (altius) vel loquatur alius pro eo.

XII   *De Loquela Regis post Pronuntiationem*

Rex post pronunciationem pro Parliamento rogare debet clericos et laicos, nominando omnes eorum gradus, scilicet archiepiscopos,   5 episcopos, abbates, priores, archidiaconos, procuratores et alios de clero, comites, barones, milites, cives, burgenses et alios laicos, quod ipsi diligenter, studiose et corditer laborent ad pertractandum et deliberandum negotia Parliamenti, prout ipsi magis et principalius hoc ad Dei voluntatem primo, et postea ad eius et eorum honores et commoda fore   10 intelligerint et sentierint.

XIII   *De Absentia Regis in Parliamento*

Rex tenetur omni modo personaliter interesse Parliamento, nisi per corporalem egritudinem detineatur et tunc potest tenere cameram suam, ita quod non iaceat extra manerium, vel saltim villam, ubi   15 Parliamentum tenetur, et tunc mittere debet pro duodecim personis de maioribus et melioribus qui summoniti sunt ad Parliamentum, duobus episcopis, duobus comitibus, duobus baronibus, duobus militibus comitatuum, duobus civibus et duobus burgensibus, ad videndam personam suam, et ad testificandum statum suum, et in eorum presentia   20 committere debet archiepiscopo loci, senescallo, et capitali iusticiario suo, quod ipsi coniunctim et divisim inchoent et continuent Parliamentum nomine suo, facta in commissione illa expressa mentione adtunc de causa absentie sue, que sufficere debet, et monere ceteros nobiles et magnates de Parliamento una cum notorio testimonio dictorum   25 duodecim parium suorum; causa est quod solebat clamor et murmur esse in Parliamento pro absentia regis, quia (res) dampnosa et periculosa est toti communitati Parliamenti et regni, cum rex a Parliamento absens fuerit, nec se absentare debet nec potest, nisi dumtaxat in casu supradicto.   30

XIV   *De Locis et Sessionibus in Parliamento*

Primo ut predictum est, sedebit rex in medio loco maioris banci et ex parte eius dextra sedebunt archiepiscopus Cantuariensis, episcopi

---

1 subscure N L A B H F; illicius = lucidius? *codd recensionis* (A); altius *codd recensionis* (B).
26 duodecim *om O E*.
27 Rex *codd recensionis* (A); res *codd recensionis* (B); *om J O*.

Londoniensis et Wintoniensis et post illos seriatim alii episcopi, abbates et priores; et in (parte) sinistra regis sedebunt archiepiscopus Eboracensis, episcopi Dunelmensis et Karlioliensis, et post illos seriatim comites, barones et domini; habita semper tali divisione inter predictos gradus et eorum loca, quod nullus sedeat nisi inter suos pares, et ad hoc 5 tenetur senescallus Anglie prospicere, nisi rex alium velit ad hoc assignare. Ad pedem regis dextrum sedebunt cancellarius Anglie et capitalis iusticiarius Anglie et socii sui, et eorum clerici qui sunt de Parliamento; et ad pedem eius sinistrum sedebunt thesaurarius, et camerarii et barones de scaccario, iusticiarii de banco et eorum clerici 10 qui sunt de Parliamento.

XV *De Principalibus Clericis Parliamenti*

Item, duo clerici principales Parliamenti sedebunt in medio iusticiariorum, qui irrotulabunt omnia placita et negotia Parliamenti. Et sciendum est quod ille duo clerici non sunt subiecti quibuscumque 15 iusticiariis, nec est aliquis iusticiarius Anglie iusticiarius in Parliamento, nec habent per se recordum in Parliamento, nisi quatenus assignata et data fuerit eis nova potestas in Parliamento per regem et pares Parliamenti, ut quando assignati sunt cum aliis sectatoribus Parliamenti ad audiendum et terminandum diversas petitiones et querelas in 20 Parliamento porrectas; sed sunt illi duo clerici immediate subiecti regi et Parliamento suo in communi nisi forte unus iusticiarius vel duo assignentur eis ad examinanda et emendanda eorum irrotulamenta. Et cum pares Parliamenti assignati sunt ad audiendum et examinandum aliquas petitiones specialiter per se, cum ipsi fuerint unanimes et 25 concordes in iudiciis suis reddendis super huiusmodi petitionibus, tunc recitabunt huiusmodi petitiones et processum super eisdem habitum et reddent iudicium in pleno Parliamento, ita quod ilii duo clerici principaliter irrotulent omnia placita et omnia iudicia in principali rotulo Parliamenti, et eosdem rotulos liberent ad thesaurarium ante 30 Parliamentum licentiatum, ita quod omni modo sint illi rotuli in Thesauraria ante recessum Parliamenti, salvo tamen eisdem clericis inde transcripto, seu contrarotulo si id habere velint. Isti duo clerici, nisi sint in aliis officiis cum rege, et feoda capiant de eo, ita quod inde honeste vivere poterint, capiant de rege per diem unam marcam pro 35

1 et post illos statim *O.*   2 parte *om Vesp.*
3 et post illos statim *O.*
9 sinistrum *om J N L A H B C F.*
29 omnia—32 in Thesauraria *om E.*

expensis suis per equales portiones, nisi sint ad mensam domini regis;
et si sint ad mensam domini regis, tunc capient praeter mensam suam
per diem dimidiam marcam per equales portiones per totum
Parliamentum.

XVI *De Quinque Clericis Parliamenti*   5

Dominus rex assignabit quinque clericos peritos et approbatos quorum
primus ministrabit et serviet episcopis, secundus procuratoribus cleri,
tertius comitibus et baronibus, quartus militibus comitatuum, quintus
civibus et burgensibus, et quilibet eorum, nisi sit cum rege et capiat de
eo tale feodum seu talia vadia quod inde possit honeste vivere, capiet de 10
rege per diem duos solidos, nisi sit ad mensam regis; et si sit ad mensam,
tunc capiet duodecim denarios per diem; qui clerici scribent eorum
dubitationes et responsiones quas facient regi et Parliamento, intererint
ad sua consilia ubicumque eos habere voluerint; et cum eis vacaverit
(iuvabunt) clericos principales ad irrotulandum.   15

XVII *De Casibus et Iudiciis Difficilibus*

Cum briga, dubitatio seu casus difficilis pacis vel guerre emergat in
regno vel extra, referatur et recitetur casus ille in scriptis in pleno
Parliamento, et tractetur et disputetur ibidem inter pares Parliamenti,
et si necesse sit, iniungatur per regem seu ex parte regis, si rex non   20
intersit, cuilibet gradui parium quod quilibet gradus adeat per se, et
liberetur casus ille clerico suo in scriptis, et in certo loco recitari faciant
coram eis casum illum; ita quod ipsi ordinent et considerent inter se
qualiter melius et iustius procedi poterit in casu illo sicut ipsi pro
persona regis et eorum propriis personis, ac etiam pro personis eorum   25
quorum personas ipsi representant, velint coram Deo respondere, et
suas responsiones et avisamenta reportent in scriptis, et omnibus eorum
responsionibus, consiliis et avisamentis hinc inde auditis, secundum
melius et sanius consilium procedatur et ubi saltim maior pars
Parliamenti concordat. Et si per discordiam inter regem et aliquos   30
magnates, vel forte inter ipsos magnates, pax regni infirmetur, vel
populus vel patria tribuletur, ita quod videatur regi et eius consilio

1 domini *om N A H.*
10 talia feoda *O.*
14 et—15 ad irrotulandum *om J*; mutabunt mittabunt *codd recensionis* (A); iuvabunt *codd
recensionis* (B).
17 in—18 regno *om N L A H B F.*
29 procedatur *om H.*
31 pars regni *N L A H.*

quod expediens sit quod negotium illud tractetur et emendetur per
considerationem omnium parium regni sui vel si per guerram rex et
regnum suum tribulentur, vel si casus difficilis coram cancellario Anglie
emergat, seu iudicium difficile coram iusticiariis fuerit reddendum, et
huiusmodi, et si forte in huiusmodi deliberationibus omnes vel saltim   5
maior pars concordare non valeant, tunc comes senescallus, comes
constabularius et comes marescallus, vel duo eorum, eligent viginti et
quinque personas de omnibus paribus regni, scilicet duos episcopos, et
tres procuratores, pro toto clero, duos comites et tres barones, quinque
milites comitatuum, quinque cives et burgenses, qui faciunt viginti   10
quinque; et illi viginti quinque possunt eligere ex seipsis, si velint,
duodecim et condescendere in eis, et ipsi duodecim sex et condescendere
in eis, et ipsi sex adhuc tres et condescendere in eis, et illi tres se in
paucioribus condescendere non possunt, nisi optenta licentia a domino
rege, et si rex consentiat illi tres possunt in duos, et de illis duobus alter   15
potest in alium descendere et ita demum stabit sua ordinatio supra
totum Parliamentum; et ita condescendo a viginti quinque personis
usque in unam solam personam, nisi numerus maior concordare valeat
et ordinare, tandem sola persona, ut est dictum, pro omnibus ordinabit,
que cum se ipsa discordare non potest; salvo domino regi et eius concilio   20
quod ipsi huiusmodi ordinationes postquam scripte fuerint examinare
et emendare valeant, si hoc facere sciant et velint, ita quod hoc fiat
ibidem tunc in pleno Parliamento, et de consensu Parliamenti, et non
retro Parliamentum.

XVIII *De Ordine Deliberandi Negotia Parliamenti*   25

Negotia pro quibus Parliamentum summonitum est debent deliberari
secundum kalendarium Parliamenti, et secundum ordinem petitionum
liberatarum (et affilatarum) nullo habito respectu ad quorumcumque
personas, sed qui prime proposuit prius agat. In kalendario Parliamenti
debent rememorari omnia negotia Parliamenti sub isto ordine; primo   30
de guerra si guerra sit, et de aliis negotiis personas regis, regine et
suorum liberorum tangentibus; secundo de negotiis communibus regni,
ut de legibus statuendis contra defectus legum originalium, iudicialium
et executoriarum, post iudicia reddita que sunt maxime negotia; tercio

---

9 duos barones *O.*
10 quinque burgenses *J O.*
18 valeat *om A H B F.*
23–4 et non retro Parliamentum *finit E.*
28 et affilatarum *om Vesp.*

debent rememorari negotia singularia, et hoc secundum ordinem filatarum petitionum, ut predictum est.

XIX *De Diebus et Horis ad Parliamentum*

Parliamentum non debet teneri diebus dominicis, sed secundis aliis diebus, illo die semper excepto, et aliis tribus, scilicet Omnium 5 Sanctorum, Animarum et Nativitatis Sancti Johannis Baptiste, potest teneri; et debet singulis diebus inchoari hora media prima, qua hora rex Parliamentum tenetur interesse, et omnes pares regni. Parliamentum debet teneri in loco publico, et non in privato, nec in occulto loco; in diebus festivis Parliamentum debet inchoari hora prima propter 10 divinum servitium.

XX *De Hostiariis Parliamenti*

Hostiarius principalis Parliamenti stabit infra magnum hostium monasterii, aulae, vel alterius loci ubi Parliamentum tenetur, et custodiet hostium ita quod nullus intret Parliamentum, nisi qui sectam 15 et eventum debeat ad Parliamentum, vel vocatus fuerit propter negotium quod prosequitur in Parliamento, et oportet quod hostiarius ille habeat cognitionem personarum quae ingredi debent ita quod nulli omnino negetur ingressus qui Parliamentum interesse tenetur; et hostiarius ille potest et debet, si necesse sit, habere plures hostiarios sub 20 se.

XXI *De Clamatore Parliamenti*

Clamator Parliamenti stabit extra hostium Parliamenti, et hostiarius sibi denunciabit clamationes suas; rex solebat assignare servientes suos ad arma ad standum per magnum spatium extra hostium Parliamenti, 25 ad custodiendum hostium, ita quod nulli impressiones nec tumultus facerent circa hostia, per quod Parliamentum impediatur, sub poena captionis corporum suorum, quia de iure hostium Parliamenti non debet claudi, sed per hostiarios et servientes regis ad arma custodiri.

XXII *De Stationibus Loquencium in Parliamento* 30

Omnes pares Parliamenti sedebunt, et nullus stabit nisi quando loquitur, ita quod quilibet de Parliamento eum audire valeat; nullus

---

1–2 secularia prelatorum et petitionum ut predictum est *post* negotia *add O.*
5 die simpliciter *O.*
7 inchoari—8 pares regni *om J.*
25 per magnum hostium *J.*

intrabit Parliamentum, nec exiet de Parliamento, nisi per unicum hostium; et quicumque loquitur rem aliquam que deliberari debet per Parliamentum, stabunt omnes loquentes; causa est ut audiantur a paribus, quia omnes pares sunt iudices et iusticiarii.

XXIII *De Auxiliis Regis*

Rex non solebat petere auxilium de regno suo nisi pro guerra instanti, vel filios suos milites faciendo, vel filias suas maritando, et tunc debent huiusmodi auxilia peti in pleno Parliamento, et in scriptis cuilibet gradui parium Parliamenti liberari, et in scriptis responderi; et sciendum est quod ad huiusmodi auxilia concedenda oportet quod omnes pares Parliamenti consentiant, et intelligendum est quod duo milites, qui veniunt ad Parliamentum pro ipso comitatu, maiorem vocem habent in Parliamento in concedendo et contradicendo, quam maior comes Anglie, et eodem modo procuratores cleri unius episcopatus maiorem vocem habent in Parliamento, si omnes sint concordes, quam episcopus ipse, et hoc in omnibus que per Parliamentum concedi, negari vel fieri debent: et hoc patet quia rex potest tenere Parliamentum cum communitate regni sui, absque episcopis, comitibus et baronibus, dumtamen summoniti sunt ad Parliamentum, licet nullus episcopus, comes vel baro ad summonitiones suas veniant; quia olim nec episcopus fuerat, nec comes, nec baro, adhuc tunc reges tenuerunt Parliamenta sua, sed aliter est econtra, licet communitates, cleri et laici, summonite essent ad Parliamentum, sicut de iure debent, et propter aliquas certas causas venire nollent, ut si pretenderent quod rex non regeret eos sicuti deberet, et assignarent specialiter in quibus articulis eos disrexerat, tunc Parliamentum nullum esset omnino, licet omnes archiepiscopi, episcopi, comites, barones et omnes eorum pares, cum rege interessent; et ideo oportet quod omnia que affirmari vel infirmari, concedi vel negari, vel fieri debent per Parliamentum, per communitatem Parliamenti concedi debent, que est ex tribus gradibus sive generibus Parliamenti, scilicet ex procuratoribus cleri, militibus comitatuum, civibus et burgensibus, qui representant totam communitatem Anglie, et non de magnatibus, quia quilibet eorum est pro sua propria persona ad Parliamentum et pro nulla alia.

3 ut videantur *O.*
13 contradicendo *om N L H B F.*
17 cum communitate—19 ad Parliamentum *om J.*
21 nec baro *om O.*
25–6 quibusdam articulis *O*; eos disrexerat *om J*; parliamentum illum *N L A B.*
27 episcopi *om J.*

XXIV *De Departitione Parliamenti*

Parliamentum departiri non debet dummodo aliqua petitio pendeat
indiscussa, vel, ad minus, ad quam non sit determinatum responsum, et
si rex contrarium permittat, periurus est; nullus solus de omnibus
paribus Parliamenti recedere potest nec debet de Parliamento, nisi   5
optenta inde licentia de rege et omnibus suis paribus et hoc in pleno
Parliamento, et quod de huiusmodi licentia fiat rememoratio in rotulo
Parliamenti, et si aliquis de paribus, durante Parliamento, infirmaverit,
ita quod ad Parliamentum venire non valeat, tunc per triduum mittat
excusatores ad Parliamentum, quod si non venerit, mittantur ei duo de   10
paribus suis ad videndum et testificandum huiusmodi infirmitatem, et
si sit suspicio, iurentur illi duo pares quod veritatem inde dicent, et si
comperiatur quod finxerat se, amercietur tanquam pro defalta, et si
non finxerat se, attornet aliquem sufficientem coram eis ad interessendum Parliamentum pro se, si voluerit nec ulterius excusari potest si sit 15
sane memorie.

Departitio Parliamenti ita usitari debet: primitus peti debet et
publice proclamari in Parliamento, et infra palacium Parliamenti, si sit
aliquis, qui petitionem liberaverit ad Parliamentum, cui nondum sit
responsum; quod si nullus reclamet, supponendum est quod cuilibet   20
metitur, vel saltim quatenus potest de iure respondetur, et tunc primo,
scilicet, cum nullus qui petitionem ea vice exhibuerit reclamet,
Parliamentum nostrum licentiabimus.

XXV *De Transcriptis Recordorum et Processuum in Parliamento*

Clerici Parliamenti non negabunt cuiquam transcriptum processus sui,   25
sed liberabunt illud cuilibet qui hoc petierit, et capient semper pro
decem lineis unum denarium, nisi forte facta fide de impotentia, in quo
casu nihil capient. Rotulum de Parliamento continebit in latitudine
decem pollices. Parliamentum tenebitur in quo loco regni regi placuerit.

XXVI *De Gradibus Parium Parliamenti*   30

Rex est caput, principium et finis Parliamenti, et ita non habet parem
in suo gradu, et ita ex rege solo est primus gradus. Secundus gradus est
de archiepiscopis, episcopis, abbatibus, prioribus, per baroniam
tenentibus. Tertius gradus est de procuratoribus cleri. Quartus gradus

---

3 terminatum *O*.
14–15 se unum aspicientem coram eis ad interessendum pro se *post* finxerat *O*.
33–4 pro baroniis tangentibus *O*.

est de comitibus, baronibus et aliis magnatibus et proceribus, tenentibus
ad valentiam comitatus et baronie, ut predictum est in titulo de laicis.
Quintus gradus est de militibus comitatuum. Sextus gradus est de
civibus et burgensibus: et ita est Parliamentum ex sex gradibus. Sed
sciendum est quod licet aliquis dictorum quinque graduum post regem 5
absens sit, dum tamen omnes premuniti sint per rationabiles summonitiones Parliamenti, nihilominus censetur esse plenum.

Explicit Modus Parliamenti.

7 Parliamenti metu inchoactione senectute esse plenius *J*; sentietur esse *O*.

The Manner of Parliament

Here is described the manner in which the parliament of the King of England and of his Englishmen was held in the time of King Edward, the son of King Ethelred. Which manner was related by the more distinguished men of the kingdom in the presence of William, Duke of Normandy, Conqueror and King of England: by the Conqueror's own command, and through his approval it was used in his times and in the times of his successors, the Kings of England.

I *The Summoning of Parliament*

The summoning of parliament ought to precede the first day of parliament by forty days.

II *Concerning the Clergy*

To parliament ought to be summoned and come archbishops, bishops, abbots, priors, and other higher clergy who hold by earldom or barony by reason of such tenure and none of the lesser clergy unless their presence and appearance be required other than on account of their tenures, either because they are of the King's Council, or because their presence is regarded as useful and necessary to parliament, and the King is bound to reimburse them their costs and expenses incurred in coming and staying at parliament, nor ought such of the minor clergy to be summoned to parliament but the King used to send equivalent writs to such persons at the same time asking them that they should attend parliament.

Also the King used to send his summons to archbishops, bishops, and other exempt persons, such as abbots, priors, deans, and other ecclesiastical persons who have jurisdictions set apart by exemptions of this sort and privileges, that they for every deanery and archdeaconry of England cause to be elected by the deaneries and archdeaconries themselves two experienced and suitable proctors from their own archdeaconry to come and attend parliament, to reply, undertake, state, and do, what each and every person from the said deaneries and archdeaconries would do if everyone of them was present personally. And that those proctors come with their warrants in duplicate sealed with the seals of their superiors, that they have been elected and sent to act as proctor; one of these letters shall be given to the clerks of parliament for enrolment and the other shall remain with the proctors themselves. And so with these two kinds of summons all the clergy ought to be summoned to the King's parliament.

III *Concerning the Laity*

Also there ought to be summoned and come every one of the earls and barons and their peers, that is say those who have lands and revenues to the value of a complete earldom, that is to say twenty knight's fees of one knight, each fee being reckoned worth twenty librates[1] which makes four hundred librates in all, or to the value of one complete barony, that is to say thirteen and a third knight's fees of one knight each fee being reckoned at twenty librates which makes in all four hundred marks, and none of the lesser laity ought to be summoned or come to parliament, by reason of their tenure, unless their presence is for other causes useful and necessary to parliament, and then in their case it should be done as has been said concerning the lesser clergy, who are not in the least obliged to attend parliament by reason of their tenure.

[IV *Concerning the Barons of the Ports*][2]

Also the King used to send his writs to the Warden of the Cinque Ports that he should cause to be elected from each Port by that Port two suitable and experienced barons, to come and be present at his parliament, to answer, undertake, state, and do that which their baronies would do, as if everyone from the baronies were himself present personally, and that such barons shall come with their warrants in duplicate, sealed with the common seal of the Ports, that they have been duly elected attorneys and sent on behalf of those baronies, one of which [letters] shall be delivered to the clerks of parliament, and the other remain with the barons themselves. And when these Port barons, having obtained permission had been about to leave parliament they usually had a writ under the Great Seal addressed to the Warden of the Cinque Ports that he should see to it that these barons shall have their reasonable expenses and costs from the community of their Port, from the first day of their coming to parliament until the day they returned home; express mention having been made in that writ of their stay in parliament, and of the day on which they came, and of the day on

---

[1] Twenty pounds a year.   [2] Reading of the (B) recension.

which they had permission to return, and sometimes mention used to
be made in this writ how much per day these barons are entitled to
receive from their communities, that is to say, some more, some less,
according to the individual's abilities and status, nor was it usual to lay
out more than twenty shillings a day for two barons when account was
taken of their stay, labour and expenses, nor are such expenses to be
allowed in a standard way by the court to any persons elected and sent
in this manner for the communities, unless these people have conducted
themselves honestly and well in parliament.

V *Concerning the Knights of the Shires*

Also the King used to send his writs to all the sheriffs of England that
each should cause to be elected from his county, and by the county, two
suitable, honest, and experienced knights to come to his parliament, in
the same manner as laid down for the Port barons and in the same
manner for [dealing with] their warrants, but for the expenses of the
two knights of a county it is not usual to pay more than one mark per
day.

VI *Concerning the Citizens*

In a similar manner orders used to be sent to the mayor and sheriffs of
London, the mayor and bailiffs or mayor and citizens of York and
other cities, that they on behalf of the community of their city should
elect two suitable, honest and experienced citizens to come and attend
at parliament in the same manner as it has been said for the barons of
the Cinque Ports and the knights of the shires, and it was customary for
the citizens to be the peers and equals of the knights of the shires in the
expenses of coming, staying and returning.

VII *Concerning the Burgesses*

Also in a similar manner orders used to be sent to the bailiffs and
worthy men of the boroughs, that they elect among themselves and on
behalf of themselves two suitable, honest, and experienced burgesses to
come and be present at the King's parliament in the same way as has
been said for the citizens; but the two burgesses did not usually receive
more than ten shillings a day for their expenses, and sometimes not
more than half a mark, and this used to be assessed by the court
according to the size and power of the borough, and according to the
status of the persons sent.

[VIII *Concerning the Manner of Parliament*][3]

It having first been shown in what way, to whom and at what time the parliamentary summons ought to be made, and who ought to come by summons and who not, it must secondly be said who ought to come on account of their office, and should be present without summons throughout the whole of parliament. It should be noticed in this connection that the two principal clerks of parliament chosen by the King and his Council, and that the other under clerks of whom and of whose offices especial mention will be given later and the chief crier of England with his under criers and the chief doorkeeper of England, which two offices, that is say the office of crier and of doorkeeper used to belong to one and the same person, these two officers are bound to attend on the first day. The chancellor of England, the treasurer, the chamberlains and barons of the Exchequer, the justices and all the King's clerks and knights together with the King's law officers, who are of the King's Council are bound to attend on the second day, unless they have reasonable excuses to show why they cannot be present, and then they ought to send adequate excuses.

IX *Concerning the Opening of Parliament*

The Lord King shall sit in the middle of the greater bench, and is bound to be present at prime on the sixth day of parliament, and the chancellor, the treasurer, the barons of the exchequer, and the justices, used to record cases of default made in parliament in the following order. On the first day the burgesses and citizens of the whole of England shall be called and if they do not come on that day a borough will be amerced at one hundred marks, and a city at one hundred pounds. On the second day the knights of the shires of the whole of England shall be called, and if they do not come on that day the county shall be amerced at a hundred pounds. On the third day of parliament the barons of the Cinque Ports shall be called, followed by the barons and then the earls; then if the Cinque barons do not come, the barony they are from shall be amerced at one hundred marks. In the same manner a baron as such shall be amerced at one hundred marks and an earl at one hundred pounds; and the same for those who are the peers of earls and barons, namely those who have lands and rents to the value of one earldom or one barony as mentioned previously under the title concerning summons [i.e. *Concerning the Laity*]. On the fourth day the

---

[3] Reading of the (B) recension.

proctors of the clergy shall be called, if they do not come their bishops shall be amerced at one hundred marks for each archdeaconry which has made default. On the fifth day shall be called the deans, priors, abbots, bishops, and lastly archbishops, it they do not come each archbishop shall be amerced at one hundred pounds, a bishop[4] holding a full barony at one hundred marks, and in the same manner for abbots, priors and others. On the first day a proclamation ought to made, first in the hall or in the monastery or in some public place where parliament is being held, and afterwards publicly in the city or town that all who wish to present petitions and plaints to parliament should deliver them during the five days following the first day of parliament.

X *Concerning the Sermon to Parliament*

An archbishop or a bishop or a higher clerk, who is discreet and eloquent, and who is selected by the archbishop in whose province parliament is held, ought to preach on one of the first days of parliament and in the King's presence, and this when parliament for the greater part is assembled and congregated, and in his sermon he should in due course enjoin the whole parliament that they with him should humbly beseech and pray God for the peace and tranquillity of the King and the kingdom, as will be more particularly mentioned in the following title concerning the declaration to parliament.

XI *Concerning the Declaration to Parliament*

After the sermon the chancellor of England or the chief justice of England, that is he who holds pleas before the King, or some fit, honest and eloquent justice or clerk chosen by the chancellor and chief justice ought to declare, standing up, the causes of parliament first in general and then in particular; and concerning which be it known that everybody in parliament, whoever he is, will stand up to speak, the King excepted, so that all in parliament shall be able to hear the speaker, and if he speaks indistinctly or low let him repeat it, and let him speak louder or let another speak for him.

XII *Concerning the King's Speech After the Declaration*

The King after the declaration to parliament ought to ask the clergy and laity naming all their grades, that is to say archbishops, bishops, abbots, priors, archdeacons, proctors, and other clergy, earls, barons, knights, citizens, burgesses, and other laymen, that they should all

[4] Reading of the (B) recension.

diligently, seriously and heartily labour to consider and deliberate on the business of parliament so that these matters shall be firstly in accordance with the will of God, and secondly to his and their honour and advantage, according as they will understand and perceive them.

XIII *Concerning the King's Absence in Parliament*

The King is in every way bound to be personally present in parliament unless he is detained by physical illness, in which case he may stay in his chamber, provided that he does not lie outside the manor or at least the vill in which parliament is held, and then he ought to send for twelve of the greater and worthier persons summoned to parliament, two bishops, two earls, two barons, two knights of the shire, two citizens, and two burgesses, to view his person, and testify to his condition. In their presence he ought to commission the archbishop of the place,[5] the steward, and his chief justice, so that they jointly and severally open and carry on the parliament in his name, stating expressly in that commission the reason for his absence which ought to be sufficient, and advising the rest of the nobles and the magnates of parliament together with the open testimony of their aforesaid twelve peers. The reason is that there used to be uproar and murmurings in parliament because of the absence of the King, because it is a damaging and dangerous matter[6] for the whole community of parliament and the kingdom when the King is absent from parliament, nor ought he nor can he absent himself from parliament except in the case mentioned above.

XIV *Concerning the Placing and Seats in Parliament*

First, as aforesaid, the King shall sit in the middle of the greater bench, and on his right side shall sit the archbishop of Canterbury, the bishops of London and Winchester, and beyond them in due order the other bishops, abbots, and priors, and on the left hand side of the King shall sit the archbishop of York, the bishops of Durham and Carlisle, and beyond them in due order the earls, barons, and the lords; and such a division being habitually observed among the aforesaid grades and their respective places, so that no one sits except among his peers, and the steward of England is bound to provide for this, unless the King wishes to assign someone else to this. At the right foot of the King shall sit the chancellor of England, and the chief justice of England and his fellow judges, and their clerks who are of parliament; and at his left

[5] i.e. the province in which parliament is being held.
[6] Reading of the (B) recension.

foot shall sit the treasurer, and the chamberlains and barons of the exchequer, justices of the bench, and their clerks who are of parliament.

XV *Concerning the Principal Clerks of Parliament*

Also the two principal clerks of parliament shall sit among the justices and shall enroll all the pleas and business of parliament. And it should be understood that these two clerks are not subject to any of the justices, nor is any English justice a judge in parliament nor do they have in themselves record in parliament unless new powers may have been assigned to them by the King and the peers of parliament, as when they have been assigned with other suitors of parliament to hear and determine diverse petitions and plaints which have been laid before parliament, but these two clerks are immediately subject to the King and his parliament jointly unless one or two of the justices should be assigned to the examination and correction of their enrolments. When the peers of parliament have been assigned to hear and examine any petitions especially by themselves, and when they are themselves unanimous and agreed in rendering their judgements on such petitions, they shall recite such petitions, and their proceedings concerning them, and render judgement in full parliament, so that these two clerks shall first and foremost enroll all pleas and all judgements on the principal roll of parliament and deliver these rolls to the treasurer before parliament is allowed to depart, so that these rolls shall certainly be in the Treasury before the recess of parliament, saving nevertheless to these clerks a transcript or a counter-roll if they wish to have it. These two clerks unless they hold some other offices from the King, and receive fees from him, allowing them a decent livelihood, shall receive from the King one mark a day in equal shares for their expenses, unless they shall be entitled to eat at the King's table and if they eat at the King's table then they shall receive in addition to their allowance half a mark a day in equal shares for the whole duration of parliament.

XVI *Concerning the Five Clerks*

The King shall assign five expert and proven clerks, of whom the first shall assist and serve the bishops, the second the proctors of the clergy, the third the earls and barons, the fourth the knights of the shire, the fifth the citizens and burgesses, and each of them, unless he is the with the King and receives from him such fees or wages which allows him a decent livelihood, shall receive from the King two shillings a day, unless he eats at the King's table and if he eats at the King's table he shall receive twelve pence per day. These clerks shall write down their queries and the answers which were made to the King and parliament, and shall be present at their consultations whenever they wish to have them there, and when they have time they shall assist[7] the principal clerks in enrolling.

XVII *Concerning Difficult Cases and Decisions*

When a dispute, doubt, or difficult case arises of peace or of war, within or without the kingdom, that case is to be referred and recited in writing in full parliament, and debated and discussed there among the peers of parliament, and if it is necessary it shall be enjoined by the King, or it shall be enjoined on his behalf if he is not present, to whichever grade of peers, so that the appropriate grade proceed itself, and the case shall be given to their own clerk in writing, and in a certain place they shall have that case read out in their presence, so that they should ordain and consider among themselves what the best and most just procedure is in that matter, just as they may be willing to answer before God for the person of the King, for their own persons, and for the persons of those persons whom they represent, and report in writing their answers and considerations, so that when all their replies, counsel, and considerations on either side have been heard, it can proceed according to the best and wisest counsel, and where at least the greater part of parliament agrees. And if there is discord between the King and some magnates, or perhaps between the magnates themselves, whereby the King's peace is undermined, and the people as well as the land is afflicted, so that it seems to the King and his Council that it would be expedient for the matter to be considered and settled by the advice of all the peers of the realm; or if the King and the kingdom is afflicted by war, or if a difficult case comes before the chancellor of England, or a difficult judgement pending before the justices needs to be rendered, and such like—if by chance in these matters all or even the greater part are not able to agree then the earl steward, the earl constable, and the earl marshal, or two of them shall elect twenty-five persons from all the peers of the kingdom, that is to say two bishops and three proctors for all the clergy, two earls and three barons, five knights of the shire, five citizens and five[8] burgesses, which make twenty-five, and these twenty-five can elect twelve from among themselves if they wish and reduce into them, and these twelve can reduce into six, and these six into three and reduce into them, but these

---

[7] Reading of the (B) recension.   [8] Reading of J.O.

three cannot reduce themselves further unless they obtain leave from the Lord King, and if the King agrees, these three may become two, and of these two one can decline into the other, and in that case only his ruling will stand above the whole parliament, and so by the reduction of twenty-five persons to one person only, unless the greater number have been able to agree and decide, then this one person, as stated, who cannot disagree with himself, shall decide for all; reserving only to our Lord the King and his Council the power to examine and amend these ordinances after they have been written, if they know how and so wish, so that it shall then be done in full parliament, and with the consent of parliament and not behind the back of parliament.

XVIII *Concerning the Order of Business of Parliament*

The business for which parliament has been summoned ought to be considered according to the calendar of parliament, and according to the order of petitions lodged and filed, without consideration of the manner of people, but who first proposes, acts first. In the calendar of parliament all parliamentary business ought to be listed in this order: first concerning war if there is a war, and other matters concerning the persons of the King, Queen, and their children; secondly matters of common concern to the kingdom, so that laws shall be enacted against the defects of customary law, the law of the courts and the executive after judgement has been given, which are the chief business; thirdly, there ought to be listed private business, and this according to the order of petitions filed, as aforesaid.

XIX *Concerning the Days and Hours of Parliament*

Parliament ought not to be held on Sundays, but it can be held on all other days, that day always excepted, and three others, namely All Saints, All Souls, and the nativity of St. John the Baptist; and it ought to begin each day at mid-prime, at which hour the King is bound to be present in parliament, and all the peers of the kingdom. Parliament ought to be held in a public and not in a private or a secret place; on feast days parliament ought to begin at prime on account of divine service.

XX *Concerning the Doorkeepers of Parliament*

The chief doorkeeper of parliament shall stand inside the great door of the monastery, hall, or other place where parliament is held, and shall guard the door so that no-one may enter parliament, except he who owes suit and appearance at parliament, or who will have been called because of business that he is transacting in parliament, and it is necessary that this doorkeeper should recognize those who ought to enter so that no-one shall be denied entry to parliament who ought to be in parliament, and the doorkeeper can and ought, if necessary, to have several assistant doorkeepers under him.

XXI *Concerning the Crier of Parliament*

The crier of parliament shall stand outside the door of parliament, and the doorkeeper shall tell him what to announce. The King used to assign his serjeants-at-arms to stand some distance outside the door of parliament to guard the doorway, so that no one should under the penalty of arrest make a demonstration or a disturbance by the door, by which parliament would be impeded. Because by law the door of parliament ought not to be closed, but be guarded by the doorkeepers and the King's serjeants-at-arms.

XXII *Concerning the Position of Speakers in Parliament*

All the peers of parliament will sit, and no one will stand except when he speaks in such a manner that everyone in parliament can hear him; no one will go in or out of parliament except by the one door. And whoever speaks on any matter which ought to be debated by parliament will stand as will all speakers. The reason for this is so that they may be heard by the peers, because all peers are judges and justices.

XXIII *Concerning Aids to the King*

The King used not to demand aid from his kingdom except for an imminent war,[9] or knighting his sons, or marrying his daughters, and then such aids ought to be requested in full parliament, and these requests delivered in writing to each grade of peers of parliament, and given a written reply. And it should be realized that for the granting of such aids it is necessary that all the peers of parliament consent. It must be understood that two knights who come to parliament for the shire, have a greater voice in granting and denying than the greatest earl of England, and in the same manner the proctors of the clergy from one diocese, if they are agreed, have a greater voice in parliament than the bishop himself, and this in everything that ought to be granted, denied, or done by parliament. And this is evident because the King can hold parliament with the community of his kingdom, without

[9] Or a war that is actually present.

bishops, earls, and barons, provided they have been summoned to parliament, even though no bishop, earl, or baron come in response to their summons; because at one time there was no bishop, no earl, no baron, and yet the Kings held their parliaments then. But it is different the other way round; allow that the communities, clerical and lay, are summoned to parliament, as by right they should, and for certain reasons are not willing to come, if, for example, they argue that the King does not govern them as he should, and mention particular matters in which he has not ruled correctly, then there would be no parliament at all, even though all the archbishops, bishops, earls and barons, and all their peers were present with the King, and therefore it is necessary that all matters which ought to be confirmed or annulled, granted, denied, or done by parliament, ought to granted by the community of parliament, which is composed of three grades or orders of parliament, that is to say the proctors of the clergy, the knights of the shire, the citizens and burgesses who represent the whole community of England, and not the magnates because each of these is at parliament for his own individual person, and for no one else.

XXIV *Concerning the Departure of Parliament*

Parliament ought not to depart as long as any petition remains undiscussed, or at least to which no reply has been determined upon, and the King breaks his oath if he allows the contrary; and no single one of the peers of parliament can or ought to leave parliament unless he has obtained permission from the King and from all his peers and this in full parliament, and a record of this license ought to be entered on the róll of parliament, and if during the course of parliament anyone of the peers falls ill, so that he is unable to attend parliament, then for three days he should send excusers to parliament, but if he does not come, two of his peers should be sent to him to see and to testify to his sickness, and if there is any suspicion, these two peers shall be sworne that they speak the truth, and if it is found that he is feigning sickness, he shall be amerced as for absence, and if he is not feigning sickness then he shall appoint as attorney some sufficient person [i.e. substitute] in their presence to attend parliament for him; even if he should wish, he cannot be further excused, if he be of sound mind.

The departure of parliament ought to be conducted in this way: first it ought to be asked and proclaimed publicly in parliament, and within the pale of parliament, whether there is anyone who has delivered a petition to parliament who has not yet received a reply, because if no-one speaks up, it must be supposed that everyone has his remedy, or at least has been replied to as far as is possible by law, and then and only then that is to say when no one who has presented a petition on that occasion objects, will we release our parliament.

XXV *Concerning Transcripts of Records and Processes in Parliament*

The clerks of parliament will not refuse anyone a transcript of his process, but will give it to anyone who asks, and they will always receive a penny for ten lines, unless a good case is made of inability to pay, in which event they will take nothing. The roll of parliament will measure ten inches in width. Parliament will be held in whatever place in the realm pleases the King.

XXVI *Concerning the Grades of Peers of Parliament*

The King is the head, the beginning, and the end of parliament, and therefore he has no peer in his grade, therefore from the King alone comes the first grade; the second grade consists of the archbishops, bishops, abbots, and priors who hold by barony; the third grade consists of the proctors of the clergy; the fourth grade of the earls, barons, and other magnates and nobility, who hold to the value of an earldom or barony, as mentioned in the title on the laity; the fifth grade consists of the knights of the shires, and the sixth of the citizens and burgesses, and so parliament is of six grades. But it must be realized that if any of the said grades below the King be absent, provided that they have all been forewarned by due and correct summons of parliament, none the less it shall be considered to be complete.

Here ends the Manner of Parliament

Historical Notes

page 67

3   The attribution of the parliamentary system to Edward the Confessor may be explained by the cult of the Confessor evident during the reign of Edward II. In particular Edward II promised by his coronation oath to confirm the laws of the Confessor, F. W. Maitland, *Constitutional History* (Cambridge, 1913), pp. 99–100.

12–14   The principle that bishops hold their possessions of the King 'sicut baroniam' is to be found in the *Constitutions of Clarendon* (Cap XI). In the time of Edward I it was argued that the archbishop of Canterbury was summoned to parliament 'like any other baron', Richardson and Sayles, *Irish Parliament*, p. 121. In the parliament of 1387 the Archbishop of Canterbury argued that the prelates holding by barony were peers of parliament, *Rot. Parl.* III 236–7. For a different view, namely that 'the episcopate attended parliament by reason of its spiritual rather than its supposed tenurial position', see Plucknett, *The English Government at Work*, ed. Willard and Morris, p. 95. On the position of the spiritual lords see L. O. Pike, *A Constitutional History of the House of Lords* (London, 1894), pp. 151–68. For the actual attendance of the bishops and abbots, J. S. Roskell, 'The Problem of the Attendance of Lords in Medieval Parliaments', *B.I.H.R.* 29 (1956), 173–5.

25–31   For a detailed discussion of this passage in the *Modus* see above, *Clerical Representation in the Modus*, pp. 41–3 The whole question of clerical representation in the *Modus* is reviewed by Clarke, pp. 15–32, 125–32, Roskell, pp. 411–42, and Plucknett, *English Government at Work*, ed. Willard and Morris, pp. 99–100. Clerical proctors rarely attended parliament after the 1330s. See above, p. 23.

page 68

8–14   The reference to twenty knights' fees of an earl, and 13⅓ fees of a baron derive ultimately from Magna Carta as modified in the *Confirmatio* of 1297. In the *Confirmatio* the relief to be paid by a baron was a hundred marks and by an earl one hundred pounds, which corresponds to the tariff of amercements for barons and earls as set out in the *Modus*, see p. 44. For the stabilization of the baronial list after 1321 see J. Enoch Powell and Keith Wallis, *The House of Lords in the Middle Ages* (London, 1968), p. 315. As they say the author of the *Modus*, 'considered that all who had landed property of the value theoretically attributed to an earl or baron . . . should be treated respectively as their "equivalents" or "peers", and that all should be summoned without exception', p. 286.

21 The phraseology in the (B) recension, 'the King is bound to send his writs', may well derive from the fact that the barons of the Cinque Ports were not summoned to parliament regularly until 1322. In 1321 the use of the *solebat* clause would have been inappropriate, see p. 25. For the general background see K. M. E. Murray, *The Constitutional History of the Cinque Ports* (Manchester, 1935).

page 69

8–10 There was no fixed rate of wages for the barons of the Cinque Ports.

14–18 Thirty-seven shires returned seventy-four county members. Before 1372 a number of knights were sheriffs and lawyers, K. Wood-Leigh, 'Sheriffs, Lawyers and Belted Knights in the Parliaments of Edward III', *E.H.R.* 46 (1931), 372–88, and 'Knights' Attendance in the Parliaments of Edward III', *E.H.R.* 47 (1932), 398–413.

19–20 The majority of manuscripts of the second recension add that *now* knights of the shire are to be paid four shillings a day. It was in 1327 that the rate was established as four shillings a day for the knights of the shire and two for the burgesses, H. M. Cam, *Liberties and Communities in Medieval England* (London, 1963), p. 237.

30 On the election of citizens and burgesses see M. McKisack, *The Parliamentary Representation of the English Boroughs During the Middle Ages* (Oxford, 1932), pp. 24–43. The list of parliamentary boroughs was not fixed in this period.

page 70

1–5 There was a good deal of variation in the wages actually paid by the boroughs, M. McKisack, *ibid*, pp. 82–99. For the payment of the Colchester burgesses in the fifteenth century see p. 193.

7–19 For a discussion of the official element in parliament see Clarke, pp. 203–10; H. G. Richardson and G. O. Sayles, 'The

King's Ministers in Parliament, 1272–1377', *E.H.R.* 46–7
(1931–2), 529–50, 194–203, 377–97. 'It is hardly possible to
imagine a medieval parliament working unless such men as
these were at the centre', Plucknett, p. 98. According to some
historians the strong professional element in the Council as
described by the *Modus* indicates a date early in the fourteenth
century, J. F. Baldwin, *The King's Council in England in the Later
Middle Ages* (Oxford, 1913), pp. 70–3.

page 70

23–34 On the tariff of amercements see above, *The Tariff of*
(and *Amercements*, pp. 44–7. The detailed tariff of amercements is
1–9, found only in the English *Modus*. Richardson and Sayles, *Irish*
p. 71) *Parliament*, pp. 137–44, have commented on these figures. See
also Roskell, 'The Problem of the Attendance of Lords in
Medieval Parliaments', pp. 153–204. It is probable that as far
as the Commons were concerned these figures remained more
theoretical than practical.

page 71

8 The (B) reading, *episcopus*, would appear to be the original one.
13–14 The time allowed for the filing of petitions was usually six
days. *Rot. Parl.* I. 182. 350; Clarke, p. 223.

15–24 The first known English parliamentary sermons were concerned with the deposition of Edward II, Clarke, p. 224. It
may be that before that time the sermon was religious rather
than political in character. The most famous parliamentary
sermon expressing a political ideology was that of Edmund
Stafford, Bishop of Exeter in the parliament of September,
1397. *Rot. Parl.* III. 347. See also Bishop Russell's drafts for his
parliamentary sermons in 1483. S. B. Chrimes, *English
Constitutional Ideas*, pp. 167–91.

25–32 The first example of the Declaration (*pronuntiatio*) on the
(and Parliament Rolls is for the Lincoln parliament of 1316. *Rot.*
1–2, *Parl.* I. 350. In the reign of Edward III it was usually delivered
p. 72) by the Chancellor or Chief Justice, although the archbishop of
Canterbury declared the cause of summons in 1332 and 1399,
(*Rot. Parl.* II. 64. 107).

page 72

3–11 It was only on very rare occasions that the King would take
part in deliberation, either as a speaker or as a hearer . . . ', W.
Stubbs, *Constitutional History* (Oxford, 1898) III. 495. Richard

II did address his parliaments, *Rot. Parl.* III. 338–9. In 1485 Henry VII addressed the Commons expounding 'with his own mouth' the justice of his title. *Rot Parl.* VI 268. See p. 179.

12–30 It is possible that the passage refers to an incident in 1313 when Edward II stayed away from parliament. 'Sed rex morbo ut putabatur ficto detentus ad diem non venit . . . ' *Vita Edwardi Secundi*, ed. N. Denholm-Young (Nelson, 1957), p. 38. See W. A. Morris, 'The date of the *Modus Tenendi Parliamentum*', *E.H.R.* 49 (1934), 410. A deputation which visited Richard II in 1386 in similar circumstances may have quoted the *Modus*, see p. 26. n. 48.

31–3 The normal seating until 1539 was as described here with the
(and clergy on the King's right, and the laity together with the
1–11, primate and bishops of the northern province on the King's
p. 73) left, Powell and Wallis, *House of Lords*, p. 545. A picture showing the seating arrangements for the parliament of 1523 is found in a herald's drawing done by or for Thomas Wriothesley, Garter King 1505–34, (Wriothesley MS. Royal Library, Windsor), Powell and Wallis, pp. 555–6. It has been suggested that the arrangements described in this paragraph were generally similar to the arrangements in the Exchequer which may have served as a model, Clarke, pp. 220–3. The *Modus* may well have been referred to in a later age as a general guide concerned among other matters with questions of seating and precedence, see p. 48. The statement that the rest of the estates shall sit in rows is found only in the (B) recension which reads, 'First, as is aforesaid, the King shall sit in the middle of the greater bench, and on his right hand shall sit the archbishop of Canterbury, and on his left hand the archbishop of York, and immediately after them the bishops, abbots, and priors in rows, always in such manner among the ranks aforesaid and their places . . . '

page 73

10 The reference to chamberlain in the singular in the (B) recension may refer to Hugh Despenser who was chamberlain from 1318, Morris, p. 418; Clarke, pp. 204–5, see also p. 24.

12–35 This account of the parliamentary clerks does not accord with
(and what is known of these officials, Richardson and Sayles, 'The
1–4, King's Ministers in Parliament, 1272–1377', pp. 529–50, 194–
p. 74) 203, 377–97. For the career of W. Ayreminne who was

'probably the clerk of parliament from 1316 onwards' see
Cuttino, 'A Reconsideration of the *Modus Tenendi Parliamentum*',
p. 33 ff. The lack of evidence concerning the number of
parliamentary clerks as described in paragraph XVI does not
mean that some scheme similar to that contained in the *Modus*
may not have been proposed or tried at some time, Galbraith,
p. 83, n. 4.

30–2   Before *c.* 1327 the parliament rolls were deposited in the
Treasury, although stored for current use in the Wardrobe.
They are known to have passed into the custody of the
Chancery by 1330, Clarke, pp. 211–13; Galbraith, p. 89;
H. G. Richardson and G. O. Sayles, 'The Early Records of the
English Parliaments', *B.I.H.R.* 6 (1929), 135–6. The statement
that the parliament rolls are to be deposited in the Treasury
dates both recensions to a period before 1327.

page 74

30–2   The wording of the (B) recension may refer to the events of
1321 when parliament met to dismiss the Despensers who
were supported by the King, see pp. 24, 107.

page 75

5–24   There is a proposal for a similar committee of twenty-five in
the Tract on the Steward, L. W. V. Harcourt, *His Grace the
Steward* (London, 1907), pp. 164–7. As regards the practical
influence of this proposal Miss Clarke suggested that the
delegation sent by parliament to notify Edward II at
Kenilworth of his deposition was a deputation of the estates of
parliament, and was based in part upon the scheme of the
Modus, Clarke, pp. 173–95. There are legitimate doubts
however, whether the deputation which went to Kenilworth
was a parliamentary delegation at all, B. Wilkinson, *Constitutional History of Medieval England 1216–1399* (London, 1960), II,
161. In 1327 contemporaries were still uncertain about the
validity of parliamentary action and Edward II was not
formally deposed by parliament, G. Lapsley, 'The Parliamentary Title of Henry IV', *E.H.R.* 49 (1934), 582; B. Wilkinson,
'The Deposition of Richard II and the Accession of Henry IV',
E.H.R. 54 (1939), 223–9.

25–34   'This was the sequence outlined in the charge to the Commons
(and   recorded on the parliament rolls at a later date, and it
1–2,   presumably formed part of the *pronuntiatio* when the author

p. 76) was writing', Harriss, p. 81. A calendar of business was
probably prepared for the parliaments of 1309 and 1311,
Richardson and Sayles ('The Early Records of the English
Parliament', p. 130) who say 'we think these statements (in the
Modus) give some inkling of what actually took place'. As
described in the *Modus* the order of business recalls the concern
with 'the common business of the kingdom' mentioned in the
Provisions of Oxford. See J. G. Edwards, *Historians and the
Medieval English Parliament* (Glasgow, 1960), pp. 17–18; 'Justice
in Early English Parliaments', *B.I.H.R.* 27 (1954), 41. The
hearing of petitions could take place at any time during the
session of parliament. For the situation in the Lincoln
parliament of 1316 see *Rot. Parl.* I. 350, v; Clarke, p. 227.

page 76

3–8 'Mid-prime was the middle of the first hour which began
either at six o'clock in the morning or in summer at sunrise',
Clarke, p. 218. This accords with the time of meeting of the
parliament of Carlisle in 1307, *Rot. Parl.* I. 189.

8–11 The concern about secret meetings of parliament away from
Westminster is found in other sources such as the Ordinances
of 1311 (*Rot. Parl.* I. 285, no. 29), and in Lancaster's comment
of 1320, 'Non enim decebat habere parliamentum in cameris,
ut dixit', *Vita Edwardi Secundi*, ed. N. Denholm-Young (Nelson,
1957), p. 104.

17–19 'It is necessary that this doorkeeper should recognize those
who ought to enter so that no-one shall be denied entry to
parliament who ought to be in parliament.' 'Archbishop
Stratford may have cited this rule when he was turned away
from parliament in 1341', Clarke, p. 228. n. 1.

22–32 These paragraphs on the crier and the position of speakers
(and stand as unique statements for which there is no corroborative
1–4, evidence. In the account of the Good Parliament of 1376 we
p. 77) hear of the knights of the shire going to the lectern with their
muttered grace before and after speaking, *The Anonimalle
Chronicle 1333–81*, ed. V. H. Galbraith (Manchester, 1927,
reprinted 1970), p. xliv.

page 77

6–34 For a discussion of the position of the Commons as described
in this paragraph see above, pp. 38–9. 'Perhaps at this date

grants were not yet made by indenture, but the *Modus* tells us that both the King's request for aid, and the response of parliament shall be in writing', Harriss, *King, Parliament, and Public Finance*, p. 82. Grants are first recorded as made by indenture in 1346, *Rot. Parl.* II. 159–60. Cuttino, pp. 42–4, stresses the appearance here of Romano-canonical principles, see Gaines Post 'Plena Potestas and Consent in Medieval Assemblies', *Traditio*, 1 (1943), 355–408; 'A Romano-Canonical Maxim, 'Quod Omnes Tangit' in Bracton', *ibid*, 4 (1946), 197–251.

page 78

2–3   'This reflected a repeated demand of the Commons and when in September 1332 the King wanted to march north immediately after parliament had granted the tax, he took pains to seek the approval of the knights', Harris, p. 82.

26–7   The charge of one penny for ten lines was said to be the custom as late as the time of Hooker, see p. 53.

28–9   On the nature of the parliament rolls see Richardson and Sayles, 'The Early Records of the English Parliaments', pp. 129–55; Clarke, pp. 211–16. There was not originally a single roll of parliament. In paragraph XV there is mention of a principal roll of parliament which may imply the existence of others. At the time of the Lincoln parliament of 1316 there developed the idea of a principal record of proceedings and this was the work of Ayreminne, *Rot. Parl.* I. 355 ff. The roll of 1316 (of which an abstract is given by Cuttino, pp. 38–40) gives 'in the form of short dated minutes, a record of parliamentary proceedings, day by day, and so enables us to get an intelligible idea of what the estates actually did', T. F. Tout, *The Place of the Reign of Edward II in English History*, (Manchester, 1936), p. 166. Richardson and Sayles do not regard the roll as a precedent for others, *The Early Records of the English Parliaments*, p. 129 ff. They refer to the statement of the *Modus*, 'And when it (the *Modus*) says that the two principal clerks of parliament enroll in the principal roll of parliament all pleas and all judgements . . . it leads us to suppose that in the earlier fourteenth century at any rate, pleas and judgements and matter of this kind were what people expected to find on a parliament roll', *Ibid.*, p. 131. It was about this time that the rolls became approximately ten inches wide, Clarke, p. 215.

30 The (A) recension has a composite title apparently endeavouring to retain the sense of the earlier titles found in (B).

31–2 The word peer is used in two senses in the *Modus*. All those
who attend parliament are peers, but the term also means as
here those 'equal in degree'. Galbraith, p. 98. n. 2; Clarke,
p. 11. The expressions, *pares parliamenti* (paragraph xv), and
pares regni (paragraph xvii) are found elsewhere in the treatise.
'In *pares parliamenti* the equality is one of membership of a
parliament irrespective of grade or income ... *Pares regni* ...
is virtually synonymous with *pares parliamenti*', *English Historical
Documents*, ed. Rothwell. III. p. 925 n. 2.

page 79

5 The grades of the *Modus* are not necessarily to be equated with
estates. See the comments of Pollard, *The Evolution of Parliament*,
particularly in the chapter entitled 'The Myth of the Three
Estates'. Pollard found in the *Modus* not too many but too few
grades, *ibid.*, p. 69. There is however a strong case to be made
for maintaining that the idea, generally held by the fifteenth
century, that the political nation of England was made up of
three estates, in which the former grades of the people merged,
had both a longer ancestry and a greater degree of general
acceptance than Pollard admitted. See Chrimes, *English
Constitutional Ideas*, pp. 115–26. The *Modus* appears to indicate
the beginning of the process of this amalgamation of the
various 'grades' into the three-fold parliamentary concept.
For a view of the English parliament as 'a concentration of
local communities rather than an assembly of estates', see
Helen Cam, 'The Theory and Practice of Representation in
Medieval England', *History* I (1953), 11–26. The term grades
appears to have an ecclesiastical origin, Clarke, p. 321.

RECENSION 'B'

G	B.L. Nero D. VI.
D	B.L. Domitian A.XVIII.
M	B.L. Add 32097.
Υ	B.L. Add 29901.
V	B.L. Vitellius C. IV.
T	B.L. Tiberius E. VIII
R	Bodleian Library, Rawlinson C. 398.
P	B.N Paris Lat. 6049.
codd.	codicum consensus recensionis B.

Modus Tenendi Parliamentum

⟨A⟩ Hic describitur modus, quomodo Parliamentum Regis Anglie et Anglicorum suorum tenebatur tempore Regis Edwardi filii Regis Etheldredi; qui quidem modus recitatus fuit per discretiores regni coram Willielmo Duce Normannie et Conquestore et Rege Anglie, ipso 5 Conquestore hoc precipiente, et per ipsum approbatus, et suis temporibus ac etiam temporibus successorum suorum regum Anglie usitatus.

⟨I⟩ *Summonitio Parliamenti*

Summonitio Parliamenti procedere debet primum diem Parliamenti 10 per quadraginta dies.
⟨II⟩ Ad Parliamentum summoneri et venire debent, ratione tenure sue, omnes et singuli archiepiscopi, episcopi, abbates, priores, et alii majores cleri, qui tenent per comitatum vel baroniam, ratione hujusmodi tenure, et nulli minores nisi eorum presentia et eventus aliunde quam 15 pro tenuris suis requiratur, ut si sint de consilio regis, vel eorum presentia necessaria vel utilis reputetur ad Parliamentum; et illis tenetur Rex ministrare sumptus et expensas suas de veniendo et morando ad Parliamentum; nec debent hujusmodi clerici minores summoneri ad Parliamentum, sed Rex solebat talibus peritis mandare 20 brevia sua rogando quod ad Parliamentum suum interessent.

Item, Rex solebat facere summonitiones suas archiepiscopis, episcopis, et aliis exemptis personis ut abbatibus, prioribus, decanis, et aliis ecclesiasticis personis, qui habent jurisdictiones per hujusmodi exemptiones et privilegia separatim, quod ipsi pro quolibet decanatu et 25 archidiaconatu Anglie per ipsos decanatus archidiaconatus eligi facerent duos peritos et idoneos procuratores de proprio archidiaconatu ad veniendum et interessendum ad Parliamentum, ad illud subeundum, allocandum et faciendum idem quod facerent omnes et singule persone ipsorum decanatuum et archidiaconatuum, si ibidem personaliter 30 interessent.

Et quod hujusmodi procuratores veniant cum warantis suis duplicatis, sigillis superiorum suorum signatis, quod ipsi ad hujusmodi procurati-

---

1 Modus tenendi parliamentum *GPDYTR (om MV)*.
4 qui quidam modus *GMPYV*; qui quidmodum *D*.
15 et eventus—17 presentia *om MPRT*.
30 personaliter *om MR*.

onem clerici missi sunt, quarum litterarum una liberabitur clericis de Parliamento ad irrotulandum et alia residebit penes ipsos procuratores. Et sic sub istis duobus generibus summoneri debet totus clerus ad Parliamentum.

⟨III⟩ *De Laicis*   5

Item, summoneri et venire debent omnes et singuli comites et barones, et eorum pares, scilicet illi qui habent terras et redditus ad valentiam comitatus vel baronie integre, videlicet viginti feoda unius militis, quolibet feode computato ad viginti libratas, que faciunt quadringentas libratas in toto, vel ad valentiam unius baronie integre, scilicet 10 tresdecim feoda et tertiam partem unius feodi militis, quolibet feodo computato ad viginti libratas, que faciunt in toto cccc marcas; et nulli minores laici summoneri nec venire debent ad Parliamentum, ratione tenure sue nisi eorum presentia aliis de causis fuerit utilis vel necessaria ad Parliamentum, et tune de illis fieri debet sicut dictum est de 15 minoribus clericis, qui ratione tenure sue ad Parliamentum venire minime tenentur.

⟨IV⟩ *De Baronibus Portuum*

Item, Rex tenetur mittere brevia sua custodi Quinque Portuum quod ipse eligere faciat et de quolibet portu per ipsum portum duos idoneos 20 et peritos barones ad veniendum et interessendum ad Parliamentum suum ad respondendum, subeundum, allegandum, et faciendum idem quod baronie sue, ac si ipsi de baroniis illis omnes et singuli personaliter interessent ibidem; et quod barones hujusmodi veniant cum warantis suis duplicatis, sigillis communibus Portuum suorum signatis, quod ipsi 25 rite ad hoc electi, et attornati sunt, et missi pro baroniis illis, quarum una liberabitur clerices de Parliamento, et alia residebit penes ipsos barones. Et cum hujusmodi barones Portuum, licentia optenta, de Parliamento recessum fecerant, tunc solebant habere breve de magno sigillo custodi Quinque Portuum, quod ipse rationabiles sumptus et 30 expensas suas hujusmodi baronibus habere faceret de communitate Portus illius, a primo die quo versus Parliamentum venerint usque ad

---

1 electi et missi sunt *codd recensionis* (A).
5 *titulus* Summonitio parliamenti ad laicos *DY*.
8 vel baronie integre (or an entire barony) *om codd recensionis* (A).
12 que faciunt in toto 300 maiores *Y*.
18 *titulus* Summonitio parliamenti ad barones quinque portuum *DY*.
19 solebat mittere *codd recensionis* (A).
21 barones ad perficiendum ibidem quod baronie sue incumbet *R*.

diem quo ad propria redierunt, facta etiam expressa mentione in brevi illo de mora quam fecerint ad Parliamentum, de die quo venerint, quo licentiati fuerint redeundi; et solebat mentio fieri aliquando in brevi quantum hujusmodi barones capere debent de communitatibus illis per diem, scilicet aliqui plus, aliqui minus, secundum personarum 5 habilitates, honestates (et respectus) nec solebat poni per duos barones per diem ultra viginti solidos, habito respectu ad eorum moras, labores et expensas, nec solent hujusmodi expense in certo reponi per curiam pro quibuscumque personis sic electis et missis pro communitatibus, nisi persone ipse fuerint honeste et bene se habentes in Parliamento. 10

⟨V⟩ *De Militibus*

Item, Rex solebat mittere brevis sua omnibus vicecomitibus Anglie, quod eligi facerent quilibet de suo comitatu per ipsum comitatum duos milites idoneos, et honestos, et peritos, ad veniendum ad Parliamentum suum, eodem modo dictum est de baronibus Portuum, et de warantis 15 suis eodem modo, sed pro expensis duorum militum de uno comitatu non solet poni ultra unam marcam per diem.

⟨VI⟩ *De Civibus*

Eodum modo solebat mandari majori et vicecomitibus Londonarium, et majori et ballivis vel majori et civibus Eborum et aliarum civitatum, 20 quod ipsi pro comitatu civitatis sue eligerent duos idoneos, honestos, et peritos cives ad veniendum et interessendum ad Parliamentum eodem modo quo dictum est de baronibus Quinque Portuum et militibus comitatuum; et solebant cives esse pares et equales cum militibus comitatuum in expensis veniendo, morando et redeundo. 25

⟨VII⟩ *De Burgensibus.*

Item, eodem modo solebat et debet mandari ballivis et probis hominibus burgorum, quod ipsi ex se et pro se eligant duos idoneos, honestos, et peritos burgenses ad veniendum et interessendum ad Parliamentum eodem modo quo dictum est de civibus; sed duo burgenses non solebant 30 percipere pro expensis suis per unum diem ultra decem solidos, et aliquando ultra dimidiam marcam, et hoc solebat taxari per curiam,

---

6 et respectus *add PYVT.*
11 *titulus* Summonitio parliamenti ad milites comitatuum *DY.*
15 eodem modo—**16** warantis suis *om V.*
18 *titulus* Summonitio parliamenti ad cives comitatuum *DY.*
26 *titulus* Summonitio parliamenti ad burgenses *DY.*

secundum magnitudinem et potestatem burgi et secundum honestatem personarum missarum.

⟨XV⟩ *De Principalibus Clericis Parliamenti*

Item, duo clerici principales Parliamenti sedebunt in medio justici-
ariorum, qui irrotulabunt omnia placita et negotia Parliamenti. Et 5
sciendum quod illi duo clerici non sunt subjecti quibuscumque
justiciariis, nec est aliquis justiciarius Anglie in Parliamento, nec habent
per se recorda in Parliamento, nisi quatenus assignata et data fuit eis
nova potestas in Parliamento per regem et pares Parliamenti, ut
quando assignati sunt cum aliis sectatoribus Parliamenti ad audiendum 10
et terminandum diversas petitiones et querelas in Parliamento correctas
et sunt illi duo clerici immediate subjecti regi et Parliamento suo in
communi, nisi forte unus justiciarius vel duo assignentur eis ad
examinanda et emendanda eorum irrotulamenta, et cum pares
Parliamenti assignati sunt ad audiendas et examinandas aliquas 15
petitiones specialiter per se, tunc cum ipsi fuerint unanimes et concordes
in judiciis suis reddendis super hujusmodi petitionibus; tunc recitabunt
et processu super eisdem habito et reddent judicia in pleno Parliamento,
ita quod illi duo clerici principaliter irrotulent omnia placita et omnia
judicia in principali rotulo Parliamenti, et eosdem rotulos liberent ad 20
thesaurarium regis antequam Parliamentum licentiatur, ita quod omni
modi sint illi rotuli in Thesauraria ante recessum Parliamenti, salvo
tamen eisdem clericis inde transcripto, sive contrarotulo si id habere
velint. Isti duo clerici, nisi sint in alio officio cum rege, et feoda capiant
de eo, ita quod inde honeste vivere poterint, de rege capiant per diem 25
unam marcam cum expensis suis per equales portiones, nisi sint ad
mensam domini regis, tunc capient preter mensam suam per diem
dimidiam marcam per equales portiones, per totum Parliamentum.

⟨XVI⟩ *De quinque Clericis*

Item, Rex assignabit quinque clericos peritos et approbatos, quorum 30
primus ministrabit et serviet episcopis, secundus procuratoribus cleri,

---

7 iusticiarius in Parliamento *V.*
11 porrectas *MR.*
17 recitabunt huiusmodi petitiones *add codd recensionis* (A).
21 ante parliamentum licentiatum *codd recensionis* (A).
24 in aliis officiis *codd recensionis* (A)
26 pro expensis *codd recensionis* (A); cum *om R.*
27 et si sint ad mensam domini regis *add codd recensionis* (A).
29 *titulus* De Quinque Clericis Parliamenti *DY.*

tertius comitibus et baronibus, quartus militibus comitatuum, quintus civibus et burgensibus, et quilibet eorum, nisi sit cum rege et capiat de eo tale feodum seu talia vadia quod inde honeste possit vivere, capiet de rege per diem duos solidos; nisi sint ad mensam domini regis, tunc capiant per diem duodecim denarios; qui clerici scribent eorum 5 dubitationes et responsiones quas faciunt regi et Parliamento, et intererunt ad sua consilia ubicumque eos habere voluerint; et, cum ipsi vacaverint, juvabunt clericos principales ad irrotulandum.

⟨XVII⟩ *De Casibus et Judiciis difficilibus*

Cum briga, dubitatio, vel casus difficilis sit pacis vel guerre, emergat in 10 regno vel extra, referatur et recitetur casus ille in scriptis in pleno Parliamento, et tractetur et disputetur ibidem inter pares Parliamenti, et, si necesse sit, injungatur per regem seu ex parte regis, si Rex non intersit, cuilibet graduum parium quod quilibet gradus adeat per se, et liberetur casus ille clerico suo in scripto, et in certo loco recitare faciant 15 coram eis casum illum; ita quod ipsi ordinent et considerent coram se qualiter melius et justius procedi poterit in casu illo, sicut ipsi pro persona regis et eorum propriis personis, ac etiam pro personis eorum quorum personas ipsi representant, velint coram Deo respondere, et suas responsiones et avisamenta reportent in scriptis, ut omnibus eorum 20 responsionibus, consiliis et avisamentis hinc inde auditis, secundum melius et sanius consilium procedatur, et ubi saltem major pars Parliamenti concordet. Ut si per discordiam inter eos et regem et aliquos magnates, vel forte inter ipsos magnates, pax regni infirmetur, vel populus vel patria (tribuletur) ita quod videtur regi et ejus consilio 25 quod expediens sit quod negotium illud tractetur et emendetur per considerationem omnium parium regni sui, vel si per guerram rex et regnum tribulentur, vel si casus difficilis coram cancellario Anglie emergat, seu judicium difficile coram justiciariis fuerit reddendum, et hujusmodi, et si forte in hujusmodi deliberationibus omnes vel saltem 30 major pars concordare non valeant, tunc comes senescallus, comes constabularius, et comes marescallus, vel duo eorum eligent viginti quinque personas de omnibus paribus regni, scilicet duos episcopos, et tres procuratores, pro toto clero, duos comites et tres barones, quinque milites comitatuum, quinque cives et burgenses, qui faciunt viginti 35

8 mittabunt clericos *J*.   10 sit *om M*.
21 responsionibus et avisamentis *G*.
23 et si per discordiam inter regem et aliquos magnates *codd recensionis* (A).
25 tribuletur *om codd recensionis* (B).   35 quinque burgenses *R*.

quinque; et illi viginti quinque possunt eligere ex seipsis duodecim et
condescendere in eis, et ipsi duodecim sex et condescendere in eis, et ipsi
sex adhuc tres et condescendere in eis, et illi tres in paucioribus
condescendere non possunt, nisi optenta licentia a domino rege, et si
rex consentiat, in tres possunt in duos, et de illis duobus alter potest in 5
alium descendere; et ita demum stabit sua ordinatio supra totum
Parliamentum; et ita condescendo a viginti quinque personis usque ad
unam personam solam, nisi numerus major concordare valeat et
ordinare, tandem sola persona, ut est dictum, pro omnibus ordinavit
que cum se ipsa discordare non potest; salvo domino regi et ejus concilio 10
quod ipsi hujusmodi ordinationes postquam scripte fuerint examinare
et emendare valeant, si hoc facere sciant et velint, ita quod hoc ibidem
tunc in pleno Parliamento, et de consensu Parliamenti, et non retro
Parliamentum.

⟨XVIII⟩ *De Negotiis Parliamenti* 15

Negotia pro quibus Parliamentum (summonitum) est debent deliberari
secundum kalendarium Parliamenti, et secundum ordinem petitionum
liberatarum, et affilatarum, nullo habito respectu ad quorumcumque
personas, sed qui prius proposuit prius agat. In kalendario Parliamenti
rememorari debent omnia negotia Parliamenti sub isto ordine; primo 20
de guerra si guerra sit, et de aliis negotiis personas regis, regine, et
suorum liberorum tangentibus; secundo de negotiis communibus regni,
ut de legibus statuendis contra defectus legum originalium, judicialium,
et executoriarum, post judicia reddita que sunt maxime communia
negotia; tercio debent rememorari negotia singularia, et hoc secundum 25
ordinem filatarum petitionum, ut predictum est.

⟨XIX⟩ *De Diebus et Horis ad Parliamentum*

Parliamentum non debet teneri diebus dominicis, sed cunctis aliis
diebus, illo die semper excepto, aliis tribus, scilicet Omnium Sanctorum,
et Animarum, et Nativitatis Sancti Johannis Baptiste, potest teneri; et 30
debet singulis diebus inchoari hora media prima, qua hora rex tenetur
Parliamentum interesse, et omnes pares parliamenti debent teneri in
occulto loco, in diebus festivis Parliamentum debet inchoari hora prima
propter divinum servitium.

1 ex seipsis si velint *add V* et *codd* recensionis (A). **6** in alium condescendere *DY*.
16 summonitum *om codd recensionis* (B). **21** aliis negotiis communibus regni *MR*.
25 tercio—**26** ut predictum est *om DY*. **28** cunctis *om M*.
33 occulto loco *om R*.

⟨XXVI⟩ *De Gradibus Parium*

Rex est caput, principium, et finis Parliamenti, et ita non habet parem in suo gradu, et ita ex rege solo est primus gradus; secundus gradus est ex archiepiscopis, episcopis, abbatibus, prioribus, per baroniam tenentibus; tertius gradus est de procuratoribus cleri; quartus de 5 comitibus, baronibus et aliis magnatibus et proceribus, tenentibus ad valentiam comitatus et baronie, sicut predictum est in titulo de laicis; quintus est de militibus comitatuum; sextus de civibus et burgensibus: et ita est Parliamentum ex sex gradibus. Sed sciendum est quod licet aliquis dictorum graduum post regem absentet, dum tamen omnes 10 premuniti fuerint per rationabiles summonitiones Parliamenti, nihilominus censetur esse plenum.

⟨VIII⟩ *De Modo Parliamenti*

Ostensa primo forma qualiter quilibet et a quanto tempore summonitio Parliamenti fieri debet, et qui venire debent per summonitionem, et qui 15 non; secundo dicendum est qui sunt qui ratione officiorum suorum venire debent, et interesse tenentur per totum Parliamentum, sine summonitione; unde advertendum est quod duo clerici principales Parliamenti electi per regem et ejus concilium, et alii clerici secundarii de quibus et quorum officiis dicetur specialius post, et principalis 20 clamator Anglie cum subclamatoribus suis, et principalis hostiarius Anglie, que duo officia, scilicet officium clamatorie et hostiarie, solebant ad unum et idem pertinere, isti officiarii tenentur interesse primo die: cancellarius Anglie, thesaurarius, camerarius, et barones de scaccario, justiciarii, omnes clerici et milites regis, una cum servientibus regis ad 25 placita, qui sunt de concilio regis, tenentur interesse secundo die, nisi rationabiles excusationes habeant ita quod interesse non possent, et tunc mittere debent bonas excusationes.

⟨IX⟩ *De Inchoatione Parliamenti*

Dominus Rex sedebit in medio majoris banci, et tenetur interesse primo, 30 sexto die Parliamenti: et solebant cancellarius, thesaurarius, barones de

---

1 *titulus* De gradibus parium *GMVRPT;* De gradibus parliamenti *DY.*
4–5 et baroniam tenentibus *DY.*
13 De Modo Parliamenti *GPMVTR;* De Ordine Parliamenti *DY.*
24 camerarii *codd recensionis* (A).

scaccario, et justiciarii recordare defalta facta in Parliamento sub ordine qui sequitur. Primo die vocabuntur burgenses et cives totius Anglie quo die si non veniant, amerciabitur burgus ad centum marcas et civitas ad centum libras: secundo die vocabuntur milites comitatuum totius Anglie, quo die si non veniant, amerciabitur comitatus unde sunt 5 ad centum libras: tertio die Parliamenti vocabuntur barones Quinque Portuum, et postea barones, et postea comites; unde si barones Quinque Portuum non veniant, amerciabitur baronia illa ad centum marcas; et comes ad centum libras; eodem modo fiet de illis qui sunt pares comitibus et baronibus, scilicet qui habent terras et redditus ad valorem 10 unius comitatus vel unius baronie, ut predictum est in titulo de summonitione: quarto die vocabuntur procuratores cleri, quo die si non venient, amerciabuntur episcopi sui pro quolibet archidiaconatu qui defaltam fecerit ad centum marcas: quinto die vocabuntur decani, priores, abbates, episcopi, demum archieposcopi, qui si non veniant, 15 amerciabitur quilibet archiepiscopus ad centum libras, episcopus tenens integram baroniam ad centum marcas, et eodem modo de abbatibus, prioribus etc. Primo die debet fieri proclamatio, primo in aula, sive monasterio, seu aliquo loco publico ubi Parliamentum tenetur, et postmodum publice in civitate vel villa, illa quod omnes illi, qui petitiones 20 et querelas liberare volunt ad Parliamentum, quod illis deliberentur a primo die Parliamenti in quinque dies proximo sequentes.

⟨X⟩ *De Predicatione ad Parliamentum*

Unus archiepiscopus, vel episcopus vel magnus clericus discretus et facundus, (electus) per archiepiscopum in cuius provincia Parliamen- 25 tum tenetur, predicare debet uno istorum primorum quinque dierum Parliamenti in pleno Parliamento et in presentia regis, et hoc quando Parliamentum pro majori parte fuerit adjunctum et congregatum, et in servicio suo consequenter subjungere toti Parliamento quod ipsi cum eo humiliter Deo supplicent, et ipsum adorent, pro pace et tranquillitate 30 regis et regni, prout dicetur specialius in sequenti titulo de (pronuntiatione) ad Parliamentum.

---

8 eodem modo amerciabitur baro per se ad centum marcas *add codd recensionis* (A).
16 archiepiscopus ad centum libras *om MR;* et quilibet tenens *codd recensionis* (A).
21 liberare voluerint *codd recensionis* (A).
21 illas deliberent *codd recensionis* (A).
25 clericus per archiepiscopum *codd recensionis* (B); discretus per archiepiscopum *V*.
27 in presentia—28 Parliamentum *om Y.*　　　31–2 predicatione *codd.*

⟨XI⟩ *De Pronuntiatione in Parliamento*

Post predicationem debet cancellarius Anglie vel capitalis justiciarius
Anglie, ille scilicet qui tenet placita coram rege, vel alius idoneus,
honestus, et facundus justiciarius, vel clericus, per ipsos cancellarium et
capitalem justiciarium electus, pronunciare causas Parliamenti, primo 5
in genere, et postea in specie, stando; et inde sciendum est quod omnes
de Parliamento, quicumque fuerit, dum loquitur stabunt, rege excepto,
ita quod omnes de Parliamento audire valeant eum qui loquitur, et si
obscure dicat vel ita basse loquitur, dicat iterato, et loquatur altius, vel
loquator alius pro eo. 10

⟨XII⟩ *De Loquela Regis post Pronuntiationem*

Rex post pronuntiationem pro Parliamento rogare debet clericos et
laicos, nominando omnes eorum gradus, scilicet archiepiscopos,
episcopos, abbates, priores, archidiaconos, procuratores, et alios de
clero, comites, barones, milites, cives, burgenses, et alios laicos, quod 15
ipsi diligenter, studiose et corditer laborent ad pertractandum et
deliberandum negotia Parliamenti, prout majus et principalius hoc ad
Dei voluntatem primo, et postea ad ejus et eorum honores, et commoda
fore intellexerint et sentierint.

⟨XIII⟩ *De Absentia Regis in Parliamento* 20

Rex tenetur omni modo personaliter interesse Parliamento, nisi per
corporalem egritudinem detineatur, et tunc potest tenere cameram
suam, ita quod non jaceat extra manerium, vel saltem villam, ubi
Parliamentum tenetur, et tunc debet mittere pro duodecim personis de
majoribus et melioribus qui summoniti sunt ad Parliamentum, scilicet 25
duobus episcopis, duobus comitibus, duobus baronibus, duobus militibus
comitatuum, duobus civibus, et duobus burgensibus, ad videndam
personam suam et testificandum statum suum, et in eorum presentia
committere debet archiepiscopo loci, senescallo, et capitali justiciario
suo, quod ipsi conjunctim et divisim inchoent et continuent Parliamen- 30
tum nomine suo, facta in commissione illa expressa mentione adtunc de
causa absentie sue, que sufficere debet, et monere ceteros nobiles et
magnates de Parliamento, una cum negotio et testimonio dictorum

3 ille *om M.*
9 loquatur alicius *R.*
25 scilicet *om M.*
6 et inde *GDYRTP.*
16 concorditer *M.*
29 archiepiscopo loci ubi parliamentum tentum fuit *R.*

duodecim parium suorum; causa est quod solebat clamor et murmur esse in Parliamento pro absentia regis, quia res dampnosa et periculosa est toti communitati Parliamenti et etiam regni, cum rex a Parliamento absens fuerit, nec se absentare debet nec potest, dumtaxat nisi in casu supradicto. 5

⟨XIV⟩ *De Loco et Sessionibus in Parliamento*

Primo, ut predictum est, rex sedebit in medio loco majoris banci, et ex parte ejus dextra sedebit archiepiscopis Cantuariensis, et ex parte ejus sinistra archiepiscopus Eborum, et post illos statim episcopi, abbates et priores linealiter, semper tali modo inter predictos gradus, et eorum 10 loca, quod nullus sedeat nisi inter suos pares; et ad hoc tenetur senescallus Anglie prospicere, nisi rex alium assignaverit; ad pedern eius dextrum sedebunt cancellarius Anglie et capitalis justiciarius Anglie, et socii sui, et eorum clerici qui sunt de Parliamento; et ad pedem ejus sinistrum thesaurarius, camerarius, et barones de scaccario, 15 justiciarii de banco, et eorum clerici qui sunt de Parliamento.

⟨XX⟩ *De Hostiario Parliamenti*

Hostiarius principalis Parliamenti stabit infra magnum hostium monasterii, aule, vel alterius loci ubi Parliamentum tenetur, et custodiet hostium, ita quod nullus intret Parliamentum, nisi qui sectam et 20 eventum debeat ad Parliamentum, vel vocatus fuerit propter negotium quod prosequitur in Parliamento, et oportet quod hostiarius ille habeat cognitionem personarum que ingredi debent si necesse sit, habere plures.

⟨XXI⟩ *De Clamatore Parliamenti* 25

Clamator Parliamenti stabit extra hostium Parliamenti, et hostiarius denunciabit sibi clamationes suas; rex solebat mittere servientes suos ad arma ad standum per magnum spatium extra hostium Parliamenti, ad custodiendum hostium, ita quod nulli impressiones nec tumultus facerent circa hostia, per quod Parliamentum impediatur, sub poena 30 captionis corporum suorum, quia de jure hostium Parliamenti non debet claudi, sed per hostiarium et servientes regis ad arma custodiri.

---

1 parium suorum una cum negocio ut testimonio dictorum *add Y.*
15 camerarii *codd recensionis* (A).
23–4 habere plures *om Y.*
29 nulli oppressiones *MR T.*

⟨XXII⟩ *De Stationibus Loquentium*

Omnes pares Parliamenti sedebunt, et nullus stabit sed quando loquitur, et loquetur ita quod quilibet de Parliamento eum audire valeat; nullus intrabit Parliamentum, nec exiet de Parliamento, nisi per unum hostium, et quicumque loquitur rem aliquam que deliberari debet per 5 Parliamentum, stabunt omnes loquentes; causa est ut audiatur a paribus, quia omnes pares sunt judices et justiciarii.

⟨XXIII⟩ *De Auxilio Regis*

Rex non solebat petere auxilium de regno suo nisi pro guerra instanti, vel filios suos milites faciendo, vel filias suas maritando, et tunc debent 10 hujusmodi auxilia peti in pleno Parliamento, et in scriptis cuilibet gradui parium Parliamenti liberari, et in scriptis responderi; et sciendum est quod si hujusmodi auxilia concedenda oportet quod omnes pares Parliamenti consentiant, et intelligendum est quod duo milites, qui veniunt ad Parliamentum pro comitatu, majorem vocem habent in 15 Parliamento in concedendo et contradicendo, quam major comes Anglie, et eodem modo procuratores cleri unius episcopatus majorem vocem habent in Parliamento, si omnes sint concordes, quam episcopus ipse, et hoc in omnibus que per Parliamentum concedi, negari vel fieri debent: et hoc patet quod rex potest tenere Parliamentum cum 20 communitate regni sui, absque episcopis, comitibus et baronibus, dumtamen summoniti sunt ad Parliamentum, licet nullus episcopus, comes vel baro ad summonitiones suas veniant; quia olim nec fuerat episcopus, nec comes, nec baro, adhuc tunc reges tenuerunt Parliamenta sua, sed aliter est econtra, licet communitates cleri et laici summonite 25 essent ad Parliamentum, sicut de jure debent, et propter aliquas causas venire nollent, ut si pretenderent quod dictus rex non regeret eos sicuti deberet, et assignarent specialiter in quibus eos non rexerat, tunc Parliamentum nullum esset omnino, licet archiepiscopi, episcopi, comites et barones, et omnes eorum pares, cum rege interessent: et ideo 30 oportet quod omnia que affirmari vel infirmari, concedi vel negari, vel fieri debent per Parliamentum, per communitatem Parliamenti concedi debent, que est ex tribus gradibus sive generibus Parliamenti, scilicet ex procuratoribus cleri, militibus comitatuum, civibus et burgensibus, qui representant totam communitatem Anglie, et non de magnatibus, quia 35

2 nisi quando loquitur *codd recensionis* (A). **4** nisi per unicum hostium *codd recensionis* (A).
12 scriptis liberari et responderi *add MR*. **15** pro ipso comitatu *codd recensionis* (A).
24 nec baro *om DY*. **27** dictus dominus *R*.

quilibet eorum est pro sua propria persona ad Parliamentum et pro nulla alia.

⟨XXIV⟩ *De Partitione Parliamenti*

Parliamentum departiri non debet dummodo aliqua petitio pendeat indiscussa, vel, ad minus, ad quam non sit determinata responsio, et si 5 rex contrarium permittat, perjurus est; nullus solus de paribus Parliamenti recedere potest nec debet de Parliamento, nisi optenta inde licentia de rege et omnibus suis paribus et hoc in pleno Parliamento, et quod de hujusmodi licentia fiat rememoratio in rotulo Parliamenti, et si aliquis de paribus, durante Parliamento, infirmaverit, ita quod ad 10 Parliamentum venire non valeat, tunc per triduum mittat excusatores ad Parliamentum, quo die si non venerit, mittantur ei duo de paribus suis ad videndum et testificandum hujusmodi infirmitatem, et si sit suspicio, jurentur illi duo pares quod veritatem inde dicent, et si comperiatur quod finxerat se, amercietur tanquam pro defalta, et si 15 non finxerat se, tunc attornet aliquem sufficientem coram eis ad interessendum ad Parliamentum pro se, nec sanus excusari potest si sit sane memorie.

Departitio Parliamenti ita usitari debet: primitus peti debet et publice proclamari in Parliamento, et infra palacium Parliamenti, si sit 20 aliquis, qui petitionem liberaverit ad Parliamentum, cui nondum sit responsum; quod si nullus reclamet, supponendum est quod cuilibet medetur, vel saltem quatenus potest de jure respondetur, et tunc primo videlicet cum nullus qui petitionem suam ea vice exhibuerit reclamet, Parliamentum vestrum licentiabimus. 25

⟨XXV⟩ *De Transcriptis Recordorum in Parliamento*

Clerici Parliamenti non negabunt cuiquam transcriptum processus sui, sed liberabunt illud cuilibet qui hoc petierit, et capient semper pro decem lineis unum denarium, nisi forte facta fide de impotentia, in quo casu nihil capient. Rotuli de Parliamento continebunt in latitudine 30 decem pollices. Parliamentum tenebitur in quo loco regni regi placuerit.

Explicit Modus tenendi Parliamentum.

3 *titulus* De Peticione Parliamenti *D.*
6 perjurus nullus est *Y.*
25 Parliamentum nostrum licentiabimus *codd recensionis* (A).
26 *titulus* De Transcriptis Recordorum et Processuum in Parliamento *codd recensionis* (A).
30 rotulum *codd recensionis* (A).

III
*Modus Tenendi Parliamenta
et Consilia in Hibernia*

The history of the *Modus* in England is not the complete story of the medieval treatise. The influence of the *Modus* in Ireland has also to be considered. Whatever significance is attached to the Irish *Modus* there can be no doubt that the English *Modus* played a part, if only a small part, in the affairs of the Irish parliament, partly through the medium of the Irish text, and partly through other sources.[1]

Although Miss Clarke believed that the influence of the English *Modus* was present in Ireland during the closing years of Edward III's reign, and at the time of William of Windsor's appointment in Ireland,[2] there is in fact no concrete evidence for this, nor is there evidence that any version of the *Modus* was known in Ireland before the time of Richard II.[3] What is certain, however, is that by the early years of the fifteenth century an Irish version of the *Modus* had been constructed. Two versions of this Irish *Modus* survive. The first may be described as the version of 1419, and is found in the exemplification of 12 January of that year.[4] This exemplification which is found in the only surviving medieval manuscript is now in the Huntington Library, California (E.L. 1699), and was once a part of the Bridgewater or Ellesmere Collection. It may have been brought to London in 1613 by Lord Gormanston when the Catholic party in the Irish parliament were petitioning the King for their grievances.[5] Its text was known to antiquaries in the early seventeenth century at a time when it was in the possession of Thomas Egerton, first Lord Ellesmere, who had been involved in the enquiry following the protest of the recusant party,[6] and it was transcribed in whole or in part in three seventeenth-century

---

[1] See pp. 124–5.

[2] Clarke, pp. 115–22. Miss Clarke believed that the *Modus* helped in the development of the Irish parliament at this time, but admitted that the evidence was circumstantial, ibid., p. 115. Her views on the importance of William of Windsor in the history of the Irish parliament, 'William of Windsor in Ireland, 1369–76', *Proceedings of the Royal Irish Academy* 41 C. (1932), 55–130, have not been accepted by Richardson and Sayles, *Irish Parliament*, pp. 80–5, nor by James Lyndon, 'William of Windsor and the Irish Parliament', *E.H.R.* 80 (1965), 252–67.

[3] The Irish *Modus* may well have been constructed at this time.

[4] The text of this Irish version may well have been constructed before 1419, but as it is found only in the exemplification of that year it is described here as the version of 1419.

[5] Clarke, *Medieval Representation and Consent*, pp. 81–6.

[6] Ellesmere may have compiled *A Discourse Upon the Exposicion and Understandinge of Statutes (1561)* which was influenced by the English *Modus*. See p. 58, n. 167.

copies. The most readily accessible of these is that by William Hakewill, the well known lawyer and antiquary, whose transcript was printed by Robert Steele.[7] A second transcript now in Trinity College, Dublin, was compiled by the authority of Daniel Molyneux, Ulster King of Arms (1597–1632), from an original at that time in the hands of Sir Robert Cotton.[8] The third transcript, found among extracts from manuscripts in the Cotton collection, is a brief fragment in the Bodleian Library (Rawlingson B. 484 f. 51ᵛ), which contains only the opening part of the text.[9] The original of all these transcripts was almost certainly the manuscript now in the Huntington Library.[10] In the Huntington MS. the Irish *Modus* is one of a group of documents of which certain refer to the election and oath of the governor.[11]

A second version of the Irish *Modus* is preserved in three seventeenth-century copies. Although the original appears to have been kept in the Treasury at Waterford in this case no medieval manuscript survives. Among the later transcripts the best known is that by Anthony Dopping, Bishop of Meath, published in 1692.[12] Another transcript of this text which was once in the possession of Sir William Domvile, Dopping's uncle, is found in B.L. Add. 35505.[13] A third transcript is in Trinity College, Dublin E. 3. 18 fos. 1–10.[14] In his *Preface to the Reader*, Dopping mentioned that the original manuscript which he transcribed 'came to my hands among other Manuscripts and Papers of my ever Honoured Uncle, Sir William Domvile, late Attorney General in this

[7] Robert Steele, *A Bibliography of Royal Proclamations of the Tudor and Stuart Sovereigns 1485–1714* (Oxford, 1910), i, pp. CLXXXVIII–CXCII. Hakewill's transcript was used for John Selden's copy in Cambridge University Library Mm. VI. 62. See also B.L. MS. Facs. Suppl. 1.

[8] T.C.D. E. 3. 18 fos. 10–15. A note at fo. 15 states that this is a true copy of the exemplification 'remayning in ye hands of Sr Ro: Cotton, Knight.' Molyneux made certain corrections to the text, O. Armstrong, 'Manuscripts of the *Modus Tenendi Parliamentum*', *Proceedings of the Royal Irish Academy* 36 C (1921–4), 258.

[9] This was compiled by the Irish historian, Sir James Ware. It contains only the first three chapters.

[10] The survival of this unique medieval copy of the Irish *Modus* became known only during the 1930s, Clarke, p. 80, n. 1.

[11] See p. 123. Certain of these documents cannot be much older than 1419, Richardson and Sayles, *Irish Parliament*, p. 324, n. 2.

[12] *Modus Tenendi Parliamenta et Consilia in Hibernia*, ed. A. Dopping (Dublin, 1692).

[13] This has a note at the end of the transcript, 'Originale huius transcripti penes Willelmum Domvile, militem, Attornatum huius regni Generalem, remanet, MDCLXXVI.' Dopping acquired the manuscript through Domvile, who as this note states, had possession of the original in 1676.

[14] For an account of the manuscripts of the *Modus* which are now in the library of Trinity College, Dublin, see Armstrong, *art. cit.* pp. 256–64.

Kingdom . . . it was bestow'd on him by Sir James Cuffe, late Deputy Vice-Treasurer of Ireland, that Sir James found it among the Papers of Sir Francis Aungier, Master of the Rolls in this Kingdom, and Sir Francis his grandson, the Right Honourable the Earl of Longford has lately told me, that Sir Francis had it out of the Treasury of Waterford.'[15] Its recovery may be due to the fact 'that the revival of political opposition under James I, acting on the new learning of officials like Davies and Molyneux and of scholars like Usher and Ware, provided a search for documents and precedents which might serve as weapons in contemporary controversy'.[16]

As regards the Waterford version there are numerous errors in Dopping's text. 'Either he was using a corrupt text or he was too ignorant to understand or to transcribe what was before him.'[17] None the less apart from these errors there are sufficient differences between what we may term the Waterford tradition and the version of 1419 to justify the assumption that they represent two different versions of the Irish *Modus*. In the first place the Waterford version lacks most of the accompanying documents to the text of 1419, that is to say the exemplification clause, the section concerning the oath of the governor, and most of the section concerning the election of a governor.[18] Again this version possesses paragraph headings not found in the Huntington manuscript, and contains substantially different material in the paragraph entitled in that version, *Sessions in Parliament*.[19] It appears therefore that in a manner similar to the English *Modus* there were two principal versions of the Irish text.[20] There is no evidence, however, that either of these versions was used in the manner of the English recensions, that is to say as legal texts for specific courts. Both Irish versions appear to have survived the Middle Ages only in a single copy. The contrast between the manuscript traditions of the English and Irish *Modus* almost certainly reflects the relative importance of the two

---

[15] Dopping, pp. 3–4. Dopping was of the opinion that the manuscript was no later than the fifteenth century. The last known person to see this manuscript was William Molyneux, who was related to the Dopping family. W. Molyneux, *The Case of Ireland's Being Bound by Acts of Parliament in England, Stated* (Dublin, 1698), p. 36.

[16] Clarke, p. 77.

[17] Ibid., p. 76. Certain of the errors noted by Miss Clarke possibly arise from printer's errors, while others are to be explained by the difficult character of the printed text. Thus Quintus and si, and not dentus and di, as Miss Clarke thought, are in fact what is printed, Clarke, p. 76, n. 3.

[18] See pp. 135–7.

[19] See p. 131.

[20] See p. 124 for a possible third version constructed after 1410.

works, and there is no evidence that the Irish *Modus* was known, even to those interested in the history of the Irish parliament, during the late sixteenth century.[21]

Much discussion of the *Modus* has been dominated by the presence of this Irish version. On the evidence available we can no longer doubt that the Irish version is derived from a form of the English *Modus*, and in particular from the French translation of the (C) text. The (C) text of the *Modus* was a version built up from the first and second recensions.[22] It survives in relatively few copies, and appears to have been a kind of lay version of the *Modus*, which instead of being a legal text for a specific court, endeavoured to reproduce the gist of both standard versions.[23] This version alone was translated into French, and copies of the French text are found in the Courtenay Cartulary (B.L. Add. 49359) and the Finch-Hatton roll (Northampton Record Society).[24] On the back of the roll is a petition to Thomas of Lancaster, the son of Henry IV, and Lieutenant of Ireland, from Richard, Archbishop of Cashel (1406–40). The text therefore clearly had Irish associations, and may well have belonged to the Archbishop of Cashel himself.[25]

From the evidence of the texts it seems almost certain that the Irish *Modus* derives from a French translation of the (C) text similar to that found on the Finch-Hatton roll. In the paragraph dealing with aids to the King (XV) one of the aids *filios suos milites faciendo* is omitted only in the Irish version and in the French translation on the Finch-Hatton roll. Alone amongst the medieval versions the French text has the phrase *en lieu appert* concerning where parliament shall be held, a phrase which is translated *aperto loco* in the Irish version (paragraph XII). The Irish compiler mislead by the word *largesse* in the French text stated that each line of writing on the parliament roll is to be ten inches in length (paragraph XVII) when he should have said that the parliament roll itself shall measure ten inches in width. The remarkable word *comensor* in the Irish version in the phrase *caput, comensor et finis Parliamenti*

[21] It was apparently unknown to John Hooker in the 1560s and to Sir John Davies in the early seventeenth century. See p. 125.

[22] See Appendix IV.

[23] Pronay and Taylor, 'Use of the *Modus* . . . in the Middle Ages', pp. 19–20.

[24] The roll which is now in the Northampton Record Office was among the collections made by Dugdale for Sir Christopher Hatton. The front of the roll contains the French text of the *Modus*. This French text was edited by T. D. Hardy, *Archaeological Journal* 19 (1862), 259 ff.

[25] On Richard O'Hedigan, archbishop of Cashel, see A. J. Otway-Ruthven, *A History of Medieval Ireland* (London, 1968), p. 360.

(paragraph VIII) clearly derives its ancestry from the French word *commenciounri* of the Finch-Hatton roll.[26] There can be no doubt moreover that the Irish version is a compressed form of the French original where 'a great deal was omitted as inappropriate to Irish conditions'. Clauses or paragraphs were run together with inconsistencies remaining in the text.[27] To suppose that this Irish version preceded the English *Modus*, 'requires the assumption of single sentences and even half sentences being torn from their context, again and again, and raised to the dignity of separate clauses in the English version'.[28]

The question arises as to how and why this Irish version was compiled. Miss Clarke associated the Irish *Modus* with William of Windsor's period of office as lieutenant and governor (1369–76), and with possible changes in the Irish parliament at that time.[29] Whatever the truth of this, it is unlikely that the Irish *Modus* could have been compiled much earlier than the reign of Richard II. The French texts appear to belong to that period. The representation of the Commons, a central feature in the Irish as in the English text, did not become a regular part of the Irish parliament until the second half of the fourteenth century.[30] It was only from 1371 that clerical proctors, mentioned in the Irish *Modus,* were regularly summoned to parliament.[31] Only by the reign of Richard II had 'the notion of a defined and limited class of peers of parliament . . . appeared in Ireland'.[32] Reshaped as it was to meet Irish conditions the text of the Irish *Modus* only makes sense therefore when viewed against the development of the Irish parliament in the second half of the fourteenth century. One possible link between the English and Irish *Modus* can perhaps be found in the person of Philip Courtenay, who was King's Lieutenant in

[26] See Clarke, pp. 86–8, and the important collation of texts at pp. 91–5, also Galbraith, pp. 95–9. Richardson and Sayles have taken the contrary view that the Irish version is the original, *Irish Parliament*, p. 137. Their views have been fully answered by Galbraith, 'The *Modus Tenendi Parliamentum*', *Journal of the Warburg and Courtauld Institutes* 16 (1953), 81–99.

[27] The emphasis on the presence of the King in parliament betrays an English original. In the Irish *Modus* paragraph V groups the citizens and burgesses together. There is therefore no justification in paragraph XVI for distinguishing them separately in the committee of twenty-five.

[28] Galbraith, pp. 97–9, to whom these comments are indebted.

[29] 'William of Windsor in Ireland, 1369–1376', pp. 55–130. Miss Clarke's views have not been accepted by Richardson and Sayles, *Irish Parliaments*, pp. 80–5, or by James Lydon, *art. cit.* p. 253.

[30] *Irish Parliament*, pp. 76–8; Otway-Ruthven, p. 171.

[31] Ibid.

[32] Ibid., p. 170.

Ireland in 1385, before being displaced by Robert De Vere. The French copy of the *Modus* found in the Courtenay Cartulary is followed almost immediately by an agreement between the Earl of Devon and Philip Courtenay. It is a reasonable assumption that either in his capacity as King's Lieutenant or as a member of the Courtenay family, Philip Courtenay had in his possession a French copy of the *Modus*. It is also worth noting that Courtenay was in trouble with the King after his replacement by De Vere as King's Lieutenant, for in 1390 he was arrested in Ireland.[33] It may be that sometime during this period Courtenay introduced the *Modus* to certain circles in Ireland.

Whatever the truth of this, by 1419 at least, an Irish version of the *Modus* had been constructed, inspired in all probability by Richard O'Hedigan, archbishop of Cashel, who according to the text of the Irish copy was to have custody of the *Modus*, and who appears to have owned the French version of the (C) text found on the Finch-Hatton roll.[34] Richard O'Hedigan was a stormy petrel in the politics of Ireland in the early part of the fifteenth century. In the parliament of 1412 he was accused by the bishop of Waterford and Lismore of various offences, 'one was that he made very much of the Irish, and that he loved none of the English nation, and that he bestowed no Benefice upon any Englishman . . . that he went about to make himselfe King of Munster . . . And he exhibited many other enormious matters against him in writing, by whom the Lords and Commons were troubled . . .'.[35] It is possible that O'Hedigan had the notion of constructing a *Modus* for the Irish parliament, and that for this text he intended a more than merely procedural significance.

If this was the case his hopes were not destined to be fulfilled. One main reason for this was that the basic political assumptions of the English *Modus* were not relevant to the Irish parliament. The English *Modus* supposes that the King, Lords, and Commons embody the omnicompetent sovereignty of the kingdom, but this was not the case with the Irish parliament. The Irish parliament was not a sovereign assembly, and Poynings' Law in the 1490s ended all claims that it could be regarded as such.[36] The relationship between the Irish Commons

[33] *C.P.R. 1388–92*, p. 349. The circumstances of this are obscure, but Courtenay sailed with Richard to Ireland in 1394, Otway-Ruthven, p. 326.

[34] See p. 120.

[35] Otway-Ruthven, p. 360.

[36] Richardson and Sayles, *Irish Parliament*, pp. 269–81. See also R. D. Edwards and T. W. Moody 'The History of Poynings, Law: Part I. 1494–1615', *Irish Historical Studies* 2 (1941), 415–24, D. B. Quinn, 'The Early Interpretation of Poynings, Law 1494–1534', ibid, 214–54.

and the Irish Lords, though it may have been similar to the relationship of the English Lords and Commons in terms of purely feudal thought, was considerably different in practice, for the Irish Lords were distinctly more powerful than the Irish Commons. As the most recent historians of the medieval Irish parliament have written, 'the essential functions of parliament are performed by the lords who are, in turn, largely actuated by the ministerial council, itself the creature of a distant king.'[37]

For this reason alone, the Irish *Modus* appears to have had relatively little procedural significance in the history of Ireland and the paucity of the surviving manuscripts testifies to this fact. The only surviving medieval copy, the exemplification of 1419, appears to be a certified copy of the version found on Sir Christopher Preston, which was intended to be sent or presented to the King and his Council in England, in connection with the examination there of Sir Christopher Preston, at the time of the arrest of Preston, Kildare, and Bedlow at Clane under suspicion of sedition.[38] The collection of documents found on Preston at the time may have carried some political significance.[39]

In connection with this it should be noted that in the copy of the exemplification now in the Huntington Library, the Irish *Modus* is in fact only one of a group of documents. After the text of the *Modus* comes the provision for providing a governor, the provision for the custody of the *Modus* in the hands of the archbishop of Cashel, the form of the oath to be taken by the Justiciar (and known to have been taken by him in 1461), the catechism associated with that oath (based upon the coronation ceremony of Edward II), the admonition of the bishops on behalf of the Church, and the reciprocal oath of fealty.[40] The Irish *Modus* survives therefore in the exemplification in company with a number of documents which relate to the position of the Justiciar, which was by definition a controversial matter.

There is little evidence to suggest that the Irish *Modus* was used during the fifteenth and sixteenth centuries. It has been suggested that the reply made in the Trim parliament of January 1447, to Richard Talbot, archbishop of Dublin, quoting the privileges, franchises and usages of Ireland since the time of Henry FitzEmpress may have

[37] Richardson and Sayles, *Irish Parliament*, p. 195.
[38] H. G. Richardson, 'The Preston Exemplification of the *Modus Tenendi Parliamentum*', *Irish Historical Studies* 3 (1942), 187–92.
[39] *C.C.R. 1413–19*, p. 472. Mr. Richardson's suggestion that the exemplification was made by Sir Christopher Preston for his own protection is not entirely convincing.
[40] See Armstrong, *art. cit.* 256–64.

contained a reminiscence of the Irish *Modus*.[41] Yet despite this the *Modus* never seems to have been consulted as a procedural guide in this century. The one piece of evidence which suggests that the Irish *Modus* was consulted occurs in the *Liber Niger* or Register of John Allen, archbishop of Dublin (1529–34), where a form of the Irish *Modus* was transcribed.[42] This transcript was apparently made in 1533, on the occasion of the Irish parliament of that year, to provide evidence to maintain Allen's claim, as archbishop of Dublin, to sit on the right hand of the throne. The text in the Register appears to be based in part upon the Waterford version, but it also incorporates material from the English *Modus*, as well as new material including a passage describing the Irish parliament as being divided into three orders or houses. The statement in the text that parliament shall not be adjourned without the consent of the three orders or houses may have been based upon proceedings in the Irish parliament of 1410[43] None the less it is significant that even in this text some phraseology is taken from the English *Modus*.

The story of the *Modus* in Ireland does not quite end, however, with the history of the Irish *Modus*. If the Irish *Modus* itself appears to have had only a limited significance in the Irish parliaments of the fifteenth century, the English *Modus* had some influence in Ireland later through John Hooker's *Order and Usage*. Despite its new material and its extensive revisions Hooker's work was influenced by the English *Modus* and incorporated passages from that work.[44] Hooker, who sat in the Irish parliament of 1569, may well have conceived the idea of writing an account of the procedure of the English parliament from his experiences in Ireland.[45] His *Order and Usage*, constructed in the tradition of the English *Modus*, was published in two editions, one of which was dedicated to Sir William FitzWilliam, lord deputy of Ireland (1571–5). Hooker's treatise was intended as a practical guide for M.P.s in both England and Ireland, and in Ireland at least it became the basis for parliamentary procedures from the late sixteenth century onwards.[46]

[41] See Richardson, *art. cit.* p. 190.

[42] M. V. Clarke, 'The Manuscripts of the Irish *Modus Tenendi Parliamentum*', *E.H.R.* 48 (1933), 597–600. Miss Clarke believed that this text possibly represented a third version of the Irish *Modus*.

[43] Ibid. p. 597.

[44] See *above*, pp. 52–3. The following comments are indebted to Snow, pp. 76–86.

[45] For an account of the Irish parliament of 1569 see V. Treadwell, 'The Irish Parliament of 1569–71', *Proceedings of the Royal Irish Academy* 65 C (1966–7), 55–89. Hooker kept a diary of this parliament, above p. 52 n. 137.

[46] For the situation in England see pp. 53–4.

The statesman instrumental in securing the adoption of *The Order and Usage* in the Irish parliament was almost certainly Sir John Perrot. A summons list for the parliament of 1585, convened by Perrott and held in Dublin, contains a fragment entitled 'Orders to be kept and observed in the Lower or Common House of Parlyament' which consists of fragments from Hooker's work.[47] The Irish *Journals of the House of Commons* contain references to the 'Rules of Parliament' which almost certainly derive from the same source. Hooker's *Order and Usage* appears therefore to have become a procedural treatise for the Irish parliament. The history of Hooker's treatise shows the complete neglect into which the Irish *Modus* itself had fallen. Hooker appears to have known nothing of that text.[48] It was the English and not the Irish *Modus* which he consulted in preparing his own treatise, and which through his work exercised some influence on the Irish parliament.

An interesting postscript to the use of the *Modus* in Ireland is the fact that a brief Scottish version also survives.[49] This document entitled, 'The order of the Haldinge of the Court of Parliament in Scotland', appears to belong to the period 1570–85, and is found in a seventeenth-century manuscript, which contains a transcript of the English *Modus* as well as copies of various state trials.[50] The document was written by a clerk 'who plainly did not understand some of the language employed'. It may well belong to the period between 1570 and 1585 for the phrase 'the remanent small Barons stands all on the flure' agrees with the situation as recorded in the conventions of 1571 and 1572.[51] Even less claim to significance can be made for the Scottish version of the *Modus*, however, than for the Irish version. It comprises only a brief fragment, and never appears to have been used in a practical way. None the less unimportant as the Scottish *Modus* was, it does describe parliamentary practice in Scotland at a time when the main elements were the clergy, the lords and lairds, and the burgesses. If it refers to conditions during the early 1570s its description of parliamentary procedure is accurate. It is possible that the work may have been composed specially for the benefit of the English government. Whatever its purpose, however, the

[47] Snow, p. 78 ff.
[48] Ibid., p. 53.
[49] It is printed by J. D. Mackie, 'The Order of the Holding of the Court of Parliament in Scotland', *Scottish Historical Review* 27 (1948), 191–3.
[50] MS. Bodley 966. This is a (B) version of the *Modus*, written in English, but with one chapter *De Mondo Loquendi in Parliamente*, in Latin. It is followed, p. 523, by a list of the principal courts in England.
[51] Mackie, *art. cit.* p. 192.

very existence of the Scottish *Modus* shows that in the sixteenth century an attempt was made to produce a treatise for the holding of parliament in Scotland, using the archetype of the English *Modus*.

THE TEXT

The transcripts of the Irish *Modus* are mentioned in the general introduction above, pp. 117–20. The text of the Irish *Modus* is printed from the *inspeximus* of 1419, Huntington E.L. 1699 (*H*), the only surviving medieval manuscript, and where appropriate the punctuation and treatment of abbreviations in Miss Clarke's edition have been preserved. In certain places this manuscript is now incomplete at the edges, and readings have been supplied from the two seventeenth-century transcripts which are based upon this copy. These are the transcript of Hakewill as printed by Steele (*A*), and the transcript compiled by the authority of Daniel Molyneux (*B*). What few differences there are between the original and the seventeenth-century transcripts can be accounted for either by errors of transcription or by the fact that Hakewill in his transcript endeavoured to correct and improve upon his original.

Another version of the Irish *Modus*, which may be termed the 'Waterford version', based upon a copy which is now missing, but which appears once to have been in the treasury at Waterford, is represented only by three seventeenth-century transcripts. These are those of Dopping (*C*), Domvile (*D*), and that found in T.C.D.E. 3. 18 (*E*). Because the 'Waterford version' contains what is essentially a second version of the text its readings are printed separately and below those of the version of 1419.

SIGLA

H	Huntington E.L. 1699.
A	Hakewill (*excudit* Steele).
B	T.C.D. E. 3. 18 fo. 10 *seq.*
C	Dopping.
D	B.L. Add. 35505 (Domvile).
E	T.C.D E. 3. 18 fo. 1 *seq.*
codd.	codicum consensus recensionis Waterford.

Modus Tenendi Parliamenta et Consilia
in Hibernia

Henricus, Dei gratia Rex Anglie et Francie et dominus Hibernie, omnibus ad quos presentes littere pervenerint salutem: INSPEXIMUS tenorem diversorum articulorum in quodam rotulo pergameneo 5 scriptorum, cum Cristoforo de Preston' milite tempore arrestacionis sue apud villam de Clane per deputatum dilecti et fidelis nostri Iohannis Talbot de Halomshire, chivaler, locum nostrum tenentis terre nostre Hibernie, nuper facti invento, ac coram nobis et consilio nostro in eadem terra nostra apud villam de Trym, nono die Ianuarii ultimo 10 preterito ostenso, in hec verba:

Modus tenendi Parliamenta.

Henricus rex Anglie, conquestor et dominus Hibernie, mittit hanc formam archiepiscopis, episcopis, abbatibus, prioribus, comitibus, baronibus, iusticiariis, vicecomitibus, maioribus, prepositis, ministris, 15 et omnibus fidelibus suis terre Hibernie, tenendi Parliamentum.

I. In primis somonicio Parliamenti procedere debet per XL dies ante Parliamentum.

II. Sommoniri et venire debent ad Parliamentum omnes archiepiscopi, episcopi, abbates, priores et alii clerici qui tenent per tenuram 20 comitatus vel baronie integre, et nulli minores custubus propriis causa tenure sue. Item, somoniri debent archiepiscopi, episcopi, abbates et priores, decani et archidiaconi, exempti et alii previlegiati, qui habent iurisdiccionem, quod ipsi de assensu cleri pro quolibet decanatu et archidiaconatu Hibernie et (pro) se ipsis decanis et archidiaconis 25 faciant eligere duos sapientes et competentes procuratores pro propriis archidiaconatibus, ad veniendum et essendum ad Parliamentum ad respondendum et supportandum, locandum et faciendum quod quilibet et omnes de deacanatibus et archidiaconatibus facerent vel faceret si personaliter interessent. Et quod procuratores veniant cum warantibus 30 suis duplicatis, sigillatis sigillis superiorum suorum, unde unum deliberetur clerico Parliamenti irrotulandum, et aliud secum remaneat, etc.

1419: **5** pargameneo *A*.   **21** custibus *B*.   **22** sominiri *B*.
23 privilegiati *A*.   **25** pro *om H B*; de se *A*.   **26** faciant *om B*.

Waterford: **13** Henricus rex Anglie *incipiunt codd.*   **15** ministris *om D E*.
17 *titulus* Summonitio *add codd.*   **18** primum diem parliamentum *add codd.*
19 *titulus* Summonitio Clericorum *add codd.*   **25** et pro se *codd.*
28 allocandum et faciendum *C*.

III. Sumoniri et venire debet etiam omnis et quilibet comes et baro et pares eorum, videlicet, qui habent terras et redditus ad valenciam unius comitatus integre, quod est viginti feoda militum, quodlibet feodum computatum ad XX libras, que facit CCCC li, vel valorem baronie integre, videlicet, tresdecim feoda militum et tercia pars feodi, 5 que faciunt CCCC marcas, et nulli minores laici vel clerici custibus propriis, causa tenure sue, nisi rex sumoneat consiliarios suos vel alios sapientes necessaria causa: quibus mittere solet precando eos, custibus ipsius regis, venire et esse in Parliamento suo, etc.

IV. Item, per breve Rex mittere debet cuilibet senescallo libertatis et 10 cuilibet vicecomiti suo Hibernie, quod faciant eligere, quilibet de assensu communitatis libertatis et comitatus sui, duos milites competentes, honestos, et sapientes, ad veniendum ad Parliamentum ad respondendum, supportandum, allocandum, et faciendum quod omnis et quilibet communitatis vel libertatis comitatus facerent vel faceret si 15 personaliter interessent. Et quod milites veniant cum warantis suis, ut supradictum est de procuratoribus, et quod sine licencia parliamenti non discendant a Parliamento. Et post licenciam, habeant breve directum senescallo vel vicecomiti, quod faciat dictos milites suos habere de communitate sua racionabiles custus et expensas suas a die 20 remocionis eorum versus Parliamentum usque racionabilem diem quo ad propria revenire a Parliamento poterunt. Et quod expensa non excedat I marcam de duobus militibus per diem, etc.

V. Item, eodem modo mittendum est maioribus, ballivis, propositis civitatum et burgorum franches', quod de communi assensu commu- 25 nium suorum elegant duos cives vel burgenses, etc., ut dictum est supra de militibus. Et quod expensa duorum civium vel burgensium non excedat dimidiam marcam per diem.

VI. Et memorandum quod rex inveniet, custibus suis, principalem clericum parliamenti ad irrotulandum communia placita et negotia 30 Parliamenti, qui tanto modo subiectus erit sine medio regi et Parliamento suo in communi. Et quando pares Parliamenti sunt assignati ad examinandum peticiones per seipsos, et sunt concordes in

1419: 1 debent *A*.   3 integri id est *A*.
5 partem feodi *A*.   6 custubus *A*.   7 sumoniat *A*.
12 comitatus et libertatis comitatus *A*.   15 comitatus vel libertas comitatus *A*.
22 poterint *A B*.   24–5 prepositis civitatum et burgensibus franchesiarum *A*.

Waterford: 1 *titulus* Summonitio Laicorum *add codd*; etiam omnes senatores et quilibet comes *C*; omnes sectatores *D E*.
4 viguit libras *C*.   5 feodi unius militis *add codd*.   10 *titulus* Milites comitatum *add codd*.
24 *titulus* Cives et Burgenses *add codd*.   29 *titulus* Principalis Clericus *add codd*.

iudicio suo, tunc clericus predictus repetet peticiones et processus super
ipsos, et pares reddent iudicium in pleno Parliamento. Et iste clericus
sedebit in medio loco iusticiariorum. Et memorandum, quod nullus
iusticiarius est in Parliamento, nec habet per ipsum recordum in
Parliamento, nisi nova potestas ei assignetur per regem et pares   5
Parliamenti in parliamento. Et dictus clericus deliberabit rotulos suos
in thesaurum ante finem Parliamenti.

    VII. Item rex assignare solet, custibus suis, unum bonum clericum
probatum ad scribendum dubitaciones et responsiones quas archiepiscopi et episcopi facere velint regi et Parliamento; et secundum clericum   10
procuratorum, eodem modo; tercium pro comitibus et baronibus et
paribus eorum, eodem modo; quartum militibus libertatum et
comitatuum, et quintum civibus et burgensibus. Qui clerici semper
predictis erunt in eorum consiliis intendentes, quod si vacaverint, vel
aliquis eorum vacaverit, adiuvare debent principalem clericum ad   15
irrotulandum. Et ad minus assignare debet unum dominis et communibus spiritualibus, et alium dominis et communibus temporalibus. Et
etiam rex assignabit cum quolibet predictorum clericorum unum
hostiarium et unum clamatorem.

    VIII. De rege solo est primus gradus Parliamenti, quia est caput,   20
comensor et finis Parliamenti. De archiepiscopis, episcopis, abbatibus,
prioribus, et pares eorum, per comitatum vel baroniam tenentibus, est
secundus gradus. Tercius gradus est de procuratoribus. Quartus gradus
de comitibus, baronibus et eorum paribus. Quintus gradus est de
militibus libertatum et communitatum. Sextus gradus est de civibus et   25
burgensibus. Et si contingat quod aliquis predictorum graduum,
excepto Rege, absens a Parliamento fuerit, et debite sumonitus fuerit,
nihilominus Parliamentum iudicatum est esse plenum.

    IX Rex tenetur semper esse in Parliamento, nisi infirmitate
impediatur, et tunc infra maneriam vel villam Parliamenti debet esse,   30
et mittere debet pro duobus episcopis, II comitibus, II baronibus, II
militibus comitatuum, II civibus, et II burgensibus ad videndum

---

1419: **2** illinc clericus *A.*   **4** nec habetur *A.*   **11** pro *om B.*
12 quartum pro militibus *A.*   **15** debeat *A.*   **22** paribus eorum *A.*
25 comitatuum *A.*   **28** iudicandum *A.*   **30** esse debet *A.*
Waterford: **4** iusticiarius nullus *codd.*
8 *titulus* Clerici Parliamenti *add codd.*   **14** meorum consiliis *codd.*
20 *titulus* Gradus Parliamenti *add codd.*   **21** secundus gradus de archiepiscopis *add codd.*
27 et debite sumonitus fuerit *om codd.*
29 *titulus* De presentia Regis et absentie eius *add codd*; personaliter *post* Parliamento *add
codd.*

personam suam, et testificandum statum suum. In quorum etiam presencia committere debet archiepiscopo loci, comitibus terre, et capitali iusticiario suo, quod incipient et continuant Parliamentum nomine suo. Et rex absentare non potest nisi modo et causa supradicta, nisi sit eorum assensu parium Parliamenti. 5

X Rex sedebit in medio principalis scamni, et ad eius dexteram archiepiscopus loci, et si extra Dublin' provinciam Parliamentum fuerit tentum, tunc ad sinistram archiepiscopus Dublin', et deinde Cassellen' et Tuamen' ex utraque parte, diende episcopi, abbates, et alii, secundum ordinem suum. Cancellarius stabit iuxta regem. Thesaurarius sedebit 10 inter barones; iusticiarii de uno banco et de altero ad pedes regis, et omnes procuratores super terram.

XI Rex cum concilio suo tenetur esse primo die in parliamento, et quarto die omnes somoniti ad Parliamentum erunt vocati, et eorum defectus recordati, et per consideracionem regis et omnium parium 15 parliamenti amerciamenta defectuum taxata.

XII Parliamentum non debet teneri diebus dominicis, nec die Omnium Sanctorum, nec die Animarum, nec in Nativitate Sancti Johannis Baptiste. Omnibus aliis diebus Rex cum gradibus Parliamenti debet esse in Parliamento media hora ante primam, festivalibus diebus 20 propter servicium divinum ad horam primam, et sit Parliamentum in aperto loco semper.

XIII Peticiones sunt affilati sicut deliberantur, et sic per ordinem legantur et respondeantur. Set primo determinentur que ad guerram pertinent, postea de persona regis et regine et pueris suis ac gubernacione 25 eorum, et postea de communibus negotiis terre, sicut est de legibus faciendis et emendandis, videlicet, originalibus iudicialibus et executoriis post iudicium redditum, et postea singulares peticiones secundum

---

1419: **2** comiti terre A.   **3** incipiant et continuent parliamentum *A.*
23 sint affilata *A.*

Waterford: **6** *titulus* Sessiones in Parliamento *add codd.*
6–12 Rex sedebit in medio principalis Scammi et ad eius dextram Archiepiscopus loci Ardmachanus vel Dublin, et si extra eorum limites Parliamentum fit, tunc a dexteris Regis Archiepiscopi Armach. et Casselen., et a sinistris Regis Archiepiscopi Dublin. et Tuamen., deinde vero a dextris Episcopi, Abbates, Priores in secunda formula secundum ordinem, a sinistris in formula Comites Barones et eorum Pares secundum ordinem ad pedem per terum (dextrum *D*). Regis sedebit Cancellarius, Capitalis Iusticiarius, cum suis sociis et eorum clericis, et ad pedem sinistrum sedebunt Thesaurarius et Camerarii et Barones de scacario: Iusticiarii de Banco et eorum clerici, si sint de Parliamento, deinde procuratores terre sedebunt. *codd.*
13 *titulus* Amerciamenta Absentium *add codd.*
17 *titulus* Dies et Horae Parliamenti *add codd.*
23 *titulus* Ordo deliberandi parliamenti *add codd.*   **25** principis suis *codd.*

quod sunt super filator'. Et primo die Parliamenti sit proclamacio facta in villa et loco Parliamenti, quod omnes qui querelas vel peticiones velint deliberare Parliamento id faciant infra quintum diem sequentem.

XIV Quarto die Parliamenti vel quinto, predicacio fiat de aliquo solempni clerico eiusdem provincie, et post predicacionem cancellarius, 5 vel alius sapiens et eloquens ac honestus per cancellarium electus, monstrabit causas Parliamenti, primo generaliter, postea specialiter, stando quia quilibet loquens in parliamento tenetur stare loquendo excepto rege ut ab omnibus audiatur. Et post promocionem Parliamenti rex debet predicare clericos et laicos quod quilibet in suo gradu 10 diligenter studiose et corditer laboret ad tractandum et deliberandum negotium Parliamenti, sicut principaliter intendunt hoc esse, primo ad voluntatem Dei, et postea ad honorem et proficuum regis et ipsorum presencium.

XV Rex non solebat auxilium petere de populo suo, nisi pro guerra 15 existente vel pro filiabus maritandis. Que peticiones in pleno Parliamento debent in scripto deliberari cuilibet gradui Parliamenti, et in scripto responderi. Unde sciendum est, quod in talibus concessionibus necessarium est ut maior pars cuiuslibet status sit ad hoc consensiens. Et sciendum, quod duo milites electi habent plus vocis in concedendo vel 20 negando pro comitatu suo quam comes eiusdem comitatus: eodem modo, procuratores clericorum plus episcopis suis in concedendo et negando; quod apparet, quia rex cum comunitate sua potest tenere parliamentum suum (sine) episcopis, comitibus et baronibus, si racionabiliter sumoniti non venirent, quia aliquando fuit quod non 25 fuerunt episcopus, comes, nec baro, et tunc reges tenuerunt Parliamenta. Et si (communes) clericorum et laicorum sint sumoniti modo debito ad Parliamentum, et pro racionabili causa venire nolunt, scilicet si assignaverint specialiter causas in quibus rex eos non recte gubernaverit, tunc Parliamentum tenebitur pro nullo, quamvis omnes alii status 30 plenarie ibidem intersint. Et ideo, necessarium est quod in omnibus concedendis, faciendis, affirmandis et donandis per Parliamentum, quod sunt concesse per communes Parliamenti, que constant ex tribus gradibus, videlicet de procuratoribus clericorum, militibus libertatum

1419: **1** super filas *A*.   **3** velunt *B*.   **10** debet precari *A*.
12 intenditur *A*.   **18** scriptis *B*.
24 sine *om H*; suum *om A*.   **27** communes *om H B*.
28–9 noluerint vel si assignaverint *A*.   **31** interfuerint *A B*.   **33** sint concessa *A*.
Waterford: **1** super filatoria *C E* filatoribus *D*.
4 *titulus* Incepcio Parliamenti *add codd*.   **5** eiusdem dioceseas *codd*.
10 precare clericos *codd*.   **15** *titulus* De Adjutoriis postulandis *add codd*.

et comitatuum, civibus et burgensibus. Et quilibet parium Parliamenti
est pro seipso in Parliamento, et omnes pares Parliamenti sunt iudices
et iusticiarii in Parliamento, et sedebunt (omnes), nisi quando locuntur,
communes vero querentes et auxilii concessores vel negatores.

XVI Si dubius casus vel durus guerre vel pacis in terra advenerit, vel 5
extra terram, ista causa sit scripta in pleno Parliamento, et sint ibidem
inter pares Parliamenti disputata et tractata, et tunc, si necesse sit, per
regem m(andetur) cuilibet gradui, quod eat qualibet gradus per se
habens clericum cum causa scripta, ubi recitabunt eandem, ita quod
ordinent et considerant inter eos in quo meliori modo et iusto procedere 10
possint in casu illo, sicut pro persona regis et seipsis, ac pro quibus
presentes sunt, velint coram Deo respondere. Et responciones eorundem
(in scriptis reportarent) ut omnibus responsionibus et consiliis auditis,
secundum melius consilium procedatur, sicut si sit discordia inter regem
et alios magnates, vel inter magnates pax terre fracta fuerit, vel inter 15
populum, ita quod videtur Parliamento quod talis causa sit per omnes
gradus terre tractanda, et per eorum consideracionem emendanda (vel
per) guerram rex et terra turbe(n)tur, vel si durus casus coram
cancellario vel iusticiario, aut durum iudicium advenerit, vel aliquis
alius similis casus, et si in talibus deliberacionibus omnes, vel saltem 20
maior pars cuiuslibet gradus, non consenserint, tunc de quolibet gradu
Parliamenti, excepto rege, eligatur unus, qui omnes vel
eorum(maior)numerus eligant duos episcopos, tres procuratores pro
toto clero, duos comites, III barones, quinque milites comitatuum, V
cives et V burgenses, qui faciunt XXV personas; et ipsi de seipsis 25
possunt eligere duodecim, et condiscendere in ipsis; et ipsi XII in sex,
et condiscendere in ipsis; et ipsi sex (in) tres, et condiscendere in ipsis;
et tunc per licenciam regis illi III in duobus, et illi duo in altero ipsorum
potest condiscendere (qui cum se ipso discordare) non possit, cuius
ordinacio erit pro toto parliamento, nisi maior numerus consentire 30
possit, salvo rege et consilio, quod ipsi tales ordinaciones, postquam

---

1419: **2** pari Parliamenti *H.*   **3** omnes *om H B.*   **8** m(andetur) *om H B.*
9 eam *B.*   **13** in scriptis reportarent *om H B.*   **13** consiliis antedictis *A.*
17–18 vel per *om H B*; turba(n)tur *A.*   **22** elegatur *A.*
23 maior *om H*; eorum maior *om B.*   **27** in *om H B.*
29 qui cum se ipso discordare *om H B.*   **30** nec maior *A.*

Waterford: **3** omnes *om codd.*
4 querentes et necessitatibus subvenientes et stabunt *C D*; et vero servitutibus subvenientes
et stabunt *E.*
5 *titulus* Iudicium casus dubii *add codd.*   **8** injungatur cuilibet *codd.*
9 recitabunt causam *codd.*   **22** extra Rege *D E.*   **23** eorum tres ad minus *codd.*
25–6 XXV personas in ipsis et ipsi sex in tres et condescendere *codd.*

scripte fuerint, examinare et corrigere, si somerint in pleno Parliamento et non alibi, ex Parliamenti assensu.

XVII Clerici Parliamenti non denegabunt alicui (transcriptum, vel processus sui,) aut recordi Parliamenti, si qui solvere voluerint pro quolibet decem lineis continentibus X polices in longitudine, que est 5 mensura rotuli Parliamenti, unum denarium.

XVIII Parliamentum erit tentum in quo loco competenti terre regi placuerit, et Parliamentum departire non debet quando aliqua peticio est pendens non determinata; quod si rex contrarium fecerit, periurus est. Et de omnibus gradibus Parliamenti nullus solus potest nec debet 10 decedere a Parliamento sine licencia regis et omnium parium Parliamenti; et hoc in pleno Parliamento, ita quod inde fiat mencio in rotulis Parliamenti. Et si aliquis Parlia(menti) durante Parliamento infirmitate detineatur, ita quod Parliamento accedere non possit, tunc infra quartum diem mittet excusatores Parliamento, quo die si non 15 venerit, mittantur ei duo de paribus suis ad videndum et testificandum infirmitatem suam, et per recordum eorum sit excusatus, vel in misericordia cum (pro defectu amercietur); quod si non ficta infirmitas sit, tunc attornabit aliquem sufficientem coram ipsis essendum pro ipso in Parliamento, quia sanus et de sana memoria non potest excusari. Ad 20 departicionem Parliamenti, primo demandari et proclamari debet in aperto in Parliamento, si aliquis deliberavit peticionem Parliamento, cui (factum non) est responsum, et si nullum reclamatum est, supponendum quod cuilibet peticioni medicina racionabilis facta est. Et tunc cancellarius, vel alius assignatus per regem et Parliamentum, 25 debet dicere alta voce: Nos damus licenciam Parliamento dissolvi. Et sic finitur Parliamentum.

XIX Et eciam rex vult quod ea(dem forma) in consiliis per somonicionem factam observetur, excepto quod pro (rege) et legibus in ipsis consiliis erunt ordinaciones, in Parliamento vero statuta. 30

1419: **1** convenerint *A*.   **3** transcriptum—**4** processus sui *om H B*; recordum *H*.
8 peticio—**9** pendens non *om B*.   **13** parliamenti *om B*.
18 pro defectu amercietur *om H B*.   **23** factum non *om H B*.   **26** Nos dedimus *A*.
28 forma *om H*.   **29** pro lege *A*.

Waterford: **3** *titulus* Transcriptum *add codd.*   **7** *titulus* Perjurus Rex *add codd.*
9 periurus est et parliamentum non debet adjornari ni de consensu omnium parium parliamenti et de omnibus gradibus parliamenti *add codd.*
12 *titulus* De fine parliamenti *post* parliamento *add codd.*
18 pro defecta quod suspicio ficta infirmiter sit tunc mittat aliquem sufficientem coram ipsis *C*.
28 *titulus* De Consiliis *add codd.*

XX Et etiam rex vult ut absente rege a dicta terra, sine procuratore vel gubernatore eiusdem terre, quocunque alio nomine censeatur per ipsum regem constituto quod statim (cum) celeritate concilium regis ibidem mittat pro archiepiscopis, episcopis, abbatibus, prioribus, comitibus, baronibus, et eorum paribus, aliisque proceribus et discretis 5 viris ad minus proximorum trium comitatuum proximi, (ut) festinius convenire possint ad certum brevem diem et locum coram ipsis essendum, ad tractandum consulendum et consensiendum (cum) iusticiario regis terre Hibernie, qui vices regis ut domini Hibernie in nomine ipsius regis in omnibus supplebit, super quo statim concilium 10 regis predictum sub magno sigillo reges terre predicte, iusticiarium Hibernie constituant terram predictam in omnibus, nomine regis, iustificandum.

XXI Hanc formam rex vult ut in terra sua Hibernie in omnibus ... observetur. Et quod in custodia archiepiscopi Cassellen., 15 tanquam in medio terre, hoc scriptum populo eiusdem terre remaneat custodiendum : Constitutus a rege custos suus terre Hibernie, quocunque nomine senciatur tactis sacrosanctis evangeliis, hoc sacramentum prestet coram cancellario, consilio et (populo) : Custodiet Deo et populo terre Hibernie, leges libertates et custumas rectas, quas antiqui reges 20 Anglie, predecessores regis nunc, et ipse rex, Deo et populo Anglie et terre Hibernie concesserunt; et quod observet Deo et sancte ecclesie clero et populo pacem et concordiam in Deo integriter, secundum potestatem suam, et quod fie(ri faciat) in omnibus iudicibus suis equam et rectam iusticiam, cum discretione, misericordia, et veritate. Et quod 25 tenebit et custodiet rectas leges et custumas quas populus terre elegerit sibi esse tenendum, et ipsas defendere et fortificare debet ad honorem Dei, pro posse suo.

XXII Et memorandum quod hoc iuramentum est a iuramento regis Anglie. 30

XXIII Et accepto iuramento, investitur iuratus potestate sibi concessa, et non antea. Finitur.

1419: **1** summus *post* terra B.   **2** sentiatur *H.*   **3** constitutus *B*; cum *om H B.*   **4** mittatur *B.*   **6** ad minus comitatus proximi, ut festinius convenire possint *A*; vel *H*   **7** locum curiae *B.*   **8** cum *A om H B.*   **11** justiciandum *A*; justificando *B.*   **12** constituat *A.*   **16—17** hoc scriptum populo eiusdem terre custodiendum *A.*   **19** cancellario *om A.* populo *om H B.*   **20** custumias B.   **23** Deo integram *A.*   **24** faciat *om H.* fieri faciat *add B*; omnibus iudiciis *A B.*   **26** elegerint *B.*   **27** sibi tenendas *A.*   **31** investitur ... Justiciarum potestate sibi concessa *B.*

Waterford: **1** *titulus* Constitution Iustic. in Hibernia *add codd.*
2 vel gubernatore *om C D*; alio nomine censeatur finiunt *codd.*

XXIV Inspeximus etiam tenorem cujusdam articuli in quadam cedula de papiro scripti, et cum predicto Christofero tempore predicto similiter inventa, ac coram predicto locum nostrum (tenente et consi)lio nostro predicto, apud dictam villam de Trym, eodem nono die Ianuarii similiter ostensa, in hec verba: 5

Electus a plebe in regem ut consecretur postquam ad idem iterum consenserint, metropolitanus electum mediocriter distinctaque interroget voce: si leges et consuetudines ab anti(quo a) regibus plebi Anglorum concessas (cum) sacramenti confirmacione, eidem plebi concedere et servare voluerit, et presertim leges et consuetudines et   10 libertates a gloriosissimo rege et sancto Edwardo clero populoque concessas. Si autem omnibus hiis assentire se velle promiserit, exponat ei metropolitanus, ita dicendo; 'Servabis ecclesie Dei cleroque populo pacem ex integro et concordiam inde secundum vires tuas?' Respondebit: 'Servabo.' 'Facies fieri in omnibus iudiciis tuis equam et rectam   15 iusticiam et discretionem in misericordia et veritate secundum vires tuas?' Respondebit: 'Faciam.' 'Concedis iustas leges ess(e) ... per te esse protegendas, et ad honorem Dei roborandas quas vulgus eligerit secundum vires tuas?' Respondebit: 'Concedo et promitto.'

Sequitur admonicio episcoporum ad regem, et legatur ab uno   20 episcopo coram omnibus clara voce, sic dicendo: 'Domine rex, a vobis perdonari petimus, ut unicuique de vobis et ecclesiis vobis (commissis canonicum privi)legium ac debitam legem atque iustitiam conservetis, et defensionem exhibeatis, sicut rex in suo regno debet unicuique suo episcopo, abbatibus et ecclesiis sibi commissis.' Respondebit: 'Animo   25 libenti et devoto promitto vobis et perdonique unicuique de vobis et ecclesiis vobis comissis canonicum privilegium, et debitam (legem atque iustitiam) servabo, et defencionem quantum potero, adiuvante Domino, exhibeo, sicut rex in suo regno unicuique episcopo, abbatibus, et ecclesiis sibi comissis per rectum exhibere debet.' Adiciantur   30 praedictis interrogacionibus que infra fuerint.

Pronunciatis omnibus supradictis, dictus princeps conservet se omnia predicta observaturum, (sacramento super) altare coram cunctis protinus prestito, rege itaque in solio suo taliter collocato, pares regni

---

1419: **3** tenente et *om H.*   **6** ut consecretur *om B.*
8 ab antiquis Regibus *B.*   **9** causa *H.*   **10** serva *B.*   **15** facias *B.*
17 esse tenendas (*Liber Regalis,* p. 99).   **21** de nobis *A* (*Liber Regalis,* p. 88).
22–3 commissis canonicum *om HB.*   **23** debitam legem iustitiam *A.*
26 promitto vobis perdonoque *A.*   **27–8** legem atque iustitiam *om H.*
31 preteritis *A*; que iusta *A.*   **33** sacramento super *om H B.*

dictum regem undique circumstantes manibus palam extentis in signum fidelitatis, offerent se ad dicti regis et dicte corone sustentacionem.

Nos autem tenores articulorum predictorum de assensu prefati (locum tenentis) et consilii nostri predicti, tenore presentium duximus 5 testificandum, in cuius rei testimonium has litteras nostras fieri fecimus patentes. Teste prefato locum nostrum tenente apud Trym, xii die Ianuarii Anno regni nostri sexto.

  Per ipsum locum tenentem et consilium.

Examinatur per Iahonnem Parsant et Willelmum Sutton, clericos.   10

1419 : **1** dictum *om B.*   **5** locum tenentis *om H.*   **7** nostro *A.*   **10** Passant *B.*

The Manner of Holding Parliaments and Councils in Ireland

Henry, by the grace of God King of England and France, and Lord of Ireland, greets all those to whom the present letters shall have come. We have examined the tenor of the various articles in a certain parchment roll of writing, lately found on Christopher Preston, knight, at the time of his arrest in the town of Clane through the intermediary of our dear and faithful John Talbot of Hallamshire, knight, our representative in our land of Ireland, and shown before us and our council in our same land at the town of Trim, on the ninth day of January last passed, in these words:

The Manner of Holding Parliaments

Henry, King of England, conqueror and lord of Ireland, sends this formula for the holding of parliament to his archbishops, bishops, abbots, priors, earls, barons, justices, sheriffs, mayors, officials and ministers, and all his faithful subjects of the land of Ireland.

I Firstly the summoning of parliament ought to precede parliament by forty days.

II To Parliament ought to be summoned and come all archbishops, bishops, abbots, priors, and other clerks who hold by a complete earldom or barony, and no lesser clerks at their own cost on account of their tenure. Also there ought to be summoned archbishops, bishops, abbots and priors, deans and archdeacons, exempted and other privileged [persons] who have jurisdiction, that they with the assent of their clergy for every deanery and archdeaconry in Ireland, and for the same deaneries and archdeaconries cause to be elected two wise and competent proctors for their own archdeaconries to come and attend in parliament in order to reply and support, arrange and do what each and all persons of the deaneries and archdeaconries would do had they been personally present. And that the proctors come with their warrants in duplicate, sealed with the seals of their superiors, of which one shall be delivered to the clerk of parliament to enroll, and the other shall remain with them, etc.

III There ought to be summoned and come any and every earl and baron and their peers, that is those who have lands and revenues to the value of an entire earldom, that is twenty knights fees, each fee being reckoned at twenty pounds, which makes four hundred pounds or the value of an entire barony, that is thirteen and a third knights' fees, which makes four hundred marks, and none of the lesser laity and clergy at their own cost by reason of their tenure unless the King summons by necessity his councillors or other wise men. It is customary to send for them, asking them that they come and be present in parliament at the cost of the King.

IV Also the King ought to send by writ to the steward of any and every franchise and to any and every of his sheriffs of Ireland, that they should cause to be elected each with the assent of the community of the franchise and his county, two suitable, honest, and experienced knights, to come to parliament to reply, support, state and do what one and all of the community of the franchise or the county would do if they were personally present. And that the knights shall come with their warrants, as mentioned above concerning the proctors, and that they shall not depart from parliament without the license of parliament. And after this license they shall have a writ directed to the steward or the sheriff, that he shall pay the aforesaid knights from the community their reasonable costs and expenses from the day they went to parliament until the day when they were able to return home from parliament. And these expenses shall not exceed one mark per day for two knights.

V Also in the same manner it shall be sent to the mayors, bailiffs and officials of the franchises of the towns and boroughs, that by the common assent of their community they shall elect two citizens or burgesses etc., as mentioned above concerning the knights. And that the expenses of the two citizens or burgesses shall not exceed half a mark a day.

VI And it is to be noted that the King shall find at his own cost, a principal clerk of parliament to enroll the pleas of the community and the business of parliament, who will be subject without intermediary only to the King and his parliament in common. And when the peers of parliament are assigned to examine petitions by themselves, and are agreed in their judgement, then the said clerk shall repeat the petitions and the process upon them, and the peers shall render judgement in full parliament. And this clerk shall sit in the middle of the bench of justices. And it should be noted that no-one is a judge in parliament nor is anyone of them a judge of record in parliament, unless new powers have been assigned to him by the King and the peers of parliament in parliament. And the said clerk shall deliver his rolls to the treasury before the end of parliament.

VII Also the King is accustomed to assign at his own cost a good and competent clerk to write down the queries and replies which the archbishops and the bishops may wish to make to the King and parliament, and similarly a second clerk for proctors of the clergy, a third similarly for the earls and barons and their peers, and a fourth for the knights of the franchises and the counties, and a fifth for the citizens and burgesses. These clerks shall always give attention to their deliberations but if they are free, or if any of them are free they ought to assist the principal clerk to enroll. And at the least one ought to be assigned to the spiritual lords and commons, and another to the temporal lords and commons. And likewise the King shall assign with the aforesaid clerks an usher and a crier.

VIII The King alone constitutes the first grade of parliament because he is the head, the beginning, and the end of parliament. The second grade consists of the archbishops, bishops, abbots, priors and their peers holding by earldom or barony. The third grade consists of the proctors. The fourth grade [consists of] the earls, barons, and their peers. The fifth grade consists of the knights of the franchises and the communities [counties]. The sixth grade consists of the citizens and burgesses. And if it should happen that any of the aforesaid grades, except the King, should be absent from parliament, and ought to have been summoned none the less the parliament shall be deemed to be full.

IX The King is bound always to be present in parliament unless he is impeded by infirmity, and then he should be in the manor or the vill of parliament, and he should send for two bishops, two earls, two barons, two knights of the counties, two citizens and two burgesses to view his person and to testify to his condition. In their presence he ought to commission the archbishop of the province, the earls of the land, and his chief justice, that they begin and continue parliament in his name. And the King cannot absent himself except in the manner and for the cause abovesaid, unless it be with the assent of those peers in parliament.

X The King shall sit in the middle of the principal bench and on his right the archbishop of the place [i.e. the province in which parliament is meeting] and if parliament is held outside the province of Dublin, then on his left the archbishop of Dublin, and then Cashel and Tuam on either side, then the bishops, abbots, and others, according to their order. The chancellor shall stand next to the King. The treasurer shall sit between the barons, the justices of one bench and the other at the foot of the King, and all the proctors on the floor.

XI The King together with his Council is bound to be present on the first day in parliament, and on the fourth day all who have been summoned will be called to parliament, and their default recorded, and by the decision of the King and all the peers of parliament they shall be amerced according to their default.

XII Parliament ought not to be held on Sundays, nor on All Saints day, All Souls day, nor the nativity of St. John the Baptist. On all other days the King together with the grades of parliament ought to be in parliament at the middle hour before prime, and on feast days because of divine service at the hour of prime, and parliament should always be held in an open place.

XIII The petitions of parliament are filed as they are considered, and according to this order they are read and replied to. But first it should be determined what pertains to war, then what to the person of the King and Queen, and their children and their government, and then to the common affairs of the kingdom such as making and amending laws, that is to say original judgements as well as sentences after judgement has been given, and then individual petitions according to the order filed. And on the first day of parliament it shall be proclaimed in the vill and the place of parliament that all who have complaints and petitions that they may wish to deliver to parliament shall do so within the next five days.

XIV On the fourth or fifth day of parliament a sermon shall be delivered by some duly constituted clerk of the same province and after the sermon the chancellor or some other wise and eloquent and honest person deputed by the chancellor shall declare the causes of the parliament first in general and then in particular, standing in order that he can be heard by everyone, because everyone who speaks in parliament must stand to speak except the King. And after the opening of parliament the King ought to declare to the clergy and laity that each in his own grade should diligently, seriously, and whole-heartedly labour to treat and deliberate the business of parliament to ensure firstly that it should be in accordance with the will of God, and after to the honour and profit of the King and those present.

XV The King used not to demand an aid from his people except for a war in progress or for the marriage of his daughters. These petitions ought to be delivered in writing to each grade of parliament, and given a written reply. Hence it must be understood that in those grants it is necessary that the greatest part of each grade should assent to it. It must be understood that two knights who are elected have a greater voice in granting and denying on behalf of a county than the earl of that county. In the same way the proctors of the clergy [have] more than their bishops in granting and denying, because it is evident that the King can hold parliament with his commonalty without bishops, earls, or barons provided they did not come after they had been duly summoned because at one time there was no bishop, earl, or baron, and still the Kings held parliaments. But if the commons of the clergy and the laity are summoned to parliament in the accustomed way, and for some reasonable cause are not willing to come, namely if they give specifically as reason that the King does not govern them rightly, then there will be no parliament at all, although all the other estates are there in full. And therefore it is necessary that all matters which have to be granted, done, affirmed, and given in parliament, ought to be granted by the commons of parliament, which is composed of these grades, that is to say the proctors of the clergy, the knights of the franchises and counties, the citizens and burgesses. And each peer of parliament is in parliament for himself. All the peers of parliament are judges and justices in parliament, and they shall all sit except when they speak, the commons are plaintiffs, and the conceders or deniers of aids.

XVI If a doubtful or difficult case arises concerning war or peace in the land or outside the land, that case is rendered in writing in full parliament, and shall be debated and discussed among the peers of parliament. Then if necessary it shall be referred by the King to each grade so that each grade by itself having a clerk with the case in writing after that case has been read out, can ordain and consider among themselves what is the best and wisest manner they can proceed in that case as they would wish to answer before God for the person of the King, and themselves, and those present. And they shall report their replies in writing, so that having heard all the replies and advice, the better plan be proceeded with, and if there is discord between the King and other magnates, or if between the magnates or between the people the peace of the land is broken, so that it seems to parliament that such a matter ought to be treated by all the grades of the land, and settled by their consideration, or if the King and the land are troubled by war or if a difficult case comes before the chancellor or a justice, or a difficult judgement arises, or any similar case, and if in these deliberations all or even the greater part of each grade do not agree, then from each grade of parliament except the King one shall be elected. Let all of them or the greater number of them elect two bishops and three proctors for all the clergy, two earls, three barons, five knights of the counties, five citizens and five burgesses, which compose twenty-five persons, and from these they themselves shall be able to elect twelve and they shall reduce themselves, and these twelve to six, and they shall reduce themselves, and these six to three, and they shall reduce themselves, and then by the licence of the King these three to two, and these two can reduce into one or the other who cannot disagree with himself, and his decision will be on behalf of the whole parliament, unless the greater number are able to agree, saving to the King and Council that these ordinances after they have been written are examined and corrected if it is so decided in full parliament and not elsewhere and with the consent of parliament.

XVII The clerks of parliament shall not deny a transcript either of his process or a record of parliament to anyone who is willing to pay a penny for every ten lines containing ten inches in length which is the measurement of a parliament roll.

XVIII Parliament will be held in any suitable place in the land which pleases the King, and parliament ought not depart so long as any petition remains undiscussed and the King breaks his oath if he allows the contrary. And of all the grades of parliament no one can or ought to leave parliament without the licence of the King and of all the peers of parliament, and this in full parliament, and this shall be mentioned in the roll of parliament. And if during parliament anyone is detained from parliament by infirmity, so that he cannot come to parliament, then within four days he should send excusors to parliament, on which day if he does not come two of his peers shall be sent to him to see and to testify to his sickness, and by their record he is to be excused, or in mercy when [he is amerced for his default]; but if he is not feigning sickness, then he shall appoint as attorney some sufficient person in their presence to attend parliament for him, but if he is well and of sound mind he cannot be excused. As regards the departure of parliament, it ought first be asked and proclaimed openly in parliament whether there is anyone who has delivered a petition to parliament who has not had his reply, and if there is no contradiction it must be supposed that a reasonable remedy has been made to every petition. And then the chancellor or someone else assigned by the King and parliament ought to say in a loud voice, We give our licence for parliament to dissolve. And so ends parliament.

XIX And also the King wills that the same forms shall be observed in the summoning of the Council, except that [the law] and laws of the same council are ordinances, while in parliament they are true statutes.

XX And also the King wills that in the absence of the King from the same land without a procurator or governor of the said land or someone by whatever other name he may be known, having been appointed by the King himself, the King's Council shall directly and speedily send for the archbishops, bishops, abbots, priors, earls, barons, and their peers, with other nobles and discreet men at least to the nearest three adjacent counties, in order that they may more quickly assemble on a certain convenient day and at a place which they decide amongst themselves for deliberating, counselling, and agreeing [concerning] a Justiciar of the King of the land of Ireland, who in place of the King, and as the lord of Ireland, and in the name of the King, shall supply all things. Upon which directly the King's Council aforesaid under the King's Great Seal for the said land may appoint him Justiciar of Ireland for governing the said land in the name of the King in all things.

XXI The King wills that this form shall be observed in all things in his land of Ireland and that this writing shall be held for the people of the aforesaid land in the custody of the Archbishop of Cashel, since it is in the middle of the land. He who is appointed by the King his keeper of the land of Ireland by whatever name he is known having touched the Holy Gospel shall swear this oath in the presence of the chancellor, Council, and people; he shall keep for God, and the people of the land of Ireland the laws, liberties, and true customs which ancient Kings of England, predecessors of the present King, and the King himself, have granted to God, the people of England, and the land of Ireland. And that he shall observe peace and concord for God, holy church, the clergy and the people, in God undiminished according to his power. And that in all his judgements he will cause equal and true justice to be done with discrimination, mercy, and truth. And that he will hold and guard the true laws and customs which the people of the land shall have chosen to be kept by him, and that he ought to defend and strengthen them to the honour of God as far as he can.

XXII And note that this oath is from the oath of the King of England.

XXIII And having taken the oath he is invested on oath with power granted to him and not before. The end.

XXIV We have also examined the tenor of a certain article written on a certain sheet of paper, which was similarly found on the aforesaid Christopher at the said time, and likewise shown in the presence of the aforesaid lieutenant and in the presence of our aforesaid Council at the town of Trim, on the ninth day of January, to the following effect:

Having been elected by the people to be King so that he should be consecrated after they have again consented to it, the metropolitan shall ask the elected quietly but distinctly whether he is willing to grant and preserve to the same people the laws and customs which the Kings in ancient times had granted and by oath confirmed to the people of England, especially the laws and customs and liberties granted by the most glorious king and saint Edward to the clergy and the people. Now if he shall have said that he is willing to agree to all these things the metropolitan shall put the matter to him speaking thus: 'Will you preserve for the church of God, for the clergy and the people, entire peace and concord so far as in you lies?' He will reply, 'I will keep them'. 'Will you cause equal and right justice to be done in all your judgements, and discretion in mercy and truth according to your power?' He will reply, 'I will do so'. 'Do you grant that the just laws which your people choose are to be [kept and] to be guarded by you, and strengthened to the honour of God, according to your power?' He will reply, 'I grant and promise'.

There follows the admonition of the bishops to the King and it is to be read by one bishop clearly in the presence of all, saying: 'Lord King, we ask that it be freely granted by you that you will keep and defend for each of your churches entrusted to you canonical privilege and right law and justice as the King in his realm ought to do for each of his bishops and abbots and for the churches entrusted to him.' He will reply: 'With a mind willing and resolved, I promise you and grant it freely, and I will keep for each one of you and for the churches entrusted to you canonical privilege and right law and justice, and I will defend you to the best of my ability to the glory of God, as the King in his realm ought rightly to do on behalf of each bishop, abbot, and the churches entrusted to him.' To the aforesaid questions may be added those things which were below.

The aforesaid propositions all pronounced, the said prince undertakes that he will observe all the aforesaid, taking the oath immediately upon the altar in the presence of all. Thus, the King having been installed on his throne in this manner, the peers of the realm surrounding the King on all sides with their open hands extended in the sign of their fealty shall proffer themselves for the sustenance of the said King and Crown.

We, however, are led to testify to the tenor of the aforesaid articles by the consent of the aforesaid lieutenant and of our aforesaid council. In testimony of which we have caused these our letters patent to be made. Witnessed by our aforesaid lieutenant at Trim on the twelfth day of January in the sixth year of our reign.

By the lieutenant himself and the Council.

Examined by John Passavant and William Sutton, clerks.

Historical Notes

6 For the history of the Preston family in Ireland see Otway-
Ruthven, *History of Medieval Ireland*, p. 355. The family came
from Preston in Lancashire and settled in Drogheda in the
early fourteenth century. Sir Christopher Preston succeeded
to his father's estates in 1396. He had for a time been connected
with the Chancery as deputy-keeper of the Great Seal. One of
his first acts when he took possession of the estates was to
'examine the contents of the muniment chest', *Calendar of the
Gormanston Register c. 1175–1397*, ed. J. Mills and M. J.
McEnery (Dublin, 1916), pp. x–xi. Christopher Preston was
arrested on 26 June, 1418, at Clane, together with the earl of
Kildare and Sir John Bedlow, and was to be examined before
the King's Council, *C.C.R. 1413–19*, p. 472. 'Perhaps their
offence was really that they were trying to send representations
against Talbot to the King. In any case they must have been
cleared, for in fact they recovered all their lands, and Preston
was one of the messengers sent to the King by the parliament
of 1421', Otway-Ruthven, p. 356. Sir Christopher was an
ancestor of Lord Gormanston who may have brought a copy
of the Irish *Modus* to England in the seventeenth century, see
p. 117.

8 Sir John Talbot of Hallamshire, Lord Furnivall, and later earl
of Shrewsbury was appointed lieutenant in Ireland in 1414.
He left Ireland in 1420. The 'conspiracy' of 1418 may have
been connected with the feud between the earl of Ormonde
and Talbot. Ormonde was Kildare's son-in-law, Otway-
Ruthven, p. 354. On Talbot see E. Curtis, *History of Medieval
Ireland*, revised edn. (London, 1938), pp. 291–7, 301–3, 307.

17 The first paragraphs preserve the order of the English *Modus*
with the omission of the paragraph on the Cinque Ports. Some
material from that section was used in paragraph IV dealing
with the knights.

20–1 All Irish bishops appear to have been regarded as barons, and
therefore as spiritual peers, but although this provided a
juristic basis for summoning bishops to parliaments in reality

they were summoned because they were bishops, Richardson and Sayles, *Irish Parliament*, pp. 121, 134.

24–30 Although representatives of the lower clergy appear in the Irish parliament by the 1370s, the independent representation of the lower clergy was not at that time fully established. Nonetheless proctors of the lower clergy did not withdraw from the Irish parliament, as they did in England, see p. 25; Richardson and Sayles, *Irish Parliament*, pp. 78–9, 118.

page 129

1 For an examination of lay magnates summoned to the Irish parliaments in the fourteenth century, Ibid. pp. 127–32. In Ireland the definition of peerage and baronage was uncertain at this time.

10–16 The Commons only succeeded in establishing themselves as an integral part of the Irish parliament in 1370. There were twenty-six constituencies returning a possible total of twenty-eight knights and twenty-four burgesses, Richardson and Sayles, *Irish Parliament*, pp. 76–8. After *et quilibet* the phrase should probably read *communitatis libertatis vel comitatus* as previously.

24–8 This paragraph groups the citizens and burgesses together and prescribes for each the same rates of pay. The English *Modus* distinguishes citizens from burgesses, as does the Irish *Modus* later in paragraph XVI. See p. 121, n. 27.

29–32 There is only one clerk prescribed to enroll the pleas as against the two of the English *Modus*, but see paragraph XVII where clerks are mentioned in the plural. These paragraphs (VI and VII) repeat the substance of paragraphs XV and XVI of the English *Modus*.

page 130

16–17 This is an addition of the Irish compiler. The wording is inconsistent with the use of the word *solet* at the beginning of the paragraph, Galbraith 'The *Modus Tenendi Parliamentum*', pp. 97–8.

17–19 The *assigning* of an usher and crier with the clerks is again a result of confusion in adapting the English version.

20–21 Apart from Richard II no English king was ever present at an Irish parliament. The use of the word *comensor* in the Latin text, which is taken from the French *commenciounri*, is one example of the manner in which the Latin text was influenced by the French original.

page 131

6–12   The information in this paragraph was adapted from paragraph XIV of the English *Modus.*

13–16   This information derives from paragraph IX of the English *Modus.* For a discussion of amercements in the text see *supra* pp. 44–7 and for amercements in the Irish parliament, Richardson and Sayles, *Irish Parliament*, p. 137 ff. The practice was well established in Ireland before the end of the thirteenth century. In the fourteenth century there was considerable variation in the fines imposed upon members of the Irish parliament. The fine usually imposed upon an absent bishop was one hundred marks, see *Cal. Rot. Pat. Hib.* p. 105 no. 102, but the amount imposed upon barons and temporal peers varied considerably, Richardson and Sayles, *Irish Parliament*, p. 142. It would have been difficult for the Irish redactor to have given a clear picture of this in a brief passage. It is none the less a remarkable fact that the tariff of amercements 'the core of the argument for the priority of the Irish *Modus*, appears not in the Irish but in the English version', Galbraith, p. 99.

21–2   Irish parliaments were held in such places as Christ Church Cathedral, Dublin, and the Franciscan house at Drogheda. The phrase itself derives from the French *en lieu appert.*

23–8   This information derives from paragraphs IX and XVIII of
and   the English *Modus.* For an analysis of the petitions in the
1–3   Hilary Parliament of 1393 see Richardson and Sayles, *Irish*
p. 132   *Parliament*, pp. 88–90. English legislation was in theory applicable to Ireland, and the King could legislate for Ireland. The only notable piece of Irish legislation in the fourteenth century was the Statute of Kilkenny (1366).

page 132

4–7   For a reference to the address of Richard Wogan to the parliament of November 1441, see Richardson and Sayles, *Irish Parliament*, p. 191, n. 102.

15–16   The compiler has missed out the phrase in the English *Modus, filios suos milites faciendo.* This is also missing in the French text of the (C) version. See p. 120.

20–1   Even by the 1370s there was a far from unified system of taxation for the whole of Ireland. 'The tradition of separate bargains with local communities is difficult to outlive', Richardson and Sayles, *Irish Parliament*, p. 113. See also the comments of J. Lydon concerning the Irish Commons and taxation. In the 1370s the Irish Commons had to give their free consent to the levying of subsidies, 'without their free consent in parliament, the subsidies were not lawful', 'William of Windsor and the Irish Parliament', *art. cit.* p. 258.

page 133

1–3 In this passage the magnates of the English *Modus* have become 'peers' who are judges and justices in parliament. This may suggest that by the time of the Irish *Modus* a House of Lords was in existence, Richardson and Sayles, *Irish Parliament*, p. 76. The number of lay magnates who were summoned to the Irish parliament in the fourteenth century may have been about thirty, but the attendance was often considerably less. Ibid., pp. 127–35.

22–31 The provision in the English *Modus* that the Marshal, Constable and Steward should appoint this committee was not included in the Irish version. It related to the conditions of Edward II's reign. See p. 25, n. 45.

page 134

3–6 This passage mentions clerks in the plural, but paragraph VI mentions only one clerk. The phrase ten inches 'in length' should be ten inches 'in width'. The error apparently came from a misreading of the French word *largesse*, see p. 120. There are no surviving parliament rolls for the fourteenth-century Irish parliament.

12 The insertion of the paragraph heading at this point in the Waterford version suggestions that the headings were originally in the margin, Clarke, p. 77.

18 The phrase *pro defectu amercietur* after *cum* is found only in the later transcripts. It may not have been present in the original manuscript, whose text is missing at this point.

22–4 Contemporary practice seems to bear out the statement that in parliament every petition would be answered, Richardson and Sayles, *Irish Parliament*, p. 92. n. 143.

29 The correct reading would appear to be *lege*.

page 135

1 This concluding section has sometimes been identified with the Statute of Henry FitzEmpress, but see Richardson and

Sayles, pp. 324–31. The clause endeavours to deal with the problem that the English king was not present in the Irish parliament, see p. 149.

3–6 The type of Council described here was not known in the fourteenth century, Richardson and Sayles, *Irish Parliament*, p. 324, n. 2.

8 The reading *cum* would mean that they took counsel with the Justiciar, which would be impossible when they were meeting to support him, O. Armstrong, *art. cit.* p. 259 n. 6. The readings of the Huntington Ms. are suspect in one or two places at this point.

15 The archbishop of Cashel at this time was Richard O'Hedigan. His connection with the French text of the *Modus* on the Finch-Hatton roll has already been mentioned, p. 122. Miss Clarke has suggested that his alliance with the Butlers may be important in this context, pp. 89–90.

17 This oath was known to have been sworn by the *custos* in 1462. *Rot. Pat. Hib.* 1. Edward IV. No. 62. O. Armstrong, *art. cit.* p. 261. n. 1. It was the oath of Lord Rowland FitzEustace, Lord Portlester, as Deputy to George, Duke of Clarence. On FitzEustace see Otway-Ruthven, pp.389, 392, 398–9.

page 136

8 The catechism is similar to that of Edward II, L. G. Wickham Legg, *English Coronation Records* (London, 1901), p. 87.

20 The admonition of the bishops is not found in the *Liber Regalis* of Edward II, but is similar to that in the *Liber Regalis* of Richard II, *English Coronation Records*, p. 88.

32 The reciprocal oath of fealty is also found in the *Liber Regalis, ibid.*, p. 99.

page 137

10 John Passavant was made clerk of the Hanaper 'in consideration of his great labours in the Irish chancery since the coronation of Henry IV', *C.P.R. 1422–29*, p. 67. William Sutton was clerk of the Common Pleas of the Exchequer of Ireland, *C.P.R. 1401–1405*, p. 377.

IV

A Rochester Account Concerning Disputes During the Parliament of 1321

The *Modus* has been held by several scholars to be associated with the events of the parliament of 1321.[1] If that was the case, it would not appear to have been because of any notable participation by the Commons in the political events of the time. Although knights, burgesses, and diocesan clergy were summoned to the parliament of July and August 1321, this account concerning the events of the summer of that year,[2] although written from outside parliament, leaves little doubt that in the political manoeuvrings of the period it was the magnates and prelates who dominated the proceedings.[3]

The parliament of 1321 met in order to put into effect the programme of opposition to the Despensers, already planned at the Sherburn assembly.[4] Because of the scanty nature of the records concerning the political proceedings,[5] this narrative, royalist in sympathy, and possibly written by a clerk in the circle of Hamo Hethe, is of considerable interest.[6] It reveals that meetings of magnates by themselves were held at various places when parliament was sitting and suggests that the

[1] See p. 24. G. P. Cuttino, 'A Reconsideration of the *Modus Tenendi Parliamentum*', *The Forward Movement of the Fourteenth Century*, ed. F. L. Utley (Columbus, 1961), pp. 31–60, has called attention to the similarity between the ideas expressed in the *Modus* and the events of the Hilary parliament of 1316.

[2] The account is found in B.L. Faustina B.V. fos. 34ᵛ–36ᵛ. A part of the chronicle was printed by H. Wharton, *Anglia Sacra* (London, 1691), pp. 356–77, but with this portion omitted. See the comments of J. R. Maddicott, *Thomas of Lancaster 1307–1322* (Oxford, 1970), pp. 269–89.

[3] None the less, as is well known, this is the period when the Commons were becoming an integral part of parliament. Out of approximately 160 parliaments between 1301 and 1485, the Commons were present on all but eight occasions, and were invariably present after 1325. On the other hand out of the 70 or so parliaments between 1258 and 1300 representatives of the shires and towns attended on only nine occasions, Cuttino, *art. cit.* p. 42.

[4] B. Wilkinson, 'The Sherburn Indenture and the Attack on the Despensers, 1321', *E.H.R.* 63 (1948), 1–28. Maddicott, pp. 269–89 gives a detailed analysis of the crisis and its sources. This study and that by J. R. S. Phillips, *Aymer de Valence* (Oxford, 1972) must now largely supersede the older accounts by Tout and Conway-Davies for the political history of the reign.

[5] Two important collections of documents at Canterbury (A) and Lambeth (B) which are examined by Wilkinson and Maddicott contain texts of the Indenture, the Despensers' Indictment, and the *Homage et sermont* declaration discussed below. See also the Canon of Bridlington's account in *Chronicles of Edward I and Edward II*, ed. W. Stubbs (R.S., 1882–3) II, 62–70, and the official indictment entered in the Close Rolls, and printed in *Statutes of the Realm* (1810) I, 182–4.

[6] It is difficult to establish the sense of the text in several places. The account may well have been dictated.

magnates wanted to settle these baronial disputes in parliament and by recognized parliamentary forms. It suggests that while the magnates considered that they constituted the decisive element in parliament they were none the less aware of the desirability of settling such issues with the consent of parliament as a whole.

The account, which preserves first hand information on events in London during the parliament of 1321, simplifies a complex story. At Clerkenwell on 27 July, some twelve days after the opening of parliament, the Marcher Lords asked the bishops and the earls of Richmond, Pembroke, Warenne and Arundel to join them in their opposition to the Despensers. This the earls did, and confirmed their action by taking an oath. The prelates refused. After further deliberations the Marchers sent, together with the earls and bishops, two knights as delegates to the King carrying their petitions. By these petitions they asked the King to have the Despensers brought to parliament, 'to reply and to restore by award of their peers that which they have destroyed'. The King asked for the credentials of the knights. When it was found that they carried none, he ordered that their authority be put in writing.

At the next meeting of the Lords held in the Carmelite friary Bartholomew Badlesmere who is described as the author of the whole undertaking asked that Hugh Despenser, the son, be arraigned as a traitor, and to further this end he produced a document which he claimed Despenser had shown to several lords. This was none other than the famous document of 1308 relating to the reasons for exiling Gaveston, of which the general preamble consisting of the *Homage et sermont* declaration and the second clause were produced.[7] The account says that withdrawing the name of Gaveston, the barons charged Hugh with using the document to colour his own deeds.[8]

The use in 1321 of the declaration of 1308 with its distinction between the allegiance due to the Crown rather than to the person of the King has been the subject of much comment. Several historians have agreed that the document was used in two ways in 1321, firstly as

---

[7] For the manuscripts in which the declaration is found see note on the text, p. 159. In addition to being found in the collections of documents at Canterbury (A) and Lambeth (B), the declaration is found in B.L. Burney 277, fos. 5ᵛ–6. It was printed from that document by H. G. Richardson and G. O. Sayles, *The Governance of Medieval England* (Edinburgh, 1963), pp. 467–8. A Latin version is also preserved in the Canon of Bridlington's account, *Chronicles of Edward I and Edward II*, II, 33–4.

[8] p. 163. In the chronicle the document is said to have been invented in 1311. We should note however that the article against Gaveston in the Ordinances 'revived the charges and the language of the declaration of 1308', G. L. Harriss, p. 168.

'a statement of baronial principles' at the assembly at Sherburn-in-Elmet called by Lancaster in early summer before the meeting of parliament, and then as a means of condemning the Despensers at the subsequent parliament of July–August 1321. The apparent double use of this document has been ascribed to weakness on the part of the magnates by Professor Wilkinson, and to convenience by Dr. Maddicott.[9] The account of this chronicle suggests a less complicated story, involving simply the search for some precedent to secure judgement against an entrenched royal favourite.

According to this account, at the meeting in the Carmelite friary Badlesmere produced the preamble of 1308 together with the next clause of that document which charged Gaveston with accroaching royal power. The chronicle says that withdrawing the name of Gaveston, the barons imputed this to Hugh the son to colour his deeds. Although the second article may have been included by 'an oversight' it is more than likely that Badlesmere knew exactly what he was doing when he produced the preamble together with the clause. He was claiming that Despenser had followed Gaveston in accroaching royal power, and had used the preamble to justify his actions. The document which had been circulating in the period after the Ordinances was clearly capable of being interpreted in more than one sense. It could be used by the magnates to dismiss ministers unacceptable to them, or alternatively the distinction drawn between allegiance due to the King in person or to the Crown as an institution could be made to serve as a pretext for a favourite to exercise royal authority. It is not impossible that following the second of these courses Despenser had attempted to extract from the preamble an objectionable interpretation.

In the two principal collections of documents relating to the crisis of 1321, those at Canterbury (A) and Lambeth (B), it is not clear exactly how the preamble was meant to be used.[10] Its position in these

---

[9] Professor Wilkinson suggests that the use of the document to condemn Despenser was 'forced on the barons by the opposition of the king', *art. cit.* pp. 17–18. Dr. Maddicott suggests that possibly Badlesmere persuaded them that 'the declaration was more useful as ammunition against the younger Despenser than as a statement of their own principles', p. 286. As he states, this account shows clearly that 'the clause recounting Despenser's use of the declaration was voluntarily produced by the barons', thus eliminating Wilkinson's theory.

[10] An analysis of these documents is given by Wilkinson, pp. 1–19, and Maddicott, pp. 270–86. Dr. Maddicott has shown that Wilkinson's theory that (A) is associated with a meeting of the northern lords at Sherburn, and (B) with a meeting of the Marchers, does not explain the evidence. He demonstrates (pp. 275–6) that the indenture in (A) is probably an amended version of (B) which omitted the northerners, 'and was presented

continued

collections and its heading in (A) 'Forma Judicii Exilii predictorum H et H' does not necessarily suggest it was included as 'a statement of baronial principles'. This uncertainty may well suggest that while the relevance of the document was apparent to all at Sherburn the use to which it might be put was still undecided. The collections of documents which survive at Canterbury and Lambeth are in the nature of working papers relating to the discussions of the magnates, almost certainly before the opening of parliament.[11] When the documents were compiled, it was still not certain what course of action was to be followed, nor in what circumstances the documents were to be used.

It is at this point that the Rochester account illuminates the course of events. It shows that in the mid-summer of 1321 the magnates were contemplating at least three courses of action. The first was to proceed against the Despensers in full parliament by a statute outlawing them. This would have required the consent of King, Commons, and prelates, which the magnates felt they might not obtain.[12] A second course, eventually followed, was to bring a suit against the Despensers which would be determined by the judgement of the peers. The third course was baronial rebellion. For these eventualities, proposed no doubt by different groups among the magnates different drafts of particular documents would be required.[13]

It is therefore possible to believe that there was no double use of the document of 1308. So far from it being 'a statement of baronial principles', if indeed it is legitimate to talk at all about the existence of such principles, it is much more likely that the preamble was included in the documents as an obvious precedent relating to the nature of allegiance. When Badlesmere produced it in the form he did, he almost certainly intended to illustrate the use to which Despenser had put the preamble, i.e. accroaching royal power in the manner of Gaveston.

---

for sealing merely to Lancaster's retainers together with a few others'. Although the dating of (A) is later than (B) this may be due to a copyist's error.

[11] Although Dr. Maddicott suggests that the version of the indictment in (B) belongs to a period between Badlesmere's deception and 14 August, p. 286, many of the documents in (B) could belong to an earlier period. We should note that (B) contains the earliest version of the indenture, while the *Appeal to the Seignurs* in that collection may belong to the Sherburn period.

[12] This account makes it clear that the prelates did not approve the magnates' action in proceeding against the Despensers. They refused to take the oath on 27 July and at the meeting on 14 August when the earls and barons gathered in the great hall at Westminister the prelates remained in another room. For the rôle of Pembroke in the events of 1321 see Phillips, *Aymer de Valence*, pp. 201–13.

[13] This may well explain the demand for an award in (B), and a statute in (A).

Badlesmere was not, however, necessarily saying that Despenser had circulated the document in exactly that form.[14]

From the point of view of parliament the importance of this account is that it shows that in 1321 disputes between the baronage and the King could still be regarded as a matter either for settlement by parliament or for the peers by themselves. In this case 'parliament merely offered an occasion for the delivery of sentence', but 'the earliest versions of the indictment leave us in little doubt that they (the magnates) would have preferred to act by way of statute . . .'[15] The preference shown by the magnates for a parliamentary settlement indicates in fact which of the two views was the prevailing one.[16] None the less the fact that in the end the magnates decided to proceed by themselves shows that in 1321 such a course of action was still possible. The *Modus*, which was probably written in this period, says that disputes of this kind should be settled by a committee of twenty-five, a proposal which may have been popular in some circles, but which was certainly not put into effect.[17] In fact, however, the unilateral action of the baronage in 1321 echoed the past, and the crisis of this year was probably one of the last major baronial disputes involving more than a clash over purely private matters, which was settled by the old method of judgement by peers.[18]

THE TEXT

The Rochester account, previously unpublished, survives only in B.L. Faustina B.V. fos. 34ᵛ–36ᵛ. Its text, which is corrupt, may have been dictated, and the sense is difficult to establish in several places. The text of the declaration of 1308, pp. 162–3, is found in various sources. The

[14] It was probably the 'mechanics' of this procedure, i.e. the fact that Badlesmere may well have placed a copy of the document in Grey's wallet, which incurred Hamo Hethe's anger. See p. 163.

[15] Maddicott, p. 288, who suggests also that this judgement is important in the history of the procedure of impeachment. Although we have proposed a different interpretation concerning the use of the document of 1308, Dr. Maddicott provides generally the best account available of this crisis.

[16] Although an award was made in parliament, this account speaks in one place of 'a statute', p. 164.

[17] See p. 33. While this account illustrates clearly the aristocratic society in which the magnates were successfully checkmating the King's prerogative, it also illustrates the fact that new thinking of the type seen in the *Modus* could only come from social groups below the magnates, and in all probability from the bureaucracy concerned with the running of parliament.

[18] L. O. Pike, *A Constitutional History of the House of Lords* (London, 1894), pp. 175 ff.

main variants only have been noted:

A Canterbury (variants printed by B. Wilkinson,
B: Lambeth   'The Sherburn Indenture and the Attack on the
        Despensers, 1321', *E.H.R.* 63 (1948), 23–4.)
S: *Statutes of the Realm* I. 182.
C: B. L. Burney 277, fos. 5ᵛ–6 (printed by H. G. Richardson and G. O.
  Sayles, *The Governance of Medieval England* (Edinburgh, 1963), pp.
  467–8).
D: *Annales Londonienses* in *Chronicles of the Reigns of Edward I and Edward
  II* (R. S., London, 1882) I. 153–4.

A short Latin version of the declaration is found in the Canon of
Bridlington in *Chronicles of Edward I and II*, II. 33–4, (see also p. 65).

A Rochester account concerning disputes during the parliament of 1321

⟨fo. 34ᵛ⟩ In parliamento supradicto oriebatur magna dissensio ac ⟨fo.
35⟩ invidia vehementer pululavit inter comitem Herford et dominum
J(ohannes) de Mouwbray ac alios magnates Regni ex parte una, et 5
dominum H(ugh) de Despenser filium Regis camerarii ex altera, pro
baronia de Breaus quia eam citius adquirere posset quam eam dictus
H(ugh) favente et domino Rege in hiis et omnibus aliis adquisivisset.
Prefatus comes cum dominis R(ogerus) et R(ogerus) de Mortuo Mari
et aliis quampluribus maioribus regni favente eis cum comite Lancastrie 10
magnum exercitum colligentes terras et castella omnia dicti H(ugh)
tam in Wallis quam in Anglia devastantes, et sub colore tali domini
H(ugh) patris ac eorum adherencium terras castrum atque loca
depredando destruxerunt asserentes quod pro utilitate regis et regni
hoc fecerunt, et in assertionem huius rei vexillum regis erectum ubilibet 15
in castris locis et terris ponentes, omnia in manibus regis verbaliter
capientes ad eius utilitatem et dicebant occupata detinebant. Huius rei
causa dominus Rex parliamentum suum apud Westmonasterium in
tres septimas sancti Johanni convocare fecit. Convocaverat prius comes
Lancastrie apud Shirbourne in Elmet omnes prelatos ultra Trentam et 20
Comitem Hereford cum maioribus supranominatis; confederantes sese
adinvicem quod H(ugh) et H(ugh) patrem et filium predictos tanquam
proditores Regni persequerentur adicientes hoc utile esse pro Rege.
Convenientibus igitur prelatis et proceribus regni apud Westmonasterium ad parliamentum citatum in tres septimas sancti Johanni Baptiste, 25
Comes Herford, domini R(ogerus) et R(ogerus) de Mortuo Mari,
J(ohannes) de Mowbray, J(ohannes) Gyffard de Bremefeld, R(ogerus)
Clifford, H(enricus) Tyeys, R(ogerus) Samory, H(enricus) Sandale,
B(artholomeus) de Badlesmere cum aliis barnettis circiter viginti
quinque sibi adherentibus miserunt ad dominum J(ohannes) de Grey 30
ac alios magnos circum vicinos et eis in auxilium venirent. Alioquin
terras et loca eorum destruerent. In secta et apparatu eorum fuerant
omnes induti tunicis viridibus quarum quarta pars brachii dextri crocei
coloris fuit quasi fuissent per predictos patrem et filium quarteronati.
Venientes igitur ad parliamentum totam patriam in itinere devastantes, 35
abbates, priores, rectores, cives, mercatores, et ditiores patrie de

17 valitatem. MS.
31–2 Alioquin terras et loca eorum destruerent precedes the following sentence. MS.

marchia astantes ad contribuendum eis ecclesias ubique et patriam depauperarunt. Applicuerunt tandem in civitate Londonii cum mille equitibus armatis et multitudine magna peditum, favente eis comite lancastrie qui semper de parliamento ⟨fo. 35ᵛ⟩ se absentavit. Die lune proximo post festum sancti Jacobi Apostoli, et accitis apud Clerkenewell 5 prelatis et Richemundie, Penbroch, Warenne, et de Arendel comitibus petebant quod ad honorem dei Regis et regni utilitatem adherent sibi, quibus libenter annuentibus, comites predicti iuramento hoc firmarunt. Prelati vero iurare negaverunt. Tractantibus illis aliquandiu delibera- runt prelatos et comites prefatos mittere ad Regem et in eorum 10 presencia duo milites quos mitterent cum suis peticionibus (ut) eas porrigerent domino Regi. Fuerunt autem hec petitiones. 'Sire nos mestres vous maundent que coux tyenent sire Hugh le Despenser Piere et le fiz vostre et du Reame enemys et tretres et pur cieux les voilent y puer. Et pur ceo vous prient que vous lez meneez en parlement en 15 respounz a resteyure par agard dez piers ceo qil ount deseruy lez facez venir et que coux soyent exile hors de terre pur touz iours et couy et lour heyrs desherytes com faus et tretres atteyns et espiones.' Hiis dictis quesivit dominus Rex a militibus an litteras credencie haberent; quibus respondentibus quod non. Rex precepit ut credenciam suam in scriptis 20 ponerent; quo facto milites recesserunt. Rege nimium anxiato. Congregatis itidem in unum prelatis et proceribus apud fratres de carmelo, B(artholomeus) de Badlesmere, dux et auctor ac inventor totius facti et consilii vice et nomine omnium proposuit quod Hugh Despenser filius proditor et inimicus Regis et regni manifeste fuit 25 approbatus pro eo quod conspiravit contra Regem confederando suos legios homines contra Regem in cuius testimonium veritatis dominos R(icardus) de Grey, J(ohannes) Giffard de Brymineffeld, barones, R(obertus) de Schirlaund, militem, testes aductavit, dicens quod dominus Hugh eis tradidit quandam cedulam cuius tenor talis est. 30 Homage et serment de ligiaunce est plus par la resoun de la coroune que par la resoun del roy, et plus se lye a la coroune qe a la persone; et ceo piert quart avant ceo que lestat de la coroune soyt descenduz nule ligiaunce est a la persone regardaunte; dount sy luy Roy, en cas ne se mene par resoun en droyt del estat de la coroune, luy liges sount liez par 35 serment fait a la coroune de remener le Roy ad amender lestat de la coroune par resoun. Autrement ne seroit poynt le serment tenuz. Outre

31–2 de la person le roy *A B C D S*; et les gentz sunt plus liez a la corone *A B*.
35 del estat *om S.*
36 remner le Roy a demender MS., ad amender *om A B C D S*.

ceo fait a demander coment hom doyt mener, ⟨fo. 36)⟩ le Roy eu par
seute de ley ou par asperte. Par suete de ley ne put hom pas redresser,
quar il nyaverent pas iuges si ceo ne fut par le Roy. En quel cas si la
volente le Roy ne se acorde a la resoun, si naveroyt il fors le errouz
meyntenuz et constrince et damages pur la corone et pur le people. Et 5
pur ceo aiugee est que la chose seyt hoste par aspertee. Il est lye par soun
serment de soy governer par (*sic*) le poeple et ly liges de governer ove
luy al ayde de luy. En droit de la persone Peres de Gaverstoun le poeple
doyt iuger numsuffrable par resoun quar il destruit la corone et lad fait
poure en son poere quil ad par soun consail hoste le roy du consail de 10
soun realme et met descord entre luy et soun poeple. Il ad attret a luy
ligiaunce des gentz par serment auxi haut come al Roy, enfesaunt
luymeismes poer au Roy et enfeblissaunt la corone. Par les biens de la
corone quil ad attret a luy par soun poer, la force de la corone issi qe en
luy nest remys qe la corone en fust desherites et luymeismes sovereyn 15
du realme par sa mavoistee et tresoun de soun lige seignur et de la
corone en contre sa foy. Adinventa fuit istra racio anno domini 1311 et
facta in ordinacionibus pro domino Petro de Gaveston. Hic tunc
subducto nomine Petri ad colorandum factum suum predicto H(ugo)
filio imputabant. Tunc episcopus Roffensis de hiis valde admirans 20
quesivit a domino R(icardus) de Grey an recepit huius cedulam de
domino H(ugh) qui dixit quod eam invenit in bursa sua inter alias
cedulas. Ab illo enim tempore episcopus roffensis facta eorum
detestabatur et suspecta habebat. Dominus Eadmundus de Wodestoke
frater regis factus fuit tunc comes Kancie ad quem comitatum 25
B(artholomeus) de Badlesmere totis viribus aspiravit. Instantissime
tunc barones per mediatorem Comitem de Penbroke et omnia verba
pro eis facientem contra regem, egerunt ut pater et filius H(ugh) et
H(ugh) in exilium deportarentur autem et eorum heredes exheredar-
entur. Ad quod cum rex respondisset hoc esse iniustum et contra 30
iuramentum suum quemquam exheredare sine responso, et melius
fuisse eos ad tempus in hibernia moraturos quousque corda magnorum
essent sedata, quia proditores nescivit licet dure se habuerant erga
magnos, dolendum tamen esse viros generosos et nobiles sic ⟨fo. 36ᵛ⟩

2 ou par asprete ou per suete de lei *A B.*
5 meyntenuz et conferme, dount il convient pur le serment sauver qe qant le Roi ne voet
chose redrescer, ne oster qest pur le commun poeple malveise et damages *add A B C D S.*
9 Desherite la coroune *C.*
14 en attreaunt a lui roial poer et roiale dignitee, come en alliaunce faire de gentz par
sermentz de vivre et morir oves qe li . . . *Rot. Parl.* I. 283.
15 fust destruit *C.*

debere iudicari, adiecit Comes Penbroch quod de duobus eligeret Rex, aut guerram suorum vel exilium duorum et quod necessario unum perficere oporteret. Rex(igitur) plebis multitudini parcere preferens quam duobus proceribus prelatorum, Comitum, Baronum, Iusticiariorum ac omnium ibidem congregatorum (precibus) non tantum 5 victus sed vi metu et necessitate compulsus quod publice protestans ad concedendum, consenciendum et annuendum peticionibus eorum transiliebatur invitus, quo facto recessit Rex amaricto animo valde dolens. Die igitur veneris in vigilia assumptionis beate marie convenientibus comitibus, baronibus in unum in magna aula Regis 10 apud Westmonasterium Rege presente, prelatis vero in magna camera remanentibus, petebant barones sicuti prius predictos H(ugh) et H(ugh) tanquam proditores et inimicos Regis et regni exulare asserentes quod si lex terre hoc non promitteret, se posse cum pares essent regni, super hoc novam edere legem et statuere in pleno parliamento de 15 consuetudine regni, quam consuetudinem statim persequentes statuerunt et decreverunt predictos H. et H. iudicaliter exilium subire sine spe redeundi ac cum heredibus suis exheredari imperpetuum. Comite Herford statutum legente, dominus H(ugh) pater cantuarie existens, statim cum hoc audivit mare transivit. Hoc facto Rex ad cameram 20 suam anxius et tristis, prelatis valefactis. Episcopum Roffensis revertendo ad prandium in crastino et ad celebrandum missam suam iunctavit protestantibus prelatis quod huius exilio nullo modo consentirent. In crastino sedenti episcopo Roffensi in mensa Regis, Rex in auribus eius dixit conquerendo quod iniuste pater et filius erant 25 iudicati; ad quod cum episcopus respondisset quod Rex potuit illum defectum totum emendare dixit Rex quod talis emenda inde fieret infra dimidium annum quod totus mundus intelligeret et perhoreret.

---

3 perfide oporteret. Rex inquam MS.

A Rochester account concerning disputes
during the parliament of 1321

In this parliament a great conflict arose over the barony of Braose and much ill feeling grew up between the Earl of Hereford, Lord John Mowbray, and other magnates of the King on the one side, and on the other side Lord Hugh Despenser, the son (of) the King's chamberlain, because he had been able to take possession of it more quickly than Hereford, for the Lord King favoured him in this and in all other matters. The Earl with Lords R(oger) Mortimer and with many other lords of the kingdom, as well as with the favour of the Earl of Lancaster, collected a large army and laid waste all the lands and castles of the said Hugh in Wales and in England. On that pretext they also plundered and destroyed lands, castles, and places belonging to Lord Hugh the father as well as to the followers of both, asserting that it was done for the good of the King and the kingdom. In support of this assertion they raised the King's banner and placed it in every castle, place, and land. They claimed that they took everything into the hands of the King, and they said they were occupying them for his profit. On account of this the King ordered his parliament to assemble at Westminster three weeks after the feast of St. John the Baptist. First, however, the Earl of Lancaster summoned to Sherburn-in-Elmet all the prelates north of the Trent, as well as the Earl of Hereford and together with the lords above mentioned, they mutually bound themselves to prosecute as traitors of the realm the aforementioned Hugh, father and son, adding that it was in the interest of the King. While the prelates and leading men of the kingdom were assembling at Westminster for the parliament appointed for the third week after the feast of St. John the Baptist the Earl of Hereford, Lords Roger and Roger Mortimer, J(ohn) Mowbray, John Giffard of Brimpsfield, Roger Clifford Henry Tyes, Roger Samory, Henry Sandale, Bartholomew Badlesmere, with about twenty-five other bannerets who supported them, sent a request to Lord J(ohn) Grey and other magnates in the vicinity that they should come to their help. In addition they laid waste their lands and places. All their supporters appeared dressed in green tunics of which a quarter part of the right arm was saffron coloured, as if they had been 'quartered' by the said father and son. Coming to parliament they destroyed all the countryside en route. The abbots, priors, rectors, citizens, merchants, and other richer people of the country being present from the Marches, were constrained to make contributions to them, empoverishing everywhere the churches and the land. They finally arrived in the city of London with a thousand mounted men, and a large multitude of footsoldiers, and helping them was the Earl of Lancaster who always absented himself from parliament. On the Monday next after the feast of St. James the Apostle, after the prelates and the Earls of Richmond, Pembroke, Warenne, and Arundel, had been summoned to Clerkenwell, they requested them that for the honour of the Lord King and for the profit of the realm they join them. After they readily assented, the earls confirmed it with an oath. The prelates, however, refused to take the oath. Having considered these matters for a considerable time they decided to send the prelates and the aforementioned earls to the King together with two knights whom they were sending along with the petitions which they were to present to the Lord King. These were the petitions. 'Sire, our masters tell you that they hold both Lord Hugh Despenser, and his son, enemies and traitors to you and to the kingdom, and for this they wish them to be removed from here. And because of this they ask you that you have them brought before parliament to answer, and to restore by award of the peers that which they have destroyed. Ensure that they come, and that they are exiled out of the land for all time and they and their heirs are disinherited as false and traitorous criminals and spies.' This having been said the Lord King asked the knights whether they had letters of authority; they replied that they had not. The King ordered that their authority be put in writing, and after this had been done the knights retired. The King was very concerned. After the prelates and lords had assembled at the Carmelite friary, Bartholomew Badlesmere, the leader and initiator of the whole undertaking, proposed on behalf of and in the name of all, that Hugh Despenser, the son, was proved to be a manifest traitor and enemy of the King and the kingdom, by the fact that he had conspired against the King, conjoining his liege men against the King. As evidence for the truth of this he brought forward as witnesses, Lord Richard Grey, John Giffard of Brimpsfield, barons, and Robert of Shirland, knight, saying that Lord Hugh had shown them a certain parchment the tenor of which was as follows: 'Homage and the oath of allegiance are more by reason of the Crown than by reason of the King, and are attached more to the Crown than to the person. And this is apparent because before the estate of the Crown has descended no allegiance is due to the person. Wherefore if the King in certain cases is not led by reason, regarding the estate of the Crown, his liege subjects are bound by the oath made to the Crown to guide the King back and to amend the estate of the Crown by reason. Otherwise the oath is not kept. Then it must be asked, how is one to guide the King, whether by form of law or by force? By the course of the law one cannot obtain redress, for there are no judges who are not made by the King. In which case, if the wish of the King does not accord with reason, he will have only the error maintained and confirmed, and damaging for the Crown and the people. And for this, it is judged that the matter be settled by force. He is bound by his oath to be governed by the people, and his liege subjects are bound to govern with him and support him. As regards the person of Piers Gaveston the people judge him not to be suffered because he destroys the Crown, and has done this for his own power. He has by his advice removed the King from the counsel of his realm, and created discord between him and his people. He has attracted to himself the allegiance of men by as solemn an oath as if he were the King, making himself the peer of the King, and enfeebling the Crown. By the wealth of the Crown which he had taken to himself through his power, the strength of the Crown has thus passed to him, so that the Crown is disinherited by this, and he himself against his oath sovereign of the realm by his wickedness and his treason to his liege lord and to the Crown'. This argument was invented in 1311, and put into the Ordinances for Piers Gaveston. Removing the name of Piers, they then imputed this to the said Hugh, the son, to colour his deeds. Marvelling greatly at this the Bishop of Rochester asked Lord Richard Grey whether he had received this parchment from Lord Hugh; he [Lord Richard Grey] said that he had found it in his wallet among other parchments. From that time the Bishop of Rochester detested their actions and held them in suspicion. The Lord Edmund Woodstock, the brother of the King, was then made Earl of Kent, to which earldom Bartholomew Badlesmere had aspired with all his heart. The barons, acting through the Earl of Pembroke, who made all his speeches in their interest and against that of the King, moved instantly that Hugh, the father and son, should be sent into exile and their heirs disinherited. The King replied that this was unjust and contrary to his oath to disinherit anyone without a hearing. It would be better that they should remain for a time in Ireland until the anger of the magnates had cooled. Although they had behaved badly towards the magnates, he did not consider them traitors. It was to be regretted that well born and noble men should have judgement passed on them in this way. Then the Earl of Pembroke replied that the King must choose one of two alternatives, either war with his people, or the exile of the two, and he must of necessity accomplish one. The King preferred to spare the mass of the people rather than the two. He was persuaded not so much by the prayers of the leading prelates, earls, barons, justices, who were assembled, as under compulsion as he publicly stated from violence, fear, and duress, and was forced against his will into conceding, agreeing to, and granting their demands. When this was done he retired, embittered and very unhappy. And so on Friday on the eve of the assumption of the Blessed Mary when the earls and barons were assembled in the great hall of the King at Westminster in the presence of the King, the prelates remaining in the large chamber, the barons as previously sought the exile of the aforementioned Hugh and Hugh on the grounds that they were traitors and enemies of the King and of the realm. They declared that if the law of the land did not make this provision, they had the power, since they were peers of the realm, to promulgate and establish a new law in full parliament in accordance with the custom of the realm, following which custom they immediately afterwards determined and decreed that the said Hugh and Hugh should be exiled by due process without hope of returning and with their heirs be disinherited for all time. After the Earl of Hereford had read the statute, Lord Hugh the father who was then at Canterbury immediately he heard this crossed the sea. After this the King, anxious and sad, went to his chamber having said farewell to the bishops. As the bishop of Rochester returned for breakfast the next day, and for celebrating his mass, the King joined him, the bishops having declared that they in no way agreed to his [i.e. Despenser's] exile. The next day when the bishop of Rochester sat at the King's table, the King whispered to him complaining that the father and son had been condemned unjustly, to which when the bishop had replied that the King could totally amend that defeat, the King said that he would within half a year make such an amend that the whole world would hear of it and tremble.

page 161

1 This opening passage refers to events in the autumn of 1320 which witnessed the disputes over Gower. Several magnates hoped to secure the lordship of Gower held by William Braose. They included Humphrey Bohun, earl of Hereford, John Mowbray who was the son-in-law of William Braose, the two Roger Mortimers, and also the younger Despenser. 'What did transform the Gower issue into a major political crisis was the degree of support that Edward II extended to the younger Despenser . . .', R. R. Davies, *Lordship and Society in the March of Wales 1282–1400* (Oxford, 1978), p. 288. Edward II attempted to seize Gower for Despenser, *C.C.R. 1318–23*, p. 268. Gower was an important cause of the war of 1321 and the exile of the Despensers. See J. C. Davies, 'The Despenser War in Glamorgan', *T.R.H.S.* 3rd ser. 9 (1915), 21–64; Maddicott, pp. 259–68.

12 The Marcher lords began the destruction of the Despenser estates on 4 May, *Flores Historiarum*, ed. H. R. Luard, (R.S., 1890), III, 344. 'The destruction in Wales lasted for about five days after which the Marchers moved on to ravage other Despenser manors in the south and Midlands', Maddicott, p. 267.

19 The parliament of 1321 met on 15 July, three weeks after the feast of St. John the Baptist (24 June). This parliament lasted from 15 July to 22 August.

20 For an account of what transpired at Sherburn-in-Elmet on and after 28 June see now Maddicott, pp. 268–84, which revises the views of B. Wilkinson, 'The Sherburn Indenture and the Attack on the Despensers, 1321', *E.H.R.* 63 (1948), 1–28. Wilkinson's theory that there were two different meetings at Sherburn, one of the northern lords, and another of the Marchers, seems now improbable, Maddicott, pp. 268–84. See the comments in the introduction to the Rochester account, p. 157, n. 10.

27 John Giffard of Brimpsfield (Gloucestershire) had been the victim of Despenser's actions in 1320, R. R. Davies, p. 242. He was present at the Sherburn assembly and came forward as a

witness to Despenser's use of the Declaration of 1308, see p. 162. He was executed in 1322 and his lands forfeited, R. R. Davies, p. 46 and note.

30 John Grey, lord of Ruthin, was justice of North Wales in 1315–16, and served on the council of 1318, T. F. Tout, *The Place of the Reign of Edward II in English History* (Manchester, 1936), pp. 110, n. 2; 335–6.

32–34 The *Brut* states that the baronial followers came to parliament in 1321 in 'armour' of green cloth, the dexter quarter being yellow with white bands so that the parliament received the name, 'parliament of the bend', *Brut or the Chronicles of England*, ed. F. W. D. Brie (Early English Text Society, Old Series, 1906–8), p. 213. See also *Johannis de Trokelowe et Henrici de Blaneforde Chronica et Annales*, ed. H. T. Riley (R.S. 1866), p. 109.

page 162

3–4 Lancaster declined to attend the York parliament of 1320 objecting to parliament being held *in cameris*, *Vita Edwardi Secundi*, p. 104. Paragraph XIX of the *Modus* should probably be seen against this background. The concern about secret meetings of parliament is also found in the Ordinances, *Rot. Parl.* I. 285, no. 29.

4–8 The consent to join the magnates given on 27 July by Pembroke and the three other earls who had remained loyal to the King may not have been given as willingly as is suggested in this account, see Maddicott, p. 280, n. 9, and Phillips, p. 210, n. 1. As Maddicott states, however, this alliance suggests that Edward was faced by a powerful opposition.

23–4 Although Badlesmere's involvement in the crisis of 1321 has always been well known, the Rochester account emphasises his central part in the events of the summer, describing him as the 'leader and initiator of the whole undertaking'. In view of these actions his later relations with Edward II are easily understood, see Tout, *Place of the Reign of Edward II*, p. 132; Maddicott, p. 293.

page 163

7 All other versions of the Declaration have the sense of *governer le poeple*. In this passage *par* may well be a scribal error for *pur*.

The French text of the clause concerning Gaveston is found only in B.L. Burney MS. 277. As suggested in the introduction to this account, p. 157, Badlesmere probably made no mistake when he produced the preamble together with the clause, but see Maddicott, p. 282.

20–24   Hamo Hethe was Bishop of Rochester from 1319 to 1352. It was previously known from the *Annales Paulini* (*Chronicles of the Reigns of Edward I and Edward II* (R.S., 1882), I, 295–7) that he was one of the bishops who attempted to mediate between the barons and the King in 1321. He later resisted the deposition of Edward II, *Registrum Hamonis Hethe*, ed. Charles Johnson (Canterbury and York Society, 1948), I. pp. xiii–xiv; K. Edwards, 'The Political Importance of English Bishops During the Reign of Edward II', *E.H.R.* 59 (1944), 311–47.

24–26   According to the continuator of Gervase of Canterbury, Edward's creation of his brother as Earl of Kent (on 26 July) was a move directed against Badlesmere, Maddicott, p. 293.

27–34   On the role of Pembroke at this time see Phillips, pp. 209–13.
and   This account states that Pembroke took an oath to support the
1–3   magnates, p. 162. According to this account and to the *Vita*
p. 164 *Edwardi Secundi*, p. 113, Pembroke was responsible for putting the baronial demands to the King. None the less the evidence suggests that he attempted to steer a middle course between the magnates and Edward II. For two different views on Pembroke at this time see *Vita Edwardi Secundi*, p. 112 which suggests that Pembroke was not wholly loyal to his oath to the magnates (Phillips, p. 210), and this account which states that he made all his speeches in the interests of the barons and against the King, p. 163.

page 164

9–18   On 14 August the magnates met in the great hall of Westminster in the presence of the King, but without the prelates. Although the magnates would have preferred to be able to effect the exile of the Despensers by the full authority of a statute it is clear that they had to be content with making an award by themselves as peers of the realm. Despite the fact that both this account, p. 164 and the *Vita Edwardi Secundi*, p.

114, speak of a statute in one place, 'the indictment of 1321 was not in fact enrolled on the statute roll but on the close roll and the Exchequer parliament roll', Maddicott, p. 285. The Despensers were to leave the country by 29 August.

It should be noted in connection with the crisis of 1321 that there is no evidence which enables us to establish the identity of the tract which the Marchers produced on their advance to London (*Annales Paulini*, p. 293). Although this tract has been identified both as the *Modus* and the Tract on the Steward, it could equally well have been a version of the declaration of 1308.

V

A Colchester Account of the Proceedings of the Parliament of 1485

by the Representatives of the Borough of Colchester,
Thomas Christmas and John Vertue

This account of the first session of the first Tudor parliament of 1485 is the earliest surviving parliamentary diary by a member of the Commons. The main interest of the account derives from two characteristics. First it is the earliest day-to-day report of what actually occurred in the Commons during a parliamentary session from its opening to its adjournment.[1] In the second place its significance lies in the fact that we have here an account written by two actual members of the Commons who left an informed record of the procedure of parliament. Compared with the scheme outlined in the *Modus* this account reveals that by the fifteenth century the procedure of parliament had inevitably evolved beyond the notions of the author of that treatise. Procedures unknown to the reign of Edward II had been devised, and almost certainly unwritten rules and customs governed the deliberations of the two houses.[2] None the less in a very real sense both parliamentary procedure and the role of the Commons had developed along the general lines envisaged by the author of the *Modus*. It can perhaps be said, therefore, that the picture of parliamentary procedure and of the activities of the Commons given in the Colchester account would not have entirely displeased the author of the *Modus* writing some one hundred and fifty years earlier.[3]

This daily account, a kind of 'journal', produced by the members for Colchester provides both a contrast and a supplement to the official record of parliament prepared by Chancery clerks and enrolled as the rolls of parliament. It contrasts most obviously with the rolls in demonstrating conclusively what has long been thought, that the rolls of parliament do not represent the order—and sometimes the form—in

[1] The Colchester account describes only the first session of this parliament. An account of this session is found in *Rot. Parl.* VI. 267–335. It is followed by the record of the second session, *Rot. Parl.* VI. 336–84. On the parliament of 1485 see S. B. Chrimes, *Henry VII* (London, 1972), pp. 61–5; *English Constitutional Ideas in the Fifteenth Century* (Cambridge, 1936), p. 130; J. Enoch Powell and Keith Wallis, *The House of Lords in the Middle Ages* (London, 1968), pp. 528–30. Also on the question of attainder J. R. Lander, *Crown and Nobility, 1450–1509* (London, 1976). pp. 127–58.

[2] See the comments concerning the Recorder of London and the 'custume of the place', pp. 178–9, 185.

[3] It would be an obvious exaggeration to suppose that parliamentary procedure during the early Tudor period was substantially determined by the 'rules' of the *Modus*. None the less it is worth noting J. D. Mackie's remark concerning this Colchester account, namely that it showed 'the rule laid down in the *Modus Tenendi Parliamentum* was substantially observed', *The Earlier Tudors* (Oxford, 1952), p. 199.

which matters came before the Commons. The Chancery grouped matters in what might have seemed to them a more logical or perhaps customary order thereby depriving posterity of a glimpse of the actual context and juxtaposition of the issues as they were seen and dealt with at the time.

For example, on the rolls a single Act containing the reversals of all the attainders passed in 1484 appears as the third item of business, followed immediately by a provisory act to the effect that no action shall be taken upon it by the restored persons until after the end of the parliament, followed directly by the act attainting those who fought Henry at Bosworth.[4] In fact as the Colchester account shows the attainders passed in 1484 were not reversed in a single act but were individually taken in the case of the bishops and noblemen concerned.[5] Again the process of considering their petitions for reversal did not even begin until some weeks after the commencement of the session; the provisory act was not passed until the very last day of the session; while the attainders of those who fought against Henry came not at the beginning of the business of parliament but rather during the last three days of the session. By contrast the act restoring Elizabeth Woodville to her possessions taken away by Richard III which appears on the rolls after all these and sixteen other acts,[6] was in fact the first item to come before the Commons immediately after the customary opening piece of business, the Subsidy Bill. In fact the only item which appears on the rolls in the same order as it was actually taken is the Subsidy Bill itself.[7]

The second point of contrast is more intriguing though less readily explicable. There are some discrepancies of fact between the two versions about what actually happened. According to the rolls of parliament the Commons were reluctant to name and present their chosen Speaker because he was, technically, a man in attaint and they required a royal command before proceeding.[8] No such series of events seemed to have been witnessed by the two members for Colchester. On the contrary in what is the most detailed account yet of just how the election of the Speaker was actually done within the walls of the Commons' chamber, the proceedings are described as entirely regular and indeed very customary.[9] The Recorder of London is quoted as

---

[4] *Rot. Parl.* VI. 273–8.   [5] See p. 187.

[6] *Rot. Parl.* VI. 288.   [7] *Rot. Parl.* VI. 268–70.

[8] Lovell had supported Henry's cause in 1483, *Rot. Parl.* VI. 246.

[9] For an account of Thomas Lovell, the Speaker in this parliament, see Roskell, *The Commons and their Speakers*, pp. 97, n. 2, 298–9, 358–9. A record of his Protestation is given *Rot. Parl.* VI. 268.

informing the Commons of the customary procedure which they then followed.[10] The most likely explanation is that there was an inner core of a quasi-professional element already within the house, the predecessors of the later Tudor core of councillors, who by themselves conducted the sensitive political or legalistic aspects of the relationship between the Commons, the Council and the King. The twenty-four knights who, according to the Recorder of London, customarily carried the nomination for the Speaker to the Chancellor, or the four 'gentlemen' who presented the Subsidy Bill on behalf of the Commons for a royal scrutiny before formally passing it may represent this element.

More puzzling still is the absence from the Colchester account of any reference to the King's personal address, recorded in the parliament rolls as having been delivered to both the Lords and the Commons.[11] Considering that the Colchester members made a note about the 'many worshipful points' made by the Chancellor in his routine opening sermon while declaring the 'causes' of parliament, it is very curious that they should not have noted being addressed by the King himself. Was that address, perhaps in French or Latin, aimed at the Lords and the record rather than at the Commons, if indeed it was made to them at all? Or was the whole business—the declaration of the King's title, his right in the words of the rolls of parliament, by heredity as well as 'verum Dei judicium' on the battlefield, which is also absent from the Colchester account—just so much empty formality to be ignored by ordinary M.P.s as matters concerning the Lords, councillors, and courtiers only?

In the same category, perhaps, comes the omission of any mention of the request by the Lords and the Commons for Henry to marry Elizabeth of York, recorded in unusually circumstantial detail on the Rolls.[12] Whether the Speaker acted on his own initiative, or with the concordance of the insiders only, or whether the request was formally gone through in the Commons, but ignored by our two M.P.s, we cannot know. However, there can be no doubt that an ordinary M.P.

---

[10] It should be noted that a copy of the *Modus*, now Harvard Law Library MS. 21, was later in the possession of William Fleetwood, a sixteenth-century Recorder of the City of London, who sat in the parliament of 1572. See p. 202.

[11] *Rot. Parl.* VI. 268.

[12] This was made on 10 December, *Rot. Parl.* VI. 278 and concluded the first session. It is worth noting that according to Polydore Vergil Henry merely 'publicly declared'—sometime while Parliament was being held—that he intended to honour his promise to marry Elizabeth. *The Anglica Historia of Polydore Vergil 1485–1537*, ed. Denys Hay (Camden Society, LXXIV, 1950), p. 5.

might well have been justified in regarding it as a mere formality, a type of political posturing which had nothing to do with him or with the job he came to do. Henry had already, during his exile on Christmas Day in Rennes cathedral, formally and solemnly promised to marry Elizabeth in what was as close to an 'election platform' declaration as the age would allow. The process of obtaining a Papal dispensation for being within the prohibited degrees was already in motion, and a Papal nuncio had been specially sent for the purpose. Apart from the fact that he needed no urging to contemplate matrimony it would have been difficult for Henry to change his mind at that stage. At the same time he could not marry until the canonical process had reached at least the conclusion of the first stage. Why Henry himself, or his Council, or some group of his Lords, wished to arrange for a public demonstration in parliament of the political desirability of the marriage we can only surmise, but it was undoubtedly not 'real' business as far as ordinary M.P.s were concerned. All the same, it is an interesting and intriguing omission from a day-to-day account, and must throw an element of doubt on the official version duly enrolled.

As intriguing as the absence of references in the diary of the Colchester M.P.s to events apparently recorded in the official version of the rolls, is the reverse situation which concerns the 'Court of Requests, The Colchester M.P.s record the passing of a 'bill for the Court of Requests that it is annulled and it shall be occupied no more'. No such act is recorded on the rolls of parliament or on the Statute Roll. Moreover (as far as we know) there was no 'Court of Requests' in existence. A *council* of requests did apparently exist by 1483 when a clerk was appointed to it, but no proceedings have been found before 1493 and it was not called at least officially a 'court' until well into or even after the time of Cardinal Wolsey.[13] It is inconceivable that the Colchester M.P.s would have invented the story, or that the Commons with a substantial number of lawyers and the Recorder of London in their midst could have acted out of ignorance in abolishing a court which did not exist. It is much more likely that they were persuaded to change their minds after the beginning of the next session—this being the last act according to the Colchester account before prorogation—and that the matter was never entered on the rolls. We do not know why this was so, and indeed the whole episode is not altogether explicable in the light of our present knowledge. We do know, however,

---

[13] See *Select Cases in the Court of Requests, 1497–1569*, ed. I. S. Leadam, (Selden Society XII, 1898); Chrimes, *Henry VII*, pp. 152–3.

that when the Court of Requests' proceedings begin to survive in a later period, the court was one of the lucrative preserves of the civil lawyers and of the Chancery masters themselves. As far as it is possible to surmise from the little evidence available it seems that the story forms a part of the, as yet, highly obscure history of the interlocking conciliar and prerogative courts flourishing in this period which had a considerable role in the revival of strong central government.[14]

The manner in which this private and daily account of the proceedings in the Commons supplements the official account of the rolls is perhaps more significant than the contrasts which it also presents. In the first place the Colchester account demonstrates much more clearly than the rolls how much the hearing of petitions from all classes of society lay at the core of the functions of the Commons in the constitution. The diary of the M.P.s for Colchester graphically illustrates the impact of the succession of petitions and petitioners. Some of the petitioners, for example the yeomen who rebelled with Buckingham and who were now seeking restoration, were in as low or even humbler position in the world as our two M.P.s, while others were at the pinnacle of the spiritual and secular hierarchy of the land. There was, for example, the Countess of Warwick who, 'shewed a pytelous compleynt and therupon she delyvered a byll',[15] followed by, amongst others, the Bishops of Ely, Salisbury and Exeter's 'bill of complaints'. It is worth noting that these and many others who according to the Colchester account appeared as individual supplicants at different times before the Commons are represented by the roll as if a single collective bill of reversal had gone through the Commons. For humble citizens such as our two M.P.s to listen to and to 'deal with' the supplications of those who were immeasurably and unreachably higher up in the social scale appears to have been their most memorable experience in this parliament. The account provides therefore a useful and illuminating extension of our perspective about these men of the commonalty when they were formed into the great court of parliament.

The Colchester account, however, supplements most significantly our view of parliament, derived perforce chiefly from the rolls, by recording what the rolls ignored most completely namely debate within the Commons. The question whether the Commons were indeed the fully political assembly envisaged by the *Modus Tenendi Parliamentum* or

---

[14] See Nicholas Pronay, 'The Chancellor, the Chancery and the Council at the End of the Fifteenth Century' in *Essays Presented to S. B. Chrimes*, ed. H. Hearder and H. R. Loyn, (Cardiff, 1974).   [15] See p. 186.

merely a rubber-stamp in all matters other than in the granting of their
own moneys, the view largely derived from the records, turns largely
upon the problem of what, if any, discussion took place in the Commons,
and what challenge there was to the Government's proposed legislation.
For the late medieval period evidence on these matters is difficult to
come by. Whether or not there ever existed a Commons Journal as
there existed some sort of journal for the Lords, we have no means of
knowing.[16] Chroniclers largely lacked the interest and probably the
information about what went on inside parliament.[17] The rolls for
their part were intended as a legal record to preserve for the use of
government and also the courts what was decided upon by each
parliament. They recorded only as much of the actual proceedings as
would show that the parliament in question had indeed observed the
forms of due process, and they were not conceived of as the minutes of
actual deliberations. Any evidence therefore, however sparse, which
helps to show how the Commons actually arrived at what are recorded
as their decisions on the rolls must be of especial historical interest.

    In this context what the Colchester account shows most clearly is that
debate and argument were indeed very much a regular and accepted
part of the activities of the Commons. For example, a whole day, 14
November, is recorded as a day spent entirely in 'arguments' which led
to 'non conclusyon'.[18] A little later (25 November) the account records
that 'there were red certayn bylls and therupon were arguments and
nothing passed that day.'[19] Alas, we do not know what the bills or the
arguments were, but the fact that debate and argument could indeed
take place and at some length is clearly illustrated in this account.

    The question whether there was a procedural basis for debate as
envisaged in the *Modus* finds at least a partial answer in this account.
The authors record that on 'the tenth day of Novembre there was red
a byll for the Subsedy betwen the kyng and the merchaunts, whiche
byll was examyned amonges us and oder divers person maters and non

---

[16] A copy of the *Modus* precedes the Lords Journals when they begin in 1510. See p.
215. For earlier fragments see W. H. Dunham, *The Fane Fragment of the 1461 Lords Journal*
(New Haven, 1935); R. Virgoe, 'A New Fragment of the Lords Journal of 1461',
B.I.H.R. 32 (1959), 83–87; W. H. Dunham, '"Books of Parliament" and "The Old
Record", 1396–1504', *Speculum* 51 (1976), 712, who argues that 'some sort of Lords
Journal in the sense of "Day Books" or perhaps registers of attendance—did exist in 1461
or 1449 and possibly earlier'.
[17] The *Anonimalle Chronicle*'s account of the Good Parliament of 1376 is unique. See.
p. 6.
[18] See p. 186.
[19] See p. 187.

conclusyon'.[20] The following day the bill was discussed again and agreed and then sent up to the Lord Chancellor. The entry indicates, though it does no more than that, that there might have been some sort of group or committee for examining the bills before the Commons.

The ability to respond in a critical and questioning way to proposals from the government is an essential criterion of a genuinely political assembly. Here the Colchester account is quite explicit, 'the ninth day (of December) came in the byll of a teynt and sore was questioned with'.[21] There are references in the text to 'questions for the commonweal' being moved, about which we are ignorant, but on the issue of the attainders of those who fought at Bosworth for their then reigning King it is possible to test the statement of the Colchester members. The Croyland chronicle records, 'Among other things (being dealt with by this parliament) proscriptions, or as they are more commonly called "attainders" were voted against thirty persons, a step which though bespeaking far greater moderation than was ever witnessed under similar cirumstances in the time of King Richard or King Edward, was not taken without considerable discussion, or indeed to speak more truly, considerable censure of the measure so adopted.'[22] Thomas Betanson writing to Sir Robert Plumpton wrote that 'there was many gentlemen agaynst it, but it wold not be, for yt was the King's pleasure'.[23]

The power to hear and deliberate upon petitions for land and justice in civil matters; to examine closely and with some measure of organization the bills before them and to ask critical questions about the measures proposed by the government; these fundamental characteristics of the English House of Commons were, on the testimony of the Colchester account, possessed by the Commons in 1485. They had indeed come some way to being the political assembly envisaged by the author of the *Modus*. The very simplicity and artlessness of the account written by two very ordinary and humble members of the borough of Colchester reinforces this point. Yet at the same time it must be recognized that these same qualities prevented the authors from giving us further insights concerning the nature of the arguments and ideas which were expressed in this assembly.

[20] See p. 186.
[21] See p. 188.
[22] *Ingulph's Chronicle of the Abbey of Croyland*, ed. H. T. Riley (London, 1854), p. 511.
[23] *Plumpton Correspondence*, ed. T. Stapleton (Camden Society, 1839), p. 49.

The text of the diary of the members for Colchester has been preserved in a volume of records pertaining to the borough of Colchester known as the Red Paper Book, and now in the custody of the Town Clerk in the Colchester and Essex Museum. It contains writs, extracts from grants and similar materials, constituting the precedents for the privileges of the borough, to which miscellaneous items broadly relating to the workings of its government were added in the fifteenth century. The Red Paper Book is in a poor state of preservation, many folios having been lost, while the condition of the surviving folios renders some parts illegible particularly near the edges. The section relating to the parliament of 1485 occupies folios 126–28. It was first transcribed by Henry Harrod in *Report on the Records of the Borough of Colchester* (Colchester, 1865) and a new transcription with notes was published by W. Gurney Benham in his edition of the volume in 1902. It appears that for some reason the manuscript had further deteriorated by 1902 and that parts which were legible to Mr. Harrod were then no longer readable. By now some further parts have become almost illegible. In the following transcript we have included in brackets those parts which are found in the 1865 and the 1902 transcripts but which cannot now be read with certainty in the original. The accuracy of the two previous transcripts suggests none the less that confidence may be placed in the majority of readings of these lost sections. Certain more conjectural early readings are included in the footnotes. Lacunae are indicated by ellipses. The text has been reproduced in the form of the original entries.

A Colchester Account of the Parliament
of 1485

⟨fo.126⟩ Maister Baillies, and all my masters. Accordyng unto our
deute we went to Westmynestr the vijth day of Novembr, the yere
aboveseid, by ix of the clocke, and there we gave a tendawnse upon the 5
Kyngs grace withyn that same oure it pleased the Kyngs high grace,
and all his lords speritualx and temporalx that was there present; soo
cam downe oucte of the parlement chambir in to the cherche of
Westmynestre, and there was seid the masse of the Holy Gost. In that
while that masse wasse a seyyng cam my Lord Stuard in to the 10
parlement chambir, and there comaunded a proclamacion for the
Kyng, that every knyght that wear chosyn for the sheris, and ever(y)
citzener for ceties, and every burgessez for borrowes that they shuld
answer be ther names; and so they ware callid and resseyved in to the
parlement chambir; and son after that doon it pleasid the Kyngs grace 15
and all his ⟨fo.126ᵛ⟩ lords spirituall and temporall cam in to the
parlement chambir ... ryall estat, and all his lords spirituall and
temporall (and all his jugges) ... Kyngs grace for to comaunde my
Lord Chaunseler for to show the ... a worshipful sermon, in that he
shewe many worshipfull points (for) ... this lond. That don, the Kyng 20
comaunded my Lord Chaunseler (that he) ... all Knyghts, settnarirs
and burgeyssys, that they shuld semble to the parlement ... The vijth
day of Novembr, be ix of the clokke, so for to procede un to a (leccion
for) ... chose a Speker. So the leccion gave hir voyse unto Thomas
Lovell, a (gen tilman) ... Lyncolnes Inne. That doon, it pleased the 25
Knyghts that there there present (for to ryse f rom) ther sets and so for
to goo to that plase where as the Speker stode and ... set hym in his sete.
That don, there he thanked all the maisters of the plase. (Than) ... the
Recorder of London for to shew the custume of the place. This was his
seyeng; ... Speker, and all my maisters, there hath ben an ordir to this 30
place in tymes (passed that) ye shuld commaunde a certeyn of Knyghts
and other gentilmen, such as it pleaseth (you) ... to the nombre of
xxiiij, and they to goo togedir un to my Lord Chaunceler, (and there)
to show unto his lordship that they have doon the Kyngs commaundement in (the chosyn) of our Speker, desyrng his lordship if that he wold 35

---

21 settnarirs: citizens. **23** a (leccion): election. **27** The missing words may
be 'brought him and ...' (Benham). **28** 'Than it pleased ...' (Benham).
30 'Maister Speker' (Benham).

shew it un to the Kyngs (grace. And) ... whan it plesith the Kyng to commaunde us when we shall present hym a fore his (high grace) Yt pleased the Kyng that we shuld present hym upon the ix day of Novembre. (That) same day, at x of the cloke, sembled Maister Speker and all the Knyghts, sitteners and burgeyses in the parlament howse,   5 and so departed in to the parliament chambir (be fore) the Kyngs grace and all his lords spirituall and temporall and all his Juggs, (and so) presented our Speker before the Kyngs grace and all his lords spirituall and temporall.

The xth day of Novembre there was red a byll for the Subsedy be   10 twen the (kyng and) the merchaunts, whiche byll was examyned amonges us and oder divers person (maters) and non conclusyon.

The xjth day of Novembre the same byll was red afore us and there passed (as) an aucte. And that doon, Maister Speker commaunded iiij gentyll men for to ber (it) to my Lord Chaunseler, desyryng his lordship   15 that he wold certifie the Kyngs (good) grace withall.

The xijth day of Novembre there cam a byll from the Qwene Elizabeth that was, (and so) red, for such certeyn desyrs for castells and for oder possessions that she was (possessed) of in King Edward's day, and so red.   20

The xiijth day of Novembre it was Sonday.

The xiiijth day there were arguments for such to non conclusyon.

The xv day of Novembre there passed a byll with Master Hawte for to have (restore) hym un to his londs, the whiche he was a teynte be awcte of parliament in Kyng Richards day.   25

The xvj day of Novembre there ware qwestionns moved for the comenwell of thise false persons whiche hath reyned many dayes amongs us, and (non) conclusyon.

The xvij day of Novembre there cam in the Counteys of Warwik, and there she shewd a pytelous compleynt, and therupon she delyvered   30 a (byll).

⟨fo. 127⟩ (The xviij day of Novembre) it pleased the Kyngs good grace to send us downe a byll that he ... ettyed with his lords be advyse of an othe that no man shuld supporte ... (un) lawfull mayntenaunce by the mene of the lyveres gevyng, neyther be non other menes.   35

(The xix day) Sir John Wynkefeld brought in a byll of suche wronges and hurts ... (he felt) hym agreved of, and so delyvered a byll.

The xx day it was Sonday.

(The xxj) day of Novembre ther passyd a byll as an awct for to

33 an illegible fraction of a word omitted before ettyed.

restore blyssed Kyng Harry and Qwene (Marget) and Prince Edward, upon such atteynt as was shewed by awct of parliament be (Kyng) Edward the iiijth. Also ther passed a byll for my lady the Kyngs moder for to restore hyr (of suche) possessyons as she was a teynt of by the parliament of Kyng Richard, Kyng in ded and (not) of ryght. Also 5 ther passed a byll the same day as an awcte for Sir Jamez Loterell, to restore (hym of) his londs suche as he was a teynt of, and all hys heirez, be awcte of parliament by (Kyng) Edward, the fyrst yer of his reigne.

(The) xxij day of Novembre ther cam in a byll by Duke of Bedford of compleynte upon a teynt, (the whiche) passed by an aucte of 10 parliament in Kyng Edwards dayes, the whiche that (is restored) of as that aute had never be made.

(The) xxiij day of Novembre ther cam in a byll of compleynt by the Bysshop of Ely and the Bysshop of Salusbury, and be the Bysshop of Excetyr. They desyred to be restored of that (they) were a teynt of, be 15 awcte of parliament, in Kyng Richards dayes; and so passed as an aucte, and so restored.

The xxiiij day of Novembre, Knights and Sqwrs and other gentyllmen and yemen of the Crowne, and with odir yomen, to the numbre of vj score, they were rest(ored) aftir the forme as is above 20 rehersed.

The xxv day of Novembre ther were red certeyn bylls, and therupon were arguments, and nothing passed that day.

The xxvj day of Novembre we gave a tendaunce in the Cheker for to dyscharge our ffe fferme with Appylton and with Tynt and Hynkley; 25 and the Chambleyn was there present.

The xxvij day it was Sonday.

The xxviij day of Novembre there was a comonyng for the comen well of all the lond for to se a remedy for this fals money which that reyneth in the lond, disseyvyng of the Kyngs leige people; and so 30 continued the xxix.

The xxx day of Novembre cam downe the Clerke of the Crowne, by the commaundement of the Kyng and his lords spirituall and temporall, with xij bylls; so resseyved and red that day.

The first day of Decembre ther passed a byll with Th. Thorp ageyn 35 John Colte for such certey(n) londs that he hath holde of his to his wronge; and so he was restored.

The second day of Decembre there passed a byll with Sir Ts.

12 had is erased.   **18** sqwrs: squires.   **24** Cheker: Exchequer.
28 comonyng: communing, meeting.   **29** that yet (Benham).   40

Wrylond, as an aucte, for certeyn londs and ten'tz of that he was a teynt of be aucte of parliament, in Kyng Edwards dayes; and there upon he was restored. The same day there passed a byll with Sir John Weynescotte, as an aucte, for to restore hym a geyn unto his londs.

⟨fo.127ᵛ⟩ The iijde day of Decembre the(r) came downe ix bylls by 5 the Kyngs . . . his lords spirituall and temporall, delyvered unto us by (the clerke of) . . . So they ware red for that day, with odir maters that ware (resoned)

The iiijth day it was Sonday.

The vth day of Decembre ther passed a byll with Sir John Gylford 10 (as anaucte) . . . hym of his londs that he was a teynt of be aucte of parliament.

The vj day of Decembre ther passed a byll, as an aucte, with therle (of Oxynf), and his brodir George Fear, and his broth Th. Fear, to restore (them of . . .) ther londs whiche as they ware a teynt of be aucte 15 of parliament, (in) Kyng Edwards day. The same day passed a byll, as an aucte, (with Lord Wells) to restore hym to all his londs that he was a teint of be aucte (of parliament). The same day passed a byll, as an aucte, with my Lord Hungerford, 10 (to restore) hym agayn to his londs that he was a teint of be aucte of parliament, in Kyng Edwards 20 dayes.

The vij day of Decembre ther passed a byll with Foster as an aucte (for to restore) hym of all his londs that he was a teint be aucte of parliament. (The same) day there passed a byll with Maister Wilby as it is above said. The same (day) there passed a byll with Maister 25 Tressom after the same manner of forme.

The viij day it was oure lady day.

The ix day came in the byll of a teynt and sore was questioned with. (The same) day cam in a byll, with the erle of Stafford and with his moder, my (lady of) Bedford, savyng hym the tytyll of his lords and his 30 moders joynter (and) so was red the same day.

The x day ther passed the same byll of a teynt. The same day passed a byll, as aucte, with therle of Stafford and with my lady his moder, to (restitucion) of there londs. The same day there passed another byll that there (should) no man take non accion a genst non of tho that had 35 eny patent, (nor) no byll assyned, nor non that was proved that had

1 ten'tz: tenements.   6 Kyngs good grace (Benham).
11 The missing words may include 'to restore' (Benham).
14 Oxynf: Oxynford (Oxford); Fear: Vere.   24 Wilby: Willoughby.
26 Tressom: Tresham.   27 Conception of the Virgin Mary (8 December).
35 tho: those.

occupied (in his) owne wronge in tyme the parliament be ended. Also
the same day (there) passed a byll for the Court of Request that it is
annulled, and it (shall) be occupied no more. The same day it pleased
the Kyng and (all) his lords for to sende for Maister Speker and all the
howse in(to the) parliament chambir. And we cam theder and wayted   5
upon his (grace). So it pleased his grace for to commaunde my Lord
Chaunseler to (proloye his) high Court of parliament in to the xxiij day
of Januarie.

Historical Notes

page 185

4   In 1485 November 7 was a Monday.

9   The mass of the Holy Ghost was the usual mass for parliament, Powell and Wallis, *House of Lords in the Middle Ages*, pp. 530 n. 27, 555.

10   The Lord Steward was Thomas Stanley, Earl of Derby and Henry VII's stepfather through marriage with Margaret Beaufort. According to Polydore Vergil (*Three Books of Polydore Vergil's English History*, ed. Sir H. Ellis (Camden Society, 1844), p. 226) he placed the crown on Henry's head after the battle of Bosworth, but see Lander, *Crown and Nobility*, p. 304.

14   Roll calls were an essential feature of the parliaments of the sixteenth century, see pp. 46–7.

19   The Lord Chancellor was John Alcock, Bishop of Worcester. He declared the cause of the summoning of parliament, *Rot. Parl.* VI. 267. On Alcock see *D.N.B.* I. 236–7.

24   On the appointment of Lovell as Speaker see Roskell, *The Commons and their Speakers*, pp. 97, n. 2, 298–9. As Professor Roskell remarks, 'with Lovell as Speaker, it is hardly surprising that this first Tudor parliament showed itself realistic and competent', p. 299.

27   This 'sete', according to Professor Roskell, 'can have been none other than the Speaker's Chair,' p. 97.

29   See the comment above pp. 178–9 concerning the Recorder of London and 'the custume of the place'. It is worth noting that a later Recorder of London, William Fleetwood, had in his possession a copy of the *Modus*, Harvard Law Library MS. 21. Fleetwood was, however, also a legal antiquarian. On Fleetwood see Snow, pp. 26, 51–2; *D.N.B.* xix. 268–9.

page 186

6   Note that the account identifies the 'parliament chambir' as the place where the Lords sat. The Commons usually met in the chapter house of Westminster Abbey. There can be no doubt that the chamber was the Painted Chamber in the palace of Westminster, Powell and Wallis, p. 530.

10   For the financial grants made to the King see *Rot. Parl.* VI. 268–70; Chrimes, *Henry VII*, pp. 63–4. In the second session of

parliament he enriched the Crown by an enormous act of resumption, not referred to in this account, *Rot. Parl.* VI. 336–84.

17   Bill concerning Queen Elizabeth, *Rot. Parl.* VI. 288.

23   Richard Hawt of Ightam (Kent) was one of the Maidstone group of rebels in Buckingham's rebellion of 1483, *Rot. Parl.* VI. 245. See Agnes E. Conway, 'The Maidstone Sector of Buckingham's Rebellion', *Archaeologia Cantiana* 37 (1925), 106–14.

31   The bill was not in fact passed in 1485. It came again before the 1487 parliament and was passed then, *Rot. Parl.* VI. 391–2.

32–35   This account is a simple man's version of the oath against maintenance as administered in this parliament, *Rot. Parl.* VI. 287–8. 'The oathtakers included minors whose names do not appear on the chancery list . . .' see Powell and Wallis, p. 531.

39   Act reversing attainder on Henry VI, *Rot. Parl.* VI. 288.

page 187

3   Act restoring estates to Margaret Beaufort as Countess of Richmond, *Rot. Parl.* VI. 284–5.

6   Act restoring Hugh Luttrell to the estates of his father, Ibid., pp. 297–8.

9   Act restoring estates to the Duke of Bedford, Ibid., 278–9. An act of 1478 deprived George Neville of the dukedom of Bedford because of insufficient means to support his dignity, *Rot. Parl.* VI. 173. Jasper Tudor was created Duke of Bedford in 1485 on the accession of his nephew, Henry VII, *The Complete Peerage*, ed. Vicary Gibbs (London, 1912) II. 73.

16   No separate petition appears on the roll. Those listed in this group of petitioners include all those attainted by Richard III including the three bishops. The list is headed by Bedford and the bishops, *Rot. Parl.* VI. 273–5.

25   It was part of the duties of the Colchester burgesses to pay in the fee farm of the town at the Exchequer, M. McKisack, *The Parliamentary Representation of the English Boroughs during the Middle Ages* (Oxford, 1932, reprinted 1962), p. 139. Colchester's due were fixed at £35, *Rot. Parl.* VI. 300.

32   It is not possible to establish what these bills might have been.

35   Thomas Thorp was a Baron of the Exchequer in the time of Henry VI and Speaker in 1453. For the act annulling Colt's recovery of the lands, *Rot. Parl.* VI. 294–5. This brief and matter of fact reference hides one of the most remarkable recorded examples of the personal feuds that could develop as a result of officials acting in their official capacity against a powerful magnate, particularly if that magnate was none other than Richard, Duke of York. Thomas Thorp, the father of Roger Thorp who was the petitioner, in his capacity as baron of the Exchequer took possession of the warlike accoutrements of York (harness and other apparatus of war) after he had fallen into the King's hands. York pursued Thorp with undying vengeance for the return of these articles. His agent in this was Thomas Colt, M.P. for Warwick in 1453–4. A Middlesex jury found for the duke in 1454, and Thorp was committed to the Fleet for a time. On Thomas Thorp see J. C. Wedgwood, *History of Parliament: Biographies of the Members of the Commons House, 1439–1509* (London, 1936), 850; Lander, p. 128; Roskell pp. 253–4, 366–7.

page 188

5 It is probable that these are the statutes listed after the end of the first session, *Rot. Parl.* VI. 335.

10 No separate petition appears on the roll. Sir John Guildford was included in the general reversal of Richard III's attainder, see p. 187.

13 Repeal of the act of attainder against the De Veres, *Rot. Parl.* VI. 281–2. John de Vere commanded the archers at Bosworth, *Complete Peerage*, X. 241.

17 The attainder of John Welles, and those of his brother and nephew were reversed in 1485, *Rot. Parl.* VI. 286–7. The Welles lands were restored to him. Among other appointments he was made Constable of Bolingbroke, *Complete Peerage*, XII. 448.

19 Act reversing attainder on Lord Hungerford, *Rot. Parl.* VI. 305–6. Lord Hungerford and Moleyns (attainted 1461) was taken prisoner and beheaded in 1464. His son, Sir Thomas, was convicted of treason in 1469 and beheaded, Lander, p. 142, n. 61. The property was divided between the heir general and the heir male.

22 Act restoring estates to John Forster, *Rot. Parl.* VI. 332.

24 Act restoring estates to Robert Willoughby, Ibid., pp. 287, 325–6. See also Powell and Wallis, p. 532; Lander, p. 145.

25 Act restoring John Tresham to estates of his father, *Rot. Parl.* VI. 317–8. On Sir Thomas Tresham, 'one of the most notorious of all Lancastrians' and Speaker in the parliament of 1459 see Roskell, *The Commons and their Speakers*, pp. 368–9.

28 Richard III and his principal supporters were attainted. Those who had opposed Henry at Bosworth were declared to be rebels, *Rot. Parl.* VI. 275–8. See p. 178.

30 Act restoring lands to Catherine, Duchess of Bedford, *Rot. Parl.* VI. 284–5. The bill was 'read' on the ninth day and 'passed' on the following day.

page 189

2 There is no evidence of any act concerning the Court of Requests. See pp. 180–1.

7 As regards the payment of the Colchester burgesses for their parliamentary duties, 'an annuity of £1. 6s. 8d. being the rent from two mills 'at the New Hythe' was set aside for Thomas Christemasse', M. McKisack, *The Parliamentary Representation of the English Boroughs*, p. 97.

VI

A Draft of the Protestation
of the Speaker

This draft of the Protestation of the Speaker, written in English, occurs in a manuscript composed of a number of items.[1] These items include a *Book of Hunting* (fos. 135–75ᵛ) and *Ordinances of Hunting* (fos. 176–8ᵛ) dedicated to the Prince of Wales, the son of Henry IV. The text of the Protestation of the Speaker follows a text of the (A) recension of the *Modus Tenendi Parliamentum* (fos. 16–20ᵛ) and a text of the Tract on the Steward (fos. 20ᵛ–2). The provenance of the volume is unknown, but the name Whittokysmede occurs in two places in such a manner as to indicate that the part of the manuscript containing the *Modus* may have been compiled by or for him.

This unique text of the Speaker's Protestation whose content has hitherto been known only from the formal entries on the parliament roll cannot be dated with absolute certainty. The text indicates that the parliament to which it refers began on a Friday, and that the Chancellor at the time was the Archbishop of Canterbury. In the period between the end of the fourteenth century and the middle of the sixteenth century, four parliaments appear to fulfil these conditions, those of 3 February, 1413, 10 February, 1447, 19 November, 1487 and 25 January, 1504. In 1447, however, the parliament which had been summoned to Cambridge in 1446, was re-summoned to Bury St. Edmunds.[2] As this document speaks twice of 'the house accustunyd', referring apparently to Westminster, it would seem not to derive from that assembly.

As regards the three parliaments that were held in 1413, 1487 and 1504, that of 3 February, 1413, is a parliament of which we have no record, and the name of its Speaker is unknown.[3] There are two reasons why it is unlikely that the document relates to this 'lost parliament' of

[1] Beinecke Rare Book and Manuscript Library, Yale University, MS. 163. fos. 22–3. The text is reproduced by permission of Yale University Library. For a description of this manuscript see *Sixth Report of the Commission of Historical Manuscripts, Part 1. Report and Appendix*, p. 289; Seymour de Ricci, *Census of Medieval and Renaissance Manuscripts in the United States and Canada* (New York, 1937), 1092–3. At the time that the manuscript was included in the Historical Manuscripts Commission's Report it was in the possession of Lord Leconfield. The authors would like to thank Professor J. S. Roskell for his assistance with this text.

[2] 'English and British Parliaments and Related Assemblies to 1832', *Handbook of British Chronology*, ed. F. M. Powicke and E. B. Fryde (London, 1961), p. 531.

[3] J. S. Roskell, *The Commons and Their Speakers in English Parliaments 1376–1523* (Manchester, 1965), p. 153.

1413. A Protestation in the English language, responded to by the Chancellor in Latin, appears to be too late for a parliament held in 1413. None the less, in view of the fact that the first extant Commons' bill in English comes from the parliament of 1414, and that its subject is the right of the King to amend the wording of submissions made through the mouth of the Commons' Speaker,[4] this particular argument is not conclusive. More important is the fact that the response in this text was made by the Chancellor on behalf of the King rather than by the King in person. According to the formal record of parliament it was the King who in the parliaments of Henry IV's latter years and the early years of Henry V, made response to the Speaker. On the other hand all save the first of the parliaments of Henry VII following the practice of the immediately preceding parliaments of Edward IV and Richard III record the response to the Speaker's Protestation as being made by the Chancellor 'per mandatum regis'. This strongly supports the view that the Protestation postdates the first half of the fifteenth century.

Most likely, therefore, in view of its phraseology is the possibility that the protestation relates either to the parliament of 1487 or to the parliament of 1504. The parliament of 25 January 1504 in which the Speaker was Edmund Dudley, Empson's co-administrator, is a distinct possibility. In particular the reference in the text to 'the yeris of youre blessyd regne' suggests a reign of a longer duration than was the case at the time of the parliament of 19 November, 1487. At that time Henry VII had reigned for little more than two years, and had previously met only one parliament. The expression, 'the yeris of youre blessyd regne' would appear to imply a reign of longer duration.[5] If, however, the text does come from 1487 the Speaker who made the Protestation was John Mordaunt.[6] Mordaunt was a member of the Middle Temple, and a J.P. for Bedfordshire. He was to become a serjeant-at-law in 1495, Chief Justice of Chester, and Chancellor of the Duchy of Lancaster.[7]

[4] Rot. Parl. IV. 22.

[5] The authors are grateful to Professor J. S. Roskell for this suggestion.

[6] On Mordaunt, see Roskell, pp. 299–300; D.N.B. xxxvii. 405; E. W. Ives, 'The Common Lawyers in Pre-Reformation England', T.R.H.S. 5th ser. 18 (1968), 157–8.

[7] The linguistic evidence of the text is consistent with a date either in the late fifteenth or in the early sixteenth century. The document is basically written in 'London English' with provincial forms in which one or two Chancery forms also appear. For example 'suche' is a characteristic Chancery form. The authors are indebted to Dr. Betty Hill for this comment. It should also be noted that the address to the King as 'most Christian prince' can be found in a parliamentary petition of 1485, Rot. Parl. VI. 289.

Apart from associating the *Modus* with parliamentary material,[8] this text has an undoubted interest in its own right for it gives for the first time the actual exchange of words between the Speaker and the Chancellor. The development and significance of the Speaker's Protestation in the history of parliament has been fully treated by Professor Roskell, and need not be summarized here.[9] Suffice it to say that the Protestation was no mere formality, John Tiptoft in 1406 'appealing to his protestations no fewer than six times'.[10] It is clear from the words preserved in this document, however, that although both parts of the Protestation, i.e. the Speaker's stress on his personal unworthiness and, when over-ruled, his request that he should be merely a servant of both King and Commons, are present in this document, as they are in the formal record, the emphasis here is more on the selection of a phrase pleasing to the King's ear rather than a ringing declaration of the Commons' rights. Indeed, the request of the Speaker that he should be subject to the correction of the Commons in whatever he said on their behalf to the King, regarded as of some constitutional significance, is here obligingly and humbly made. The clerks of parliament who summarized the Protestation on the parliament roll in the words of the long established and by this time traditional legal formulae, added more point and precision than the Speaker would actually have cared to say aloud to a sovereign of the stamp of Henry VII.

[8] An English translation of the (A) recension of the *Modus* (B.L. Harley MS. 930) compiled in the middle of the fifteenth century was later in the possession of the clerk of parliament, while in the early sixteenth century a new version of the *Modus* prefaced the House of Lords Journal. See p. 215.

[9] Roskell, pp. 31–58. See the comments on Thomas Lovell, Speaker in the parliament of 1485, p. 190. His Protestation is given *Rot. Parl.* VI. 268. Because the office of Speaker developed after the *Modus* was written an account of the office is one notable omission in its text.

[10] Roskell, p. 32.

Prelucutio ad regem in Parliamento

fo. 22. Most xpian prynce replete with all vertue and grace our alle
souereigne lord hit hath plesyd youre heghnesse by the aduyse of youre
lordys spū ell and temporell of youre grete counsel for diuersez maters
and urgent causez consernyng and touchyng youre most roial person,   5
the chirch of thus youre roialme and for the welfare of alle youre true
lege pepyll of the same to lece calle and sumune thus youre hygh court
of parlement to be gynne, etc. and by the weche aduyse youre wryttez
royalle hauyth be seuerally directyd to euery of youre shyryffez of thus
youre sayde royalme comaundyng to euery of them to chese of euery of   10
your shirys 2 knyghtez, of youre cittes accus(t)umyd 2 citezyns, of
burghs in leke wyse 2 bugeys to appere byfore youre hignes on fryday
last passyd the weche youre hyght comaunden'ct youre sayd sheryffez
hauen obseruyd, obedyd, and kept youre wryttez receuyd in youre
chauncery and youre sayd kyghtez, citezyns and burgeys apperyd on   15
the sayd fryday byfore youre highnes at the wiche day hit was openyd
shuyd and claryd most notable by the mouthe of the sulf reverent fadyr
in God the archbisshopp of Caunterbery, youre chaunceller of thus
youre roialme by youre comandement diuersez and notabill causez etc
and yn especial etc, thonkyng the welfare of your most blessyd person   20
and of this youre riolme the weche in no wyse my insuffis canne (fo.
22ᵛ) declare or shewe and furthirmore hit was comawndyd by youre
highnesse that we youre sayd comes shuld go vnto the house accustunyd
and there to chese a speker of one of them to opyn, shewe, and declare
vnto youre hyghnesse suche maters as by them ther suld be comund the   25
weche youre hyghn comaundement they have as lewely as euer dede
lige pepill obbeyd obseruyd and kept, and me most vnhabill, lest of
connyng and indigne have chosyn to be ther speker. Most blessyd
prynce oure alle soueraigne lorde plese it to your magnificence to
consyder my symplenesse and myne vnkunnyng, havyng none eloquens   30
to yeve in comawndement vn to vs your saide comyns to go agen vnto
the saide hous accustumyd and ther to renovel ther election and to
chese suche a person the wyche is con yyng and in eloquens habill, and
vn to youre most heighnesse acceptabill and vn to youre most douttyd
person and to this youre roialme profitable.   35

17 notable: notably. sulf is the western form of self: self same.
21 insuffis: insufficiency.   **23** comes: commons.

Responsio cancellarie per mandatum regis rex vult habere te in prelocutorem sciens te habilis.

Most graciouse benigne and tredouttyd prince seth hit hath plesyd youre heighnesse þat y, most unhabill, schalle accept and take this 5 occupacoun of speker, y beseche you as louly and humbely as euer dede creature, to haue and to stonde vnder youre blessyd favour and socour, and to haue and enjoie in the name of alle my maystres, felowes and me all pryuelegiez, libertes, ymyunytes, and fraunchisez as any other persone or personez þat hath had and usyd byfore me and in the yeris 10 of youre blessyd regne and in the yeris of youre blessyd progenitours, and þat my protestacoun may be entryd and enactyd in this youre hye court of parlement and by autorite of the same parlement so þat no thyng may passe nor excede fro me but that y may euer be fauorid vnder youre highnesse and to reporte vnto my maystres and ffelowys 15 to reforme, adde, and mynne in suche maters as may be profitable vn to youre heighnesse and to the welfare of thus youre roialme.

Cancellarius per mandatum regis respondit quod protestatio illa irrotulari debet in parliamento auctoritate parliamenti, cum autem sicut fuit tempore suo et temporibus progenitorum et modo ampliori, 20 etc.

5 unhabill: unable.   16 mynne: diminish.

Appendix I
Manuscripts and Transcripts
of the English *Modus*

Medieval Manuscripts of the *Modus*

MSS.	PROVENANCE/OWNERSHIP	DATE
LATIN		
(A) VERSION		
Boston		
Harvard Law Library		
No. 21	William Fleetwood[1]	XV cent.
No. 29–30	Richard Pigott[2]	XV cent.
London,		
British Library		
Vespasian B. VII[3]		XIV cent.
Nero C I	Thomas Jakes[4]	XV cent.
Lansdowne 522	William Aylesbury	XV cent.
Julius B. IV	Cinque Ports[5]	XV cent.
Add. 24097		XV cent.
Norfolk,		
Holkham Hall		
MS. 232		XV cent.

[1] William Fleetwood was Recorder of the City of London in 1589 and a noted antiquarian. In this volume the *Modus*, which is incomplete, appears at the end of the manuscript together with the 1297 reissue of Magna Carta.

[2] The obit of Richard Pigott, sergeant-at-law, is given in the almanac at the beginning of the volume. Gray's Inn may be the original provenance of this MS. for the family spelt the name somewhat differently. At a latter date it appears to have been in the possession of the Crispe family, who had London connections. *C.P.R. 1494–1509*, pp. 170, 281.

[3] For a description of this MS. see p. 62 and Pronay and Taylor, 'Use of the *Modus Tenendi Parliamentum* in the Middle Ages', pp. 12–14. Its provenance is unknown.

[4] Thomas Jakes was Clerk of Warrants and Estreats during the reigns of the Yorkist kings. The office entailed the keeping of the records of the Court of Common Pleas. He was also the possessor of a fine library of his own including a manuscript Yearbook of Edward II. Margaret Hastings, *The Court of Common Pleas in the Fifteenth Century* (New York, 1947), pp. 140–1; *Year Book of Edward II*, vol. vi. ed. G. J. Turner (Selden Soc., XXVI, 1914), pp. li–lii.

[5] This volume contains the laws and customs of the Cinque Ports.

MSS.	PROVENANCE/OWNERSHIP	DATE
Oxford, Bodleian Library Oriel 46	London Guildhall[6]	XV cent.
Pennsylvania, Free Library of Philadelphia No. 9	Sir Thomas Molyneux[7]	XV cent.
Yale University,[8] Beinecke Library Ms. 163		XV cent.

(B) VERSION

MSS.	PROVENANCE/OWNERSHIP	DATE
London, British Library Nero D. VI	Thomas Mowbray[9]	XIV cent.
Add. 32097	William Lambarde (1571)[10]	XV cent.
29901	William Lambarde	XV cent.
Domitian XVIII	Lawrence Nowell, Dean of Lichfield (1576)	XV cent.
Vitellius C. IV		XV cent.
Tiberius E. VIII	John Tiptoft, Earl of Worcester[11]	XV cent.

[6] This was once a part of a collection of documents, the *Liber de Veteribus Legibus Angliae*, which belonged to the London Guildhall. It may have been the work of Andrew Horn, for it incorporates items of antiquarian interest only, Pronay and Taylor, *art. cit.* p. 15.

[7] The volume may have belonged to Thomas Molyneux (1440–1506), or more likely his grandfather, Thomas Molyneux of Horton, Notts., who married the daughter of a legal family connected with Gray's Inn, and who was himself J.P. in Nottinghamshire after 1446, and served on a number of local commissions, *Readings and Moots at the Inns of Court in the Fifteenth Century*, ed. S. E. Thorne, (Selden Soc. lxxi, 1954), p. xl.

[8] For Edmund Dudley's connection with this volume, see p. 198. The authors have been informed by David M. Sills that what appears to be an (A) recension of the *Modus* in Latin is to be found in the Newberry Library, Chicago.

[9] The evidence for Mowbray's connection with this manuscript is discussed by J. H. Round, *Commune of London* (London, 1899), pp. 302 ff.; Clarke, pp. 352–5. See also the comments of N. Denholm-Young, *The Country Gentry in the Fourteenth Century* (Oxford, 1969), p. 86, and Margaret Rickert, *The Reconstructed Carmelite Missal* (London, 1952), p. 76. The MS. belonged at one time to William Detheck, Garter King at Arms.

[10] This copy was given to Lambarde by Richard Atkins, of Lincoln.

[11] John Tiptoft, Earl of Worcester, was Constable of England in 1463–7 and again in 1470. He was also Steward of the Royal Household (1463–7). See Charles Ross, *Edward IV* (London, 1974), p. 80.

MSS.	PROVENANCE/OWNERSHIP	DATE

Oxford,
  Bodleian Library
    Rawlinson C. 398
	Sir John Fortescue[12]	XV cent.

Paris,
  Bibliothèque Nationale
    Lat. 6049
	Louis de Gruthuyse
	    (1422–1492)[13]
		XV cent.

(c) VERSION		

California,
  Huntington Library
    E.L. 35. B. 61
	Sir Thomas Egerton[14]	XV cent.

Dublin,
  Trinity College
    MS. E. 4.5
	Register of Writs	XV cent.

Durham,
  Dean and Chapter
    Registrum I. part 1
	Durham, Dean and
	    Chapter
		XV cent.

London,
  Inner Temple
    Petyt 511, vi
	Robert Fulwode[15]	XV/XVI cent.

LATIN TEXT IN LORDS JOURNAL

Lords Journal, 1510[16] XVI cent.

[12] This copy belongs to the collection of miscellaneous legal material collected by Sir John Fortescue.

[13] Gruthuyse was an expert in the art of courtly chivalry. He was a friend of Edward IV, created earl of Winchester in 1472, and took part in many of the ceremonies of the English court. See Cora L. Schofield, *The Life and Reign of Edward IV* (London, 1967), II, 39; C. L. Kingsford, *English Historical Literature in the Fifteenth Century* (Oxford, 1913), pp. 379–88.

[14] This was once a part of the Bridgewater Library, formed by Sir Thomas Egerton, first Lord Ellesmere, who owned transcripts of the Irish *Modus*, see p. 117.

[15] Robert Fulwode was a bencher of the Inner Temple, and Lent Reader in 1506. See *Readings and Moots at the Inns of Court in the 15th Century*, ed. Thorne, p. xiii; *A Calendar of the Inner Temple Records*, ed. F. A. Inderwick (London, 1896) I, 4. 54. Fulwode's name is written in this manuscript. The appearance of lawyers' names in MSS. is a complicated question. Fulwode may have been the owner or the client, see A. W. B. Simpson, 'The Circulation of Yearbooks in the Fifteenth Century', *Law Quarterly Review* 73 (1957), 505.

[16] This text may have been the work of John Taylor, clerk of the parliament at the time. For comments on this text, and its value as a procedural guide see G. R. Elton, 'The Early Journals of the House of Lords', *E.H.R.* 89 (1974), 505, and A. F. Pollard, 'The Authenticity of the "Lords Journals" in the Sixteenth Century', *T.R.H.S.* 3rd ser. 8 (1914), 36–7.

MSS.	PROVENANCE/OWNERSHIP	DATE

ENGLISH

(A) VERSION

London,
   British Library
      Harley 930 — Clerk of Parliament[17] — XV cent.

(B) VERSION

Cambridge,
   University Library
      IV. 207 (3.29) — Henry Colling (XVII cent). — XV cent.

London,
   British Library
      Add. 15091 — Robert Dudley, Earl of Leicester (1532–88)[18] — XVI cent.

London,
   Society of Antiquaries
      58 — — XV cent.

FRENCH

(C) VERSION

London,
   British Library
      Add. 49359 — Courtenay Cartulary[19] — XIV/XV cent.

Northampton,
   Northampton Record Society
      Finch-Hatton 2995. — Archbishop of Cashel[20] — XV cent.

---

[17] We know from a transcript, B.L. Add. 25457, that in the sixteenth century this particular copy belonged to a clerk of parliament. It may have been used later to construct the copy in the House of Lords Journals, *E.H.R.* 34 (1919), 212–4.

[18] This copy was furnished with an index. This suggests that it was intended to be used in a practical way.

[19] This is one of the few surviving examples of a fourteenth-century lay cartulary. It appears to be a type of record collection intended to be used by the council of a great estate, *Pronay and Taylor, art. cit.* pp. 19–20.

[20] For an account of this MS. see pp. 120–1, 215. It belonged in all probability to Richard O'Hedigan, archbishop of Cashel, and may well be the archetype from which the Irish version was constructed.

Provisional List of Transcripts

MSS.	PROVENANCE/OWNERSHIP	DATE

LATIN

(A) VERSION

Dublin,
  Trinity College
    E. 3. 18   XVI/XVII cent.?

London,
  British Library
    Harley 305 — Sir Simonds D'Ewes — XVII cent.
    Harley 2233 — XVII cent.
    Harley 4717 — XVI/XVII cent.
    Stowe 329 — Note by Twysden — XVI/XVII cent.
    Lansdowne 872 (fragment) — XVI cent.

(B) VERSION

Cambridge,
  Pepysian library
    2516 — Sir Edward Coke (1597) — XVI cent.
London, British library
    Add. 38139 — Robert Dudley, Earl of
      Leicester (1532–88) — XVI cent.
    Harley 1576 — XVI cent.
    Stowe 140 — The arms of Henry,
      Prince of Wales — XVI cent.
    Lansdowne 171 — XVI cent.

London,
  The House of Lords
    Braye 34 — XVII cent.

Sheffield,
  Central Library — Wentworth-Woodhouse
    Collection — XVII cent.

(C) VERSION

Norfolk,
  Holkham Hall
    678 — Sir Edward Coke — XVI cent.

MSS.	PROVENANCE/OWNERSHIP	DATE

ENGLISH

(A) VERSION

London,
British Library
Add. 25457 — (Transcript of B.L. Harl. 930) — XVI cent.
Harley 2115 (fragment) — XVI cent.
Lansdowne 484 — XVII cent.

(B) VERSION

California,
Huntington Library
E.L. 7976 — — XVII cent.
Dublin,
Trinity College
852 (H) — Jerome Alexander — XVI cent.

London,
College of Arms
Vincent 25 — Ralph Sheldon (1684) — XV/XVI cent.
Arundel XLI (H) — John Hooker — XVI cent.
2M2 — — XVI/XVII cent.

London,
British Library
Harley 1309 — — XVI cent.
2208 (H) — John Hooker[21] — XVI cent.
3504 — — XVI cent.
7371 — — XVI cent.
Add. 12, 227 — — XVI cent.
Add. 48, 020 (H) — Robert Beale/Christopher Yelverton — XVI cent.
48, 025 (H) — Robert Beale/Christopher Yelverton — XVI cent.
Egerton 985 — — XVI cent.

Oxford,
Bodleian Library
Ashmolean 865 — Sir John Maynard (1602–90) — XVII cent.

(H) Hooker's translation.
[21] Possibly a preprinter's copy, Snow, p. 55. It was purchased by Edward Harley from Nathaniel Noel in 1724, C. E. Wright, *Fontes Harleiani* (London, 1972), pp. 253–5.

MSS.	PROVENANCE/OWNERSHIP	DATE
Bodley 966	(see Scottish *Modus*) (One chapter in Latin)	XVII cent.

FRENCH

(C) VERSION

London,
  British Library
    Harley 305[22]   Sir Simonds D'Ewes   XVII cent.

TRANSCRIPTS OF THE LATIN TEXT IN THE LORDS JOURNAL (1510)

California,
  Huntington library
    E.L. 8446   XVI/XVII cent.

Cambridge,
  University Library
    MM. VI. 62   XVII cent.

London,
  British Library
    Harley 813   XVII cent.

    Harley 2235   XVII cent.

Provisional List of Untraced Manuscripts

1. Bromley-Davenport MSS. Hist. Manuscripts Comm. Third Report, p. 108.
2. Countess Cowper and Baroness Lucas MSS. Hist. Manuscripts Comm. Second Report, p. 8.
3. Lord Culthorpe, Grosvenor Square. MSS. Hist. Manuscripts Comm. Second Report, p. 40.
4. Leconfield MSS. Hist. Manuscripts Comm. Sixth Report, p. 301. This copy was at one time in the possession of Edward Seymour (1506–52), High Steward of England for Edward VI's coronation, and Earl Marshal.
5. Northumberland MSS. Hist. Manuscripts Comm. Third Report, p. 108.
6. Marquess of Ripon MSS. Hist. Manuscripts Comm. Sixth Report, p. 248.

---

[22] There are two transcripts in B.L. Harley 305 at fos. 275–85, and 284–93. See list of transcripts of (A) text in Latin.

7. M. Wilson Esq., Eshton Hall, York. Hist. Manuscripts Comm. Third Report, p. 298.
8. A copy belonging to Sir Francis Winnington, Stamford Court, Worcester was almost certainly destroyed in the fire of 1882.
9. There was a copy of the *Modus*, No. 333 in the library of Sir Edward Coke, which was bound up with a copy of the tract on the office of the Earl Marshal.
10. The copy of the *Modus Tenendi Parliamentum* in the Chapter Library of Westminster Library perished in the fire of 1694. See J. A. Robinson and M. R. James, *Manuscripts of Westminister Abbey* (Cambridge, 1909), pp. 26–62.
11. The first reference to the *Modus* comes in a library catalogue of Titchfield Abbey, compiled about 1400. R. M. Wilson, 'Library Catalogue of Titchfield Abbey', *Proceedings of the Leeds Philosophical and Literary Society* 5, part IV, p. 260. This copy of the *Modus* may have come from William of Wykeham who had connections with the abbey.

Appendix II
Manuscripts and Transcripts of the Irish and Scottish *Modus*

MMS.	PROVENANCE/OWNERSHIP	DATE
IRISH MODUS		
1. EXEMPLIFICATION OF 1419		
California, Huntington Library E.L. 1699	Sir Christopher Preston	XV cent.
Cambridge, University Library MM. VI. 62	John Selden (taken from Hakewill)	XVII cent.
Dublin, Trinity College E. 3. 18	Daniel Molyneux, Ulster King at Arms (1597–1632)	XVII cent.
London, British Library Ms. Facs. Suppl. I	John Selden (taken from Hakewill)	XVII cent.
New York (privately owned) Mr. Voynitch	William Hakewill	XVII cent.
Oxford, Bodleian Library Rawlinson B. 484 (fragment)	Sir James Ware	XVII cent.
2. WATERFORD TRADITION (based on A. Dopping's printed version of 1692)		
Dublin, Trinity College E. 3. 18		XVII cent.
London, British Library Add. 35505	Sir William Domvile	XVII cent.
SCOTTISH MODUS		
Oxford, Bodleian Library Bodley 966		XVII cent.

Appendix III
Note on the Translations and Transcripts
of the English *Modus*

Evidence of the interest taken in the *Modus*, and of the persistence of the (A) and (B) recensions into the seventeenth century is to be seen in the numerous translations and transcripts which were made during that period. Among medieval and post-medieval English translations of the *Modus*, translations of the (B) recension are always to be found in greater numbers than those of (A). Yet although for the purposes of translation (B) remained the more popular version it is worth noting that few of the English translations of (B) contain a perfect text. In particular all the medieval translations of (B) have certain (A) readings. Thus all say that the clerks of parliament shall have a mark a day for and not with their expenses; as in (A) they all mention discord 'between the king and the magnates'; and they all omit the phrase as to where parliament shall be held. All the medieval English texts of (B) have therefore signs of (A) influence. In his own translation of the (B) text Hooker made certain slight changes which have been noted by Professor Snow.[1] For example Hooker omitted the paragraph, *Concerning the Position of Speakers in Parliament*, and elsewhere he divided up paragraphs, making the last sentence of the paragraph *Concerning the Opening of Parliament* a separate paragraph entitled *Of the Proclamations*. He also added a small concluding paragraph of his own.

Among the later transcripts B.L. Lansdowne 484, a seventeenth-century English translation, deserves perhaps some further comment for it was taken by Miss Hodnett and Miss White to represent a new version of the *Modus*, midway between (A) and (B). In fact Lansdowne 484 is an English translation of the (A) recension. It has the (A) sequence of paragraphs with the single exception that paragraphs XXIII to XXVI come between paragraphs XVIII and XIX. As regards the text it is a normal (A) text with two exceptions. The first exception is the interpolation of a brief passage beginning, 'After the general congregation', and ending 'this godly order hath been devised', in the paragraph entitled *Concerning the Opening of Parliament* after the account of the fifth day of parliament. This interpolation appears to be a seventeenth-century addition. The second exception is that in the paragraph entitled *Concerning Difficult Cases and Decisions* this version gives as the composition of the committee of twenty-five, two bishops, two earls, two barons, two clerks for the clergy, five knights for the shires, six citizens, and six burgesses. There is no warrant for these figures in any of the medieval manuscripts, and there can be no doubt that they are a seventeenth-century addition. The text in Lansdowne 484 therefore, appears to be not so much an early form of the *Modus* as a seventeenth-century variation of the text.

[1] *Parliament in Elizabethan England*, pp. 53–4.

A note at the end of the text in B.L. Harley 1576 casts some light upon the historical knowledge of certain of these transcribers. 'In the ligier booke of the late Abbot of St. Edmonds Bury in Suffolk which is in the hands of Sir Edward Coke is cited a parliament holden in the first year of Canute's reign which is exemplified in the preface to his ninth booke, which he saith doth give credit to this auncient Treatise intitled Modus Tenendi Parliamentum.'

Appendix IV
Minor Versions of the English *Modus*

The (C) Version

The (C) version of the *Modus* has already been mentioned in connection with the Irish version of the text.[1] Only the (C) version of the *Modus* was translated into vulgar French, and this version alone was found in the possession of non-professional owners. Although it survives in a relatively few numbers of copies, the construction of this version is, however, of some interest.

As the manuscripts themselves show, the first and second recensions survived side by side, possibly at first only in a single copy, until the reign of Richard II. Probably at that time what can only be described as a new version of the *Modus* was constructed from these two texts. This was the version which we now call (C) and which borrowed readings from both (A) and (B). Examples of (C) are to be found in four manuscripts, London, Inner Temple, Petyt 511; Huntington Library, E.L. 35. B. 61; Durham, Dean and Chapter, Registrum I. Part I; Trinity College, Dublin, Ms. E. 4. 5.[2] In these manuscripts there are readings from both the (A) and (B) recensions but it is difficult to know at any place why the readings of one recension have been preferred to the other, and upon what method of selection the scribe has proceeded. It we take the text in Hunt. E.L. 35. B. 61 as one example, this begins as a form of (A), it then proceeds to the readings of (B), and ends with readings taken from both (A) and (B). The paragraph *Concerning the Doorkeepers of Parliament* has, for example, the readings of (A), although most of the readings in the later paragraphs come from (B). The sequence of paragraphs is mainly that of (B) with the exception that the paragraph *Concerning the Grades of Peers* comes at the end of the text, and that the paragraph *Concerning the Opening of Parliament* is subdivided into two, the new paragraph having the heading, *Concerning the Proclamation of Parliament*. The text in Petyt 511 agrees almost exactly with this, although there are certain slight differences between the two. In the paragraph, *Concerning the Departure of Parliament* Petyt 511 has *parliamentum nostrum* where the Huntington copy has *parliamentum vestrum*. In addition the Huntington copy omits a phrase in the paragraph, *Concerning the Principal Clerks of Parliament*, which reads *ut quando assignati sunt cum aliis sectatoribus parliamenti*.

These clearly are minor differences, and both manuscripts give what is essentially a (C) version of the text built up from (A) and (B). At certain key places the readings of (C) come from (A). Thus (C) says that the King used (*solebat*) to send his writs to the Warden of the Cinque Ports, and in the paragraph, *Concerning Difficult Cases and Decisions* the (C) version speaks only of

[1] See pp. 120–1.
[2] The last eight paragraphs of the Trinity College MS. are missing.

conflict between the King and the magnates. On the other hand in the paragraph, *Concerning the Placing and Seats in Parliament* (C) has chamberlain in the singular which is the reading of (B), and like (B) it makes the error of stating that parliament shall be held '*occulto loco*'.

The copy in the Durham Register is, like Petyt 511 and the Huntington copy, a copy of (C), and its readings agree in the main with theirs. In one or two places, however, this copy differs from the others and at these places its readings suggest that the Durham copy represents a different stage in the development of (C). In the paragraph, *Concerning Difficult Cases and Decisions* it omits the word *tribuletur* after *vel populus vel patria*, which is omitted in (B) but is present in the other versions of (C). It has chamberlains in the plural in the paragraph, *Concerning the Manner of Parliament*, which is the wording of (A), but is not the wording of the other versions of (C). In the paragraph, *Concerning the King's Absence in Parliament* it omits both *res* (B) and *rex* (A), and says simply *quia dampnosa et periculosa est*. Finally in the paragraph, *Concerning the Departure of Parliament* it has *Quo si non venerit*, which is a combination of the texts of (A) and (B). The Durham copy reinforces the conclusion that (C) was made up from (A) and (B), and that in this particular text the scribe, at several places, preferred an alternative reading to that found in the other copies of (C).

A transcript of (C) is found also in Ms. 678, fos. 60–2 among the manuscripts of Lord Leicester at Holkham Hall. Written during the late sixteenth or early seventeenth century this transcript may have been prepared for Sir Edward Coke whose interest in the *Modus* is well known. A comparison of this transcript with the other copies of (C) reveals quite clearly that it was taken from the text in Huntington E.L. 35. B. 61. In all cases where the Huntington text differs from the other copies of (C) this transcript follows the wording of the Huntington copy. Thus it omits the phrase in the paragraph, *Concerning the Principal Clerks of Parliament* which is omitted also in the Huntington text. Although the transcript contains one or two errors it is on the whole a reasonably accurate copy of what may well have been regarded as an interesting version of the *Modus*.

Much of the importance of (C) comes from the fact that it is the form of the Latin *Modus* from which the French copies were made which now survive in the Courtenay Cartulary (B.L. Add. 49359) and the Finch-Hatton roll. As Hardy, who edited this French text stated, the French version has all the marks of having been translated from a Latin original.[3] Thus it omits phrases which are present in the Latin text and it has errors which are not to be found in the Latin copy. The Latin version from which it was taken was (C), for both the French texts have the particular readings of (A) and (B) found only in (C), with the exception that they do not have the error about parliament being held *occulto loco* and that like the Durham copy of (C) they have the term *chamberlains*

---

[3] 'On the Treatise entitled *Modus Tenendi Parliamentum*" *Archaeological Journal* 19 (1862) 259ff. See pp. 120–1.

in the plural and not the singular. In the Courtenay Cartulary the paragraph, *Concerning the Opening of Parliament* is sub-divided in the manner of the Huntington copy.

Of the two French versions, the text in the Courtenay Cartulary is undoubtedly the better. Although it omits certain phrases, it gives on the whole a full and accurate translation of the Latin original. On the other hand the French text in the Finch-Hatton roll is full of errors and omissions. It omits the paragraph, *Concerning the Citizens*, and a part of the paragraph *Concerning the Grades of Peers*, as well as a number of words and phrases. It has several errors. In the paragraph, *Concerning the Order of Business of Parliament* it has, 'if there is no war' for 'if there is war', and on more than one occasion it has *evesque* for *ovesque*.

The Version in the House of Lords Journal

Yet another attempt to fuse the texts of (A) and (B) into a single version is to be found in the Latin copy of the *Modus* transcribed in the House of Lords Journal.[4] This text is mainly a text of (A), but with additions from (B). It is not as Miss Hodnett and Miss White have stated a text of (B).[5] In the first place the sequence of paragraphs is that of (A) with the exception that the paragraph, *Concerning the Grades of Peers* appears at the beginning of the text. The sequence is then exactly that of (A) with the single further exception that the paragraph, *Concerning the Manner of Parliament* occurs twice, once in its normal position in the (A) text, and once again at the place after the paragraph, *Concerning the Days and Hours of Parliament* where the section, *Concerning the Grades of Peers* would have occurred in (B).

As in the medieval texts the change in the sequence of paragraphs announces a mixed text taken from both (A) and (B). None the less, this is not a mixed text on the pattern of (C). Most of the text is taken from (A), and only the last seven paragraphs have the readings of (B). The paragraph, *Concerning the Days and Hours* has the (B) reading that parliament shall be held *occulto loco*, and after that the readings of the remaining paragraphs are uniformly those of (B). These final paragraphs have been corrected in the margin from (A), and it was these marginal corrections which lead Miss Hodnett and Miss White to suppose that the whole work was a (B) text which had been corrected from (A). In fact the copy in the House of Lords Journal is mainly (A).[6]

[4] The form of the *Modus* in the House of Lords Journal is also found in Hunt. E.L. 8446. Other copies are found in B.L. Harley 813 at fo. 4 transcribed on three sheets which have been attached to this volume; in B.L. Harley 2235 after fo. 26; and C.U.L. MM. VI. 62.

[5] Hodnett and White, *art. cit.* p. 214.

[6] The copy in the House of Lords Journal has also certain minor peculiarities. The compiler omitted the last part of the paragraph *Concerning the Barons of the Cinque Ports*, although this is present in both the (A) and (B) recensions. This part was added later. In B.L. Harley 2235 there is a marginal note, 'Hic Modus tenendi parliamentum sumebatur ex ipso Libro itinerario Henry VIII ubi recordatur unde authoritas pendeat, 1509'.

Appendix V
Printed Versions of the English *Modus*

The first printed text of the *Modus* was the English translation by John Hooker published in the two editions of 1572, the Exeter edition of 3 October, and the FitzWilliam edition shortly after that.[1] Hooker who printed the text of the *Modus* together with his own account of parliament, translated a text of the (B) recension. In view of the prevalence of the (A) recension in legal and parliamentary circles until the beginning of the sixteenth century it is difficult to know why Hooker chose to translate a (B) version of the text. His choice may possibly be explained by his limited knowledge of the manuscripts of the *Modus*, and by the fact that chivalric codices containing the (B) text remained in use substantially longer than the common law volumes. Hooker made his own translation and did not simply reproduce one of the medieval English versions.[2] His English translation was included in the 1751 edition of *Somers' Tracts*, and was reprinted by Sir Walter Scott in his 1809 edition of the same work.[3] Another English translation of the (B) text precedes Hooker's version in that edition.[4]

A French text of the *Modus* taken from the Finch-Hatton roll, and consisting of a French translation of the (C) text, was printed by T. D. Hardy in the *Archaeological Journal* in 1862.[5]

As regards printed versions of the Latin *Modus*, apart from Hakewill's treatise of 1641 which included a text of the (A) recension, the earliest printed versions were invariably based upon the (B) recension. The source of several of these texts was D. L. D'Achery's collection of documents in *Spicilegium* (Paris, 1677) xii, 557 ff. which included a text of the (B) recension taken from Paris, Bibliothèque Nationale Ms. Lat. 6049, once in the Gruthuyse collection. This same manuscript formed the basis of the text printed by T. D. Hardy for the Record Commission in 1846 although Hardy included readings from other manuscripts. Excerpts from Hardy's edition were reprinted by Stubbs in his *Select Charters*.[6] Not until Miss Clarke printed her version of the *Modus* as an Appendix to *Medieval Representation and Consent* was an (A) version, although one which contained certain (B) readings, available in a recent edition.

[1] Snow, pp. 28–38.
[2] Ibid., p. 54.
[3] *Somers Tracts*, 2nd edn. by Sir Walter Scott (London, 1809) I. 175–82.
[4] Ibid., 7–15.
[5] *Archaeological Journal* 19 (1862), 266–74.
[6] 9th edn. by H. W. C. Davis (Oxford, 1929), pp. 500–6.

Select Bibliography

Printed Sources

Bibliography of Royal Proclamations of the Tudor and Stuart Sovereigns (Bibliotheca Lindesiana, vol. 5), ed. Robert Steele (Oxford, 1910).

Brief Register, Kalendar and Survey of the Several Kinds and Forms of All Parliamentary Writs, William Prynne, 4 vols (London, 1659–64).

A Calendar of the Inner Temple Records, ed. F. A. Inderwick, 3 vols. (London, 1896–1901).

Anglia Sacra, ed. H. Wharton, 2 vols. (London, 1691).

Anglica Historia of Polydore Vergil, 1485–1537, ed. Denys Hay (Camden Society, lxxiv, 1950).

Anonimalle Chronicle, 1331–81, ed. V. H. Galbraith (Manchester, 1927, reprinted 1970).

Archeion, ed. C. H. McIlwain and P. L. Ward (Harvard University Press, 1957).

Bracton, De Legibus Angliae, ed. G. D. G. Hall (London, 1965).

Brut or the Chronicles of England, ed. F. W. D. Brie (Early English Text Society, Original Series, 131, 136. 1906–8).

Calendar of Close Rolls (London, 1892–   ).

Calendar of Patent Rolls (London, 1891–   ).

Calendar of the Gormanston Register c. 1175–1397, ed. J. Mills and M. J. McEnery (Dublin, 1916).

Chronicles of the Reigns of Edward I and Edward II, ed. W. Stubbs, 2 vols. (Rolls Series, 1882–3).

Chronicon Angliae, ed. E. M. Thompson (Rolls Series, 1874).

Chronicon Henrici Knighton, ed. J. R. Lumby, 2 vols. (Rolls Series, 1889–95).

Commons Debates 1621, ed. W. Notestein, F. H. Relf and H. Simpson, 7 vols. (Yale, 1935).

De Prerogativa Regis, ed. S. E. Thorne (New Haven and London, 1949).

De Republica Anglorum, Sir Thomas Smith (London, 1583).

Discourse upon the Exposition and Understandinge of Statutes, ed. S. E. Thorne (San Marino, 1942).

Documents Illustrative of English History in the Thirteenth and Fourteenth Centuries, ed. H. Cole (London, Record Commission, 1844).

Early Registers of Writs, ed. Elsa de Haas and G. D. G. Hall (Selden Society, lxxxvii, 1970).

English Coronation Records, ed. L. G. Wickham Legg (London, 1901).

English Historical Documents, vol. III, 1189–1327, ed. H. Rothwell (London, 1975).

English Historical Documents, vol. IV, 1327–1485, ed. A. R. Myers (London, 1969).

Expedicio Billarum Antiquitus : An Unpublished Chapter of the Second Book of the Manner of Holding Parliaments in England, ed. C. S. Sims (Louvain, 1954) (see *Manner of Holding Parliaments in England*).

Fane Fragment of the 1461 Lords Journal, ed. W. H. Dunham (New Haven, 1935).

Fleta, ed. H. G. Richardson and G. O. Sayles (Selden Society, lxxii, lxxxix, 1953, 1972).

Holinshed's Chronicles (London, 1586).
Hooker, John, Order and Usage, ed. Vernon F. Snow (Yale University Press, 1977) (see Snow, *Parliament in Elizabethan England*).
Ingulph's Chronicle of the Abbey of Croyland, ed. H. T. Riley (London, 1854).
Johannis de Trokelowe et Henrici de Blaneforde Chronica et Annales, ed. H. T. Riley (Rolls Series, 1866).
Journals of all the Parliaments During the Reign of Queen Elizabeth, Sir Simonds D'Ewes (London, 1682).
Liverpool Tractate, ed. Catherine Strateman (New York, 1937).
Manner of Holding Parliaments in England, Henry Elsyng (London, 1671).
Manuscripts of the House of Lords, ed. Maurice F. Bond (London, 1953).
Memoranda de Parliamento, ed. F. W. Maitland (Rolls Series, 1893).
Mirror of Justices, ed. W. J. Whitaker (Selden Society, vii, 1895).
Modus Tenendi Parliamenta et Consilia in Hibernia, ed. A. Dopping (Dublin, 1692).
Modus Tenendi Parliamentum, ed. T. D. Hardy (London, Record Commission, 1846).
Mum and the Sothsegger, ed. Mabel Day and Robert Steele (Early English Text Society, Original Series, 199, 1936).
Parliamentary Writs, ed. F. Palgrave, 2 vols. in 4 (London, 1827–34).
Parliaments and Councils of Medieval Ireland, ed. H. G. Richardson and G. O. Sayles (Dublin, Irish Mss. Commission, 1947), Vol. I.
Political Poems and Songs, ed. T. Wright, 2 vols. (Rolls Series, 1859).
Plumpton Correspondence, ed. T. Stapleton (Camden Society, iv, 1839).
Proceedings in Parliament 1610, ed. Elizabeth R. Foster (Yale, 1966).
Radulphi de Hengham Summae, ed. W. H. Dunham (Cambridge, 1932).
Readings and Moots at the Inns of Court in the Fifteenth Century, ed. S. E. Thorne (Selden Society, lxxi, 1954).
Red Paper Book of Colchester, ed. W. G. Benham (Colchester, 1902).
Report from the Lords Committees . . . for all matters touching the Dignity of a Peer, 4 vols. (London, 1820–9).
Report on the Records of the Borough of Colchester, Henry Harrod (Colchester, 1865).
Rotuli Parliamentorum, 7 vols. (London, Record Commission, 1783–1832).
Rotuli Parliamentorum Angliae Hactenus Inediti, ed. H. C. Richardson and G. O. Sayles (Camden Society, li, 1935).
Scalacronica of Thomas Grey, ed. J. Stevenson (Maitland Club, Edinburgh, 1836).
Select Cases in the Court of the King's Bench, ed. G. D. Sayles (Selden Society, 1936–71).
Select Cases in the Court of Requests 1497–1596, ed. I. S. Leadam (Selden Society, xii, 1898).
Select Charters of English Constitutional History, ed. W. Stubbs, revised by H. W. C. Davies (Oxford, 1929).
Somers Tracts, 2nd edn. by Sir Walter Scott (London, 1809), Vol. I.
Spicilegium, ed. D. L. D'Achery (Paris, 1675), Vol. XII.
Statutes and Ordinances and Acts of the Parliament of Ireland, King John to Henry V, ed. H. F. Barry (Dublin, 1907).
Statutes of the Realm (London, Record Commission, 1810), Vol. I.
Stilus Curie Parlamenti, Guillaume du Breuil, ed. F. Aubert (Collection de Textes pour servir à l'Etude et à L'Enseignment de L'Histoire, Paris, 1909).

Vita Edwardi Secundi; The Life of Edward II by the So-called Monk of Malmesbury, ed.
  N. Denholm-Young (London, 1957).
*William Lambarde's Notes on the Procedures and Privileges of the House of Commons
  (1584)*, ed. Paul L. Ward (London, Stationery Office, 1977) (see Ward,
  William Lambarde's Notes).
Year Book of Edward II, ed. G. J. Turner (Selden Society, xxvi, 1914), vol. vi.
Year Books, 14–15 Edward III, ed. L. O. Pike (Rolls Series, 1889).

SECONDARY WORKS

Album Helen Maud Cam (Louvain, 1960–1) 2 vols. (Studies Presented to the
  International Commission for the History of Representative and Parliamen-
  tary Institutions).
Armstrong, Olive, 'Manuscripts of the "Modus Tenendi Parliamentum" in the
  Library of Trinity College, Dublin', *Proceedings of the Royal Irish Academy*, 36C
  (1921–4), 256–64.
Baldwin, J. F., *The King's Council in England in the Later Middle Ages* (Oxford,
  1913).
Cam, H. M., *Liberties and Communities in Medieval England* (Cambridge, 1944,
  reprinted 1963).
Chrimes, S. B., *English Constitutional Ideas in the Fifteenth Century* (Cambridge,
  1936, reprinted 1966).
— *Sir John Fortescue, De Laudibus Legum Angliae* (Cambridge, 1942).
— *English Constitutional History*, 3rd edn. (London, 1961).
— *Henry VII* (London, 1972).
Clarke, M. V., *Medieval Representation and Consent* (London, 1936, reprinted
  1964).
— 'Irish Parliaments in the Reign of Edward II', *T.R.H.S.* 4th Ser. 9 (1926)
  29–62.
— 'William of Windsor in Ireland, 1369–76', *Proceedings of the Royal Irish
  Academy*, 41 C (1932), 55–130.
— 'The Manuscripts of the Irish *Modus Tenendi Parliamentum*', *E.H.R.* 48 (1933),
  576–600.
Curtis, E., *History of Medieval Ireland* (London, 1923, revised edition, 1938).
Cuttino, G. P. 'A Reconsideration of the *Modus Tenendi Parliamentum*', *The
  Forward Movement of the Fourteenth Century*, ed. F. L. Utley (Columbus, 1961),
  pp. 31–60.
Davies, J. C., *The Baronial Opposition to Edward II* (Cambridge, 1918).
— 'The Despenser War in Glamorgan', *T.R.H.S.* 3rd ser. 9 (1915), 21–64.
Davies, R. R., *Lordship and Society in the March of Wales, 1282–1400* (Oxford,
  1978).
Deighton, H. S., 'Clerical Taxation by Consent 1279–1301', *E.H.R.* 68 (1953),
  161–92.
Denholm-Young, N., *Collected Papers of N. Denholm-Young* (Cardiff, 1969).
— *The Country Gentry in the Fourteenth Century* (Oxford, 1969).
Dunham, W. H., 'The Books of Parliament' and 'The Old Record', 1396–
  1504', *Speculum*, 51 (1976), 694–712.
Edwards, Sir J. G., *The Commons in Medieval English Parliaments* (London, 1958).

— *Historians and the Medieval English Parliament* (Glasgow, 1960, reprinted 1970).
— 'The Personnel of the Commons in Parliament under Edward I and Edward II', *Essays in Medieval History Presented to Thomas Frederick Tout* (Manchester, 1925), pp. 197–214.
— 'The *Plena Potestas* of English Parliamentary Representatives', *Oxford Essays in Medieval History Presented to H. E. Salter* (Oxford, 1934), pp. 141–54.
— 'Justice' in Early English Parliaments', *B.I.H.R.* 27 (1954), 35–53.
Edwards, Kathleen, 'The Political Importance of English Bishops During The Reign of Edward II', *E.H.R.* 59 (1944), 311–47.
Elton, G. R., 'The Early Journals of the House of Lords', *E.H.R.* 89 (1974), 481–512.
Evans, E., 'Of the Antiquity of Parliaments in England: Some Elizabethan and Early Stuart Opinions', *History* 23 (1938), 206–21.
Foster, Elizabeth Read, 'The Painful Labour of Mr. Elsyng', *Transactions of the American Philosophical Society*, new ser. 62 (Philadelphia, 1972).
Fryde, E. B., and Miller, E., *Historical Studies of the English Parliament*, 2 vols. (London, 1970).
Galbraith, V. H., 'The *Modus Tenendi Parliamentum*', *Journal of the Warburg and Courtauld Institutes* 16 (1953), 81–99.
Goodman, A., 'Sir Thomas Hoo and the Parliament of 1376', *B.I.H.R.* 41 (1968), 139–49.
Grassi, J. L., 'William Airmyn and the Bishopric of Norwich', *E.H.R.* 70 (1955), 550–61.
Harcourt, L. W. V., *His Grace the Steward* (London, 1907).
Hardy, T. D., 'On the Treatise entitled *Modus Tenendi Parliamentum*', *Archaeological Journal* 19 (1862), 259–74.
Harriss, G. L., *King, Parliament and Public Finance in Medieval England to 1369* (Oxford, 1975).
— 'The Commons' Petitions of 1340', *E.H.R.* 78 (1963), 625–54.
Hastings, Margaret, *The Court of Common Pleas in the Fifteenth Century* (New York, 1947).
Hill, Christopher, *Puritanism and Revolution* (London, 1958).
Hodnett, D. K. and White, W. P., 'The Manuscripts of the *Modus Tenendi Parliamentum*', *E.H.R.* 34 (1919), 209–24.
Ives, E. W., 'The Common Lawyers in Pre-Reformation England', *T.R.H.S.* 5th Ser. 18 (1968), 145–73.
Kemp, E. W., *Counsel and Consent* (London, 1961).
Kingsford, C. L., *English Historical Literature in the Fifteenth Century* (Oxford, 1913).
Lander, J. R., *Crown and Nobility, 1450–1509* (London, 1976).
Lapsley, G. T., 'The Interpretation of the Statute of York', *E.H.R.* 56 (1941), 22–49, 411–46.
Lord, R. B., 'The Parliaments of the Middle Ages and the Early Modern Period', *Catholic Historical Review* 16 (1930), 125–44.
Lowry, E. C., 'Clerical Proctors in Parliament and Knights of the Shire 1280–1374', *E.H.R.* 48 (1933), 443–55.
Lydon, James, 'William of Windsor and the Irish Parliament', *E.H.R.* 80 (1965), 252–67.

McFarlane, K. B., 'Parliament and "Barrstard Feudalism"', *T.R.H.S.* 4th Ser. 26 (1944), 53–79.

McKisack, M., *The Parliamentary Representation of the English Boroughs During the Middle Ages* (Oxford, 1932, reprinted 1962).

Mackie, J. D., *The Earlier Tudors* (Oxford, 1952).

— 'The Order of the Holding of the Court of Parliament in Scotland', *Scottish Historical Review* 27 (1948), 191–3.

Maddicott, J. R., *Thomas of Lancaster, 1307–1322* (Oxford, 1970).

Maitland, F. W., *Constitutional History* (Cambridge, 1913).

Mélanges Julien Havet (Paris, 1895).

Morris, W. A., 'The Date of the *Modus Tenendi Parliamentum*', *E.H.R.* 49 (1934), 407–22.

— 'Magnates and the Community of the Realm in Parliament, 1264–1327', *Medievalia et Humanistica* 1 (1943), 58–94.

Morris, W. A. and Strayer, J. R., *The English Government at Work 1327–1336*, vol. ii (Cambridge, Mass., 1947).

Murray, K. M. E., *The Constitutional History of the Cinque Ports* (Manchester, 1935).

Myers, A. R., *Parliaments and Estates in Europe to 1789* (London, 1975).

— 'The English Parliament and the French Estates General in the Middle Ages', *Album Helen Maud Cam* (Louvain, 1961), II, 139–53.

— 'The Parliaments of Europe and the Age of Estates', *History* 60 (1975), 11–27.

Neale, J. E., *The Elizabethan House of Commons* (London, 1954).

— 'Commons Journals of the Tudor Period', *T.R.H.S.* 4th Ser. 3 (1920), 136–170.

Otway-Ruthven, A. J., *A History of Medieval Ireland* (London, 1968).

Phillips, J. R. S., *Aymer de Valence, Baronial Politics in the Reign of Edward II* (Oxford, 1972).

Pike, L. O., *A Constitutional History of the House of Lords* (London, 1894, reprinted 1964).

Plucknett, T. F. T., *Statutes and their Interpretation in the First Half of the Fourteenth Century* (Cambridge, 1922).

— *A Concise History of the Common Law*, 5th edn. (London, 1956).

— *Early English Legal Literature* (Cambridge, 1958).

— 'Parliament 1327–36' in *The English Government at Work, 1327–1336*; ed. J. F. Willard and W. A. Morris (Cambridge, Mass., 1940), I, 82–128.

— 'The Origin of Impeachment', *T.R.H.S.* 4th ser. 24 (1942), 47–71.

Pococke, J. G. A., *The Ancient Constitution and the Feudal Law* (Cambridge, 1957).

Pollard, A. F., *The Evolution of Parliament* (London, 1920, revised 1926).

— 'The Authenticity of the "Lords' Journals" in the Sixteenth Century', *T.R.H.S.* 3rd ser. 8 (1914), 17–39.

Pollock, F. and Maitland, F. W., *The History of English Law Before the Time of Edward I*, 2 vols., 2nd edn. with introduction by S. F. C. Milsom (Cambridge, 1968).

Post, G., *Studies in Medieval Legal Thought* (Princeton, 1964).

Powell, J. E. and Wallis, K., *The House of Lords in the Middle Ages* (London, 1968).

Pronay, N. and Taylor, J., 'The Use of the *Modus Tenendi Parliamentum* in the Middle Ages', *B.I.H.R.* 47 (1974), 11–23.

Redlich, J., *The Procedure of the House of Commons*, 3 vols. (London, 1908).

Richardson, H. G., 'The Preston Exemplification of the *Modus Tenendi Parliamentum*', *Irish Historical Studies* 3 (1942), 187–92.

Richardson, H. G. and Sayles, G. O., *The Irish Parliament in the Middle Ages* (Philadelphia and Oxford, 1952).

— *The Governance of Medieval England* (Edinburgh, 1963).

— 'The Early Records of the English Parliaments', *B.I.H.R.* 5 (1928), 71–88; 6 (1929), 129–55.

— 'The King's Ministers in Parliament under Edward I', *E.H.R.* 46 (1931), 529–50.

— 'The Parliaments of Edward III', *B.I.H.R.* 8 (1930–1), 55–82; 9 (1931–2), 1–18.

— 'The King's Ministers in Parliament under Edward II', *E.H.R.* 47 (1932), 194–203.

— 'The King's Ministers in Parliament under Edward III', *E.H.R.* 47 (1932), 377–97.

Roskell, J. S., *The Commons in the Parliament of 1422* (Manchester, 1954).

— *The Commons and Their Speakers in English Parliaments, 1376–1523* (Manchester, 1965).

— 'The Problem of the Attendance of the Lords in Medieval Parliaments', *B.I.H.R.* 29 (1956), 153–204.

— 'A Consideration of Certain Aspects and Problems of the English *Modus Tenendi Parliamentum*', *B.J.R.L.* 50 (1968), 411–42.

Ross, Charles, *Edward IV* (London, 1974).

Round, J. H., *Commune of London* (London, 1899).

Sayles, G. O., *The King's Parliament of England* (London, 1975).

Schofield, Cora L., *The Life and Reign of Edward IV*, 2 vols. (London, 1967).

Simpson, A. W. B., 'The Circulation of Yearbooks in the Fifteenth Century', *Law Quarterly Review* 73 (1957), 492–505.

Snow, Vernon, F., *Parliament in Elizabethan England* (Yale University Press, 1977) (see *Hooker, John, Order and Usage*).

Squibb, G. D., *The High Court of Chivalry* (Oxford, 1959).

Stones, E. L. G. and Blount, Margaret, N., 'The Surrender of King John of Scotland to Edward I in 1296, Some New Evidence', *B.L.H.R.* 48 (1975), 94–106.

Strayer, J. R., 'The State of York and the Community of the Realm', *American Historical Review* 47 (1941), 1–22.

Stubbs, W., *Constitutional History of Medieval England*, 3 vols., reprinted in 9th edn., by H. W. C. Davis (Oxford, 1929).

Studies Presented to S. B. Chrimes, ed. H. Hearder and H. R. Loyn (Cardiff, 1974).

Taylor, J., 'The Manuscripts of the *Modus Tenendi Parliamentum*', *E.H.R.* 83 (1968), 673–88.

Tout, T. F., *Chapters in the Administrative History of Medieval England*, 6 vols. (Manchester, 1920–33).

— *Collected Papers of Thomas Frederick Tout*, 3 vols. (Manchester, 1932–4).

— *The Place of the Reign of Edward II in English History*, 2nd edn. by H. Johnstone (Manchester, 1936).

Unwin, George, 'The Estates of Merchants' in *Finance and Trade under Edward III* (Manchester, 1918).

Vinogradoff, Paul G., *Essays in Legal History* (London, 1913).

Virgoe, R., 'A New Fragment of the Lords Journal of 1461', *B.I.H.R.* 32 (1959), 83–7.

Wagner, A. R., *Heralds and Heraldry in the Middle Ages* (Oxford, 1956).

Ward, Paul L., *William Lambarde's Notes on the Procedure and Privileges of the House of Commons (1584)* (London, Stationery Office, 1977) (introduction and commentary).

Weske, D. B., *Convocation of the Clergy* (London, 1937).

Wilkinson, B., *Studies in the Constitutional History of the Thirteenth and Fourteenth Centuries* (Manchester, 1937).

— *Constitutional History of Medieval England, 1216–1399*, 3 vols. (London, 1948–58).

— 'The Sherburn Indenture and the Attack on the Despensers, 1321', *E.H.R.* 63 (1948), 1–28.

Willard, J. F., and Morris, W. H., ed. *The English Government at Work, 1327–1336*. vol. I (Cambridge, Mass., 1940).

Wood-Leigh, K., 'Sheriffs, Lawyers and Belted Knights in the Parliaments of Edward III, *E.H.R.* 46 (1931), 372–88.

— 'Knights' Attendance in the Parliaments of Edward III', *E.H.R.* 47 (1932), 398–413.

Winfield, Percy, H., *The Chief Sources of English Medieval History* (New York, 1925).

Index

C3